THE FALL OF
THE RUSSIAN EMPIRE

MAJOR ISSUES IN HISTORY

Editor

C. WARREN HOLLISTER

University of California, Santa Barbara

THE FALL OF
THE RUSSIAN EMPIRE

EDITED BY

Edward Chmielewski

Professor of History
University of Tennessee

John Wiley & Sons, Inc.
New York • London • Sydney • Toronto

Library of Congress Cataloging in Publication Data:
Chmielewski, Edward.
  The fall of the Russian Empire.

  (Major issues in history)
  Includes bibliographical references.
    1. Russia—History—Nicholas II, 1894–1917—Addresses, essays, lectures.
    2. Russia—History—Nicholas II, 1894–1917—Sources. I. Title.
DK255.C48   947.08   72-8876
ISBN 0-471-15600-0
ISBN 0-471-15601-9 (pbk.)

Printed in the United States of America

10 9 8 7 6 5 4 3 2 1

SERIES PREFACE

The reading program in a history survey course traditionally has
consisted of a large two-volume textbook and, perhaps, a book of
readings. This simple reading program requires few decisions and little
imagination on the instructor's part, and tends to encourage in the
student the virtue of careful memorization. Such programs are by no
means things of the past, but they certainly do not represent the wave
of the future.

The reading program in survey courses at many colleges and universities today is far more complex. At the risk of oversimplification,
and allowing for many exceptions and overlaps, it can be divided into
four categories: (1) textbook, (2) original source readings, (3) specialized
historical essays and interpretive studies, and (4) historical problems.

After obtaining an overview of the course subject matter (textbook),
sampling the original sources, and being exposed to selective examples
of excellent modern historical writing (historical essays), the student
can turn to the crucial task of weighing various possible interpretations of major historical issues. It is at this point that memory gives way
to creative critical thought. The "problems approach," in other words, is
the intellectual climax of a thoughtfully conceived reading program
and is, indeed, the most characteristic of all approaches to historical
pedagogy among the newer generation of college and university
teachers.

The historical problems books currently available are many and
varied. Why add to this information explosion? Because the Wiley
Major Issues Series constitutes an endeavor to produce something new
that will respond to pedagogical needs thus far unmet. First, it is a
series of individual volumes—one per problem. Many good teachers
would much prefer to select their own historical issues rather than be tied
to an inflexible sequence of issues imposed by a publisher and bound
together between two covers. Second, the Wiley Major Issues Series
is based on the idea of approaching the significant problems of history
through a deft interweaving of primary sources and secondary analysis,
fused together by the skill of a scholar-editor. It is felt that the essence
of a historical issue cannot be satisfactorily probed either by placing a
body of undigested source materials into the hands of inexperienced
students or by limiting these students to the controversial literature of
modern scholars who debate the meaning of sources the student never
sees. This series approaches historical problems by exposing students to
both the finest historical thinking on the issue and some of the evidence
on which this thinking is based. This synthetic approach should prove

far more fruitful than either the raw-source approach or the exclusively second-hand approach, for it combines the advantages—and avoids the serious disadvantages—of both.

Finally, the editors of the individual volumes in the Major Issues Series have been chosen from among the ablest scholars in their fields. Rather than faceless referees, they are historians who know their issues from the inside and, in most instances, have themselves contributed significantly to the relevant scholarly literature. It has been the editorial policy of this series to permit the editor-scholars of the individual volumes the widest possible latitude both in formulating their topics and in organizing their materials. Their scholarly competence has been unquestioningly respected; they have been encouraged to approach the problems as they see fit. The titles and themes of the series volumes have been suggested in nearly every case by the scholar-editors themselves. The criteria have been (1) that the issues be of relevance to undergraduate lecture courses in history, and (2) that it be an issue which the scholar-editor knows thoroughly and in which he has done creative work. And, in general, the second criterion has been given precedence over the first. In short, the question "What are the significant historical issues today?" has been answered not by general editors or sales departments but by the scholar-teachers who are responsible for these volumes.

University of California   *C. Warren Hollister*
Santa Barbara

CONTENTS

THE FALL OF
THE RUSSIAN EMPIRE

CHAPTER I

INTRODUCTION

The controversial last decades in the life of Imperial Russia continue to engage historical interest and arouse lively debates in interpretation. Even if the revolutions of 1917 had not occurred, or perhaps had occurred in a modified form had it not been for the agonies experienced by Russia during World War I, the period of Russian history from 1890 to 1914 was one of such animated and many-sided change and achievement that its effect on Russian history in the twentieth century was bound to be deep and lasting. And the Soviet system that emerged from the ruins of the old regime of Nicholas II had always related to its predecessor; sometimes furthering, sometimes distorting, and sometimes repressing the major developments of that critical age that witnessed an immense acceleration in Russia's historical passage from a relatively backward, agrarian society to a relatively modern, industrialized one.

In the sphere of high culture, the early twentieth century has been characterized as Russia's silver age or even renaissance, in that all areas of cultural and spiritual life were encompassed. In art, literature, philosophy, music, and ballet, the period was one of great fecundity, vitality, and variety. Russia's cultural contributions to Europe were of the highest level. Moreover, the brilliant and sophisticated cultural climate of the age demonstrated that the educated public was departing from the simplistic, dogmatic, materialistic, narrow-minded outlook so characteristic of the nineteenth-century intelligentsia. The followers of older traditions, like Lenin and his zealous disciples, were beginning to appear old-fashioned and increasingly out-of-date. Russia's cultural efflorescence was admittedly confined to a narrow elite, but the period also witnessed dramatic gains in the field of educa-

1

tion, particularly in the primary schools. Whereas the census of 1897 revealed a literacy rate of only 21 percent for the Empire, by 1914 it was approximately 44 percent.

Economically, although Russian backwardness had not disappeared by the eve of war, it was certainly diminishing. The period was one of an industrial boom and the tempo of growth was among the highest in the world. The state of Russian agriculture was less promising. Under Peter A. Stolypin, Imperial Russia's last statesman, chairman of the council of ministers from 1906 to 1911, a government program was launched to break up the ancient peasant communes and to turn the land over to individual property owners. Controversy remains alive to this day whether Stolypin's peasant policy was practical and whether it would, in time, have produced greater agrarian efficiency and called into being a middle class of well-to-do private farmers that would have supported and strengthened the existing regime. In any case, this new government policy marked a departure from official apathy and support of the traditional and stagnant communal system of agriculture.

However, it is the political and institutional developments in Russia, particularly after 1905, that continue to arouse the strongest debates. Before the outbreak of the Russo-Japanese War followed by the 1905 revolution, there existed the phenomenon of "the two Russias"—the entrenched autocracy sustained by the bureaucracy, the official church, the army, and much of the nobility, and, in opposition, the educated and alienated intelligentsia: individuals committed to a liberalization of the regime. They ranged in ideology from liberalism to socialism, varying in methods from peaceful to the most violent, and drawing active or passive support from elements of the middle class, nobility, workers, peasants, and the oppressed but increasingly self-conscious minorities of the Empire. The main problem of Russian political life after 1905 was whether the traditional polarization between the government and educated society could be overcome and whether, over a period of time and on the basis of the first constitution in Russian history, the two Russias would be able to merge into a single functioning one. Certainly the constitution had been wrested by force from an unwilling autocracy badly shaken by military defeat. The constitution as granted was also much more limited in concessions than the one promised in the days of revolution. A good deal of the traditional and hierarchical state structure remained untouched. Furthermore, there continued in existence and in opposition even to the modified autocracy a broad spectrum of political opinion from socialists to liberals (see Chapter II).

Consequently, the question is invariably posed whether the imperial regime could have survived even if the war had not intervened. Were developments after 1905 narrowing the gulf between the two Russias and contributing to the workability of the constitutional system in a meaningful and effective way? Certainly the fiery trial of war revealed in the most overt way that the tsarist political system was unable or unwilling to accommodate itself to the institutions that had emerged after 1905. The question, however, still remains open whether the long war in itself overstrained tsarism; caused its collapse, ensuing anarchy, and inevitable Bolshevik seizure of power; or whether the final outcome resulted from the inane and blind conduct of the war by Nicholas, Alexandra, and their incompetent and isolated government.

Beyond this question lies another: whether under any circumstances—peace or war—the regime could have endured, given its altered structure from 1905 to 1914 and after or whether its overthrow or collapse was inevitable. Consequently, an examination of the relationship between Russian government and society after the revolution of 1905 can illuminate the prospects facing the country. And, in the context of Russian history, this means the viability of alternatives to the revolution that was violently accomplished in 1917 (see Chapter VIII).

At the very best, there were exceedingly few prerequisites for a representative form of government in Russia's historical legacy. An ancient autocracy, a huge and rigidly entrenched bureaucracy, a largely illiterate country of many nationalities, no legal political parties or trade unions, a weak middle class, a nobility in economic decline, and a peasantry emancipated from serfdom only since 1861—none of these phenomena foretold success for a constitutional monarchy. The weak, vacillating, and fatalistic emperor, Nicholas II, and his wife, Alexandra, both detested the idea of any curtailment of the autocratic power that they considered theirs by divine right and, as such, untouchable. Nicholas consented to the publication of the October Manifesto of 1905 that provided the basis for a constitutional regime only with the greatest reluctance. He was persuaded to accede by Sergius Witte (see Chapter III, Reading A). A brilliant but prejudiced and opinionated personality, Witte had been the dynamic minister of finance during the reign of Alexander III (1881–1894), Nicholas' strong and willful father. Removed from this post in 1903 by the jealous and resentful Emperor who was bent on the adventurous foreign policy in the Far East that led directly to the debacle of the Russo-Japanese War, Witte had been recalled to head the Russian delegation that signed the lenient peace treaty ending the war. Witte believed that, because of the inadequacies of Nicholas as an autocrat and because of the danger presented by the revolutionary situation in 1905, the grant of a constitution was the only way to save the monarchy. He himself composed the October Manifesto (see Chapter III, Reading B) and was appointed chairman of the new council of ministers. After his appointment, Witte made a serious attempt to include members of the liberal opposition in the new cabinet. However, this first effort to bridge the gulf between the "two Russias" failed. The dogmatic insistence of the liberals on the convocation of a constituent assembly that would decide the political destiny of Russia was clearly unacceptable to the government. A purely bureaucratic cabinet was formed; any role that the liberals might have played in the creation of the new constitutional system was now precluded, and the natural conservatism of the old ruling class and its proclivity to turn the clock back were strengthened.

Between December 1905 and April 1906 when the First State Duma was convoked, the structure of the new constitutional system was worked out by the authorities and the principal legislation was codified in the so-called Fundamental Laws issued in April 1906 (see Chapter III, Reading C). This legislation, while it did create the first representative assembly in modern Russian history, violated the promises made by the October Manifesto. Not only were the powers of the Duma seriously circumscribed, but also the Fundamental Laws themselves might not be revised except on the initiative of the emperor. And it was exactly a radical extension of the powers of the Duma, which had been so narrowly defined by the government, that the entire opposition movement had in mind. Consequently, a confrontation between the "two Russias" was inevitable in the political arena of the new legislature.

The first sacrifice was Witte. Attacked on all sides and exposed to Nicholas' resentment and hostility, he resigned as chairman of the council of ministers five days before the opening of the Duma and was replaced by an aging and apathetic bureaucrat, I. L. Goremykin. P. A. Stolypin, a former provincial governor and newcomer to the bureaucracy of the capital, became the new minister of the interior.

The Kadets constituted the largest political party in the First Duma, called the Duma of National Hopes. Representing the left-wing liberals and led by P. N. Miliukov, they were criticized by moderates like V. A. Maklakov (see Chapter IV) for their readiness to cooperate with the socialists, their unwillingness to modify their strict oppositional stand to the government, and their insistence that the Fundamental Laws be revised in favor of a true parliamentary democracy. To the right of the Kadets were the Octobrists, headed by the dynamic A. I. Guchkov, who took their stand on the October Manifesto as the basis for Russia's proper constitutional development. However, the Duma was dominated by the Kadets and the radical groups to the left who demanded concessions going far beyond anything the government was willing to yield: universal suffrage, ministerial responsibility to the Duma, abolition of the upper house, personal inviolability, a broad political amnesty, and the expropriation of the large landed estates. The outcome was the dissolution of the Duma in July and the appointment of the energetic and forceful Stolypin as president of the council of ministers (see Chapter III, Readings E and F). While generally desirous of acting within the existing constitutional framework, Stolypin possessed an authoritarian temper and was not inclined to endure opposition to his own policies. His principal land law was issued in November 1906 under Article 87 of the Fundamental Laws and he employed strong measures in 1906 and 1907 to put an end to antigovernmental violence in the wake of the revolution of 1905 (see Chapter III, Reading D).

The Second Duma, the Duma of Popular Anger, met in 1907 and was even more extremist and hostile to the government than the First had been. Its brief existence was largely devoted to attempts to discredit the government and Stolypin's use of Article 87 to suppress revolution and social disorder (see Chapter III, Reading G). The Duma also refused to support Stolypin's agrarian reforms and delayed confirmation of the budget. At this juncture, the government sought a convenient pretext to dissolve the Duma. It charged the 55 Social Democratic Deputies with being involved in a plot to organize a popular uprising and demanded that the Duma deprive them of parliamentary immunity and hand them over to the police. A special investigating committee of the Duma found the evidence supplied by the government inadequate. The government followed the Duma's failure to comply with its demand by dissolving the legislature. This time, however, the dissolution was accompanied by the promulgation, in violation of the Fundamental Laws, of a new electoral law on June 3, 1907 (see Chapter III, Reading H). This law was designed to reduce the representation of the liberal and radical opposition by weighing elections more heavily in favor of the landowning and propertied classes at the expense of the workers, peasants, and non-Russian minorities of the Empire.

The Third Duma, known as the Masters' Duma, was the only one to complete its full term of five years, 1907–1912. It was dominated by conservatives. This was even truer of the Fourth Duma. The strongest party was that of the Octobrists with whom Stolypin hoped to collaborate (see Chapter III, Readings I and J). He was at first successful. The Duma approved his agrarian reforms and passed measures to modernize the armed forces and expand educational opportunities (see Chapter III, Reading K). Stolypin also was able to obtain the support of a center-right majority of the Duma for a series of nationalist measures directed against the non-Russian western borderlands of the Empire. The autonomy of Finland was narrowed, a new Russian province of Chełm was created out of two of Russia's Polish provinces (see Chapter VI), and, in 1911, a bill was passed to introduce institutions of local self-government (zemstvos) in Russia's western provinces. Polish landowners were influential in the area but the bill was framed to guarantee Russian control of the institutions. However, the bill was rejected by the upper house on the basis of conservative sympathy for the Polish nobility as well as intrigues against Stolypin at court. In anger, Stolypin cajoled the reluctant Emperor into adjourning both houses for three days and introducing the zemstvos on the basis of Article 87 of the Fundamental Laws. Guchkov, the president of the Duma, resigned in protest and both the upper and lower houses condemned Stolypin's action. Indeed, as with his predecessor Witte, Stolypin's position was being undermined by the time of the zemstvo crisis. The Emperor had come to resent Stolypin's eminence, the Empress disliked him because he opposed the influence of Rasputin, and the right wing considered him superfluous now that the revolutionary crisis had been overcome. Stolypin would probably have been removed from office had he not been assassinated in September 1911 (see Chapter VII).

Stolypin's successor, his minister of finance, V. N. Kokovtsov, was still an honest and able figure, although rather unimaginative and limited. Generally conservative, he advocated modest social and administrative reforms sponsored by the government, and introduced gradually a policy that suited neither the right nor the left. However, Kokovtsov felt obliged to pursue his predecessor's nationalist program, as in the matter of Chełm, although he professed to be a moderate in nationality questions. Furthermore, he was unable to dominate or unify his colleagues in the ministries and was increasingly opposed by rightist elements, including the Empress, because of his unwillingness to increase official subsidies to rightist politicians and newspapers as well as his criticisms of Rasputin. Rasputin's growing political influence became apparent in 1911 when a favorite of his was appointed chief procurator of the Holy Synod.

Finally, in January 1914, Kokovtsov, after having negotiated a loan from France, was dropped from office and replaced by the futile and aged Goremykin, the embodiment of bureaucratic ossification (see Chapter VIII). What recommended him was his undeviating loyalty to the monarchy and his acceptance of the role of Rasputin. Under Goremykin, Russia drifted into war in 1914, a war that dealt the death blow to the constitutional system and to the autocracy that had reluctantly introduced it, weakened it, and finally abandoned it (see Chapter III, Reading L).

The readings that follow illustrate the key problems faced by the Russian monarchy in its final years. The readings show how tsarism and its opponents viewed these problems, how and to what extent they understood them, how they faced or avoided them, and, finally, how they were overwhelmed by them. The door was ultimately left open to Lenin and the Bolsheviks. The readings begin with an examination of the historically deep-seated confrontation between the regime and the educated opposition. They continue with an analysis of the overt conflict precipitated by the revolution of 1905. They then describe the new constitutional system extorted from the government and then circumscribed by it. The readings go on to demonstrate the flaws and confusion in the Russian liberal movement and the grave and ultimately insoluble issues faced by the last statesman of imperial Russia, Stolypin. One of the underlying causes of the collapse of the monarchy was surely its failure to conciliate its national minorities. One of the readings considers a case study in which the Poles, the most important of the minorities, were seriously affronted in their national self-consciousness and assaulted by militant Russian nationalism. The readings then graphically evoke the breakdown of the central Russian government in the remaining years following the assassination of Stolypin. They conclude with a severe assessment of the Russian autocracy and a summation of the basic factors contributing to its demise.

CHAPTER II

FROM   *Sidney Harcave*
The Russian Revolution of 1905

In his study of the origins and consequences of the Russian Revolution of 1905, Professor Harcave examines the tradition of the autocracy in Russian history and the static, archaic, tsarist conception of Russian society. Discussing the "two Russias," he contrasts bureaucratic officialdom with the educated and alienated opposition intelligentsia, both liberal and radical. He then demonstrates how war and revolution obliged the unwilling autocracy to issue the October Manifesto and, later, the Fundamental Laws that significantly modified the concession promised the year before. He points out that the government and the opposition movement were dissatisfied with the settlement following the revolution and concludes that, while the constitutional experiment was not predestined to failure, the extremes of the "two Russias" made compromise on a middle ground difficult to attain.

THE "TWO RUSSIAS"

"There exist two Russias. . . . Were I to label these two Russias, I should designate the one as the Russia of Leo Tolstoy, the great

SOURCE. Sidney Harcave, *The Russian Revolution of 1905* (New York: The Macmillan Company, 1964), pp. 11–18, 26–30, 32–35, 244–250, 260–262. Reprinted with permission of The Macmillan Company and The Bodley Head, London.

9

writer; and the other as that of Plehve, the late minister of the interior. The former is the Russia of our "intellectuals" and of the people; the latter is official Russia. One is the Russia of the future, as dreamed of by members of the liberal professions; the other is an anachronism, deeply rooted in the past, and defended in the present by an omnipotent bureaucracy. The one spells liberty; the other, despotism."

—Paul Milyukov (Russian historian and liberal leader), *Russia and its Crisis, 1905*

"Among the falsest of political principles is the principle of the sovereignty of the people. . . . Thence proceeds the theory of Parliamentarism, which, up to the present day, has deluded much of the so-called "intelligence," and unhappily infatuated certain foolish Russians. It continues to maintain its hold on many minds with the obstinacy of a narrow fanaticism, although every day its falsehood is exposed more clearly to the world."

—Constantine Pobedonostsev (Over-Procurator of the Holy Synod of the Russian Orthodox Church and adviser to Nicholas II), *Reflections of a Russian Statesman* (trans. of *Moskovskii Sbornik,* 1896)

A critical test of the positions stated above was made in 1905. The popular uprising which occurred in Russia at that time may properly be termed the first revolution in the country's history: "first" because there had previously been no such mass action having both organization and a political program; "revolution" because it succeeded in forcing a change in the monarchy's traditionally autocratic rule. The groups that worked to bring about the Revolution of 1905 pursued various and often conflicting ultimate goals; but they accepted a common immediate goal, the fundamental need to curb the power of the autocracy. It was clear that, whatever the ultimate goals—all of which involved change of some kind—they would remain unattainable as long as the regime held absolute power and used it to prevent change.

TSARISM AND BUREAUCRACY

At the beginning of the twentieth century, more power was concentrated in the hands of the ruler of Russia than in those of any other person on earth. The ruling Tsar, Nicholas II, who had come to the throne in 1894, exercised unlimited sovereignty over some 135 million subjects living in an area that included over a seventh of the world's surface; and he was resolutely committed to administer that sovereignty in such a manner as to preserve and perpetuate the political, social, and economic order he had inherited from his father, Alexander III. He was of the firm belief that autocracy was the only political system suited to the Russians and that, with the final touches added by his father, it was an inherently sound, though admittedly not perfect, form of government. To make any major changes in it would only result in making Russia dangerously susceptible to revolution, the dread disease that had been appearing sporadically in Europe for more than two hundred years, ravaging monarchy after monarchy— England, France, Prussia, Austria, Spain—and was still an infection against which a monarch should watchfully guard his country. Moreover, Nicholas II thought of himself as a guardian answerable only to God for his stewardship:

"In the sight of my Maker I have to carry the burden of a terrible responsibility and at all times, therefore, be ready to render an account to him of my actions. I must always keep firmly to my convictions and follow the dictates of my conscience."

Foremost among the institutions supported by the Tsar's conscience and convictions was autocracy, a basis of government established by the Fundamental Laws of the Russian Empire:

"The Emperor of all the Russias is an autocratic and unlimited monarch. Not only fear, but also conscience commanded by God Himself, is the basis of obedience to His supreme power."

Though autocracy, by definition, is intolerant of constitutional limitations on the power of the ruler—such as might be expected, for instance, from legislative bodies deriving their authority from his subjects—it does not preclude recourse to elective advisory bodies. Yet Nicholas II opposed the latter also, reasoning that they might prove to be breeding grounds for the germs of change which could develop into the ideas of elective representation in other areas. Within his government, the body most nearly advisory in nature was the State Council, made up of experienced and respected bureaucrats whose opinions he might—or might not—seek, and whose judgments he might—or might not—accept. The council members, appointed by the Tsar, could be depended upon to uphold autocracy, not to limit it. To sustain this regime inviolate, the ruler, as a matter of course, opposed any movement that allowed either criticism of the existing order or united action for the purpose of changing it. Accordingly, the time-honored system persisted; only the organizations of the nobility, acting through their respective marshals, were allowed even to petition the tsar; and the evidence of four centuries of autocratic rule in Russia warned them against the imprudence of presenting political petitions.

Traditionally, the tsar exercised his power through a large and consequential bureaucracy, hierarchically organized, uniformed in grand style, and secure in positions commanding servile attention from the public. Two classes of bureaucrats were particularly powerful: the ministers, who directed the various branches of the central government; and the governors-general, governors, and prefects, who directed the chief geographical subdivisions of the empire.

The ministers sitting collectively as the Committee of Ministers, a body instituted in 1802 for the consideration of routine administrative problems, had only very limited jurisdiction; but individually they could handle the duties of their positions with considerable freedom as long as they retained the confidence of the tsar. Among them the most important was the minister of interior, whose office was concerned with many of the vital aspects of the imperial rule; it administered the provinces into which the country was divided, also the districts into which the provinces were divided; it regulated the services of the land captains, members of the nobility who controlled the local administration of peasant affairs; it supervised the work of the associations of the nobility; it operated the postal and telegraphic services, the office of the censorship, and the department of police; and it exercised veto power over the zemstvos. Whenever problems were outside the scope of ministerial routine and were of such a nature that the tsar's approval was required, he might, if he wanted to hear a discussion of them, call a meeting of the Council of Ministers. This body, established in 1857 and always presided over by the tsar, was composed of the ministers, other high officials, and special appointees of the tsar; and in it the ministers, as well as other members, were advisors only.

Extensive authority was delegated to the governors-general, governors, and prefects, each of whom was appointed by the tsar and required to report to the minister of interior. A governor-general administered a group of provinces, over which he exercised both civilian and military control; at the time of Nicholas II, there were nine of these groups, the populace in most of them being mainly non-Russian. A governor administered one of the ninety-six provinces of the empire. And a prefect administered one of the four cities specifically exempt from provincial jurisdiction: St. Petersburg, Odessa, Kerch, and Sevastopol. These officials exercised arbitrary power when the tsar, using the authority decreed by the Law of Exceptional Measures, of 1881, placed a city, province, or district under "reinforced protection," which gave its administrator limited emergency power to deal with any condition or situation that he considered a threat to law and order; or under "extraordinary protection," which extended the administrator's emergency power to include the right on his own authority to banish persons from the area, to close newspapers and factories, to arrest and fine individuals, and to prohibit any kind of private gathering. By the beginning of 1904, more than half of Russia, including most of her major cities, was under some form of "protection."

The police, subordinate to the Ministry of Interior, likewise exercised a direct and powerful control. There were political police and regular police, city police and rural police, factory police and railroad police. Nowhere in Europe were the police as numerous, as venal, or as powerful as those of Russia. Most unrestricted in their authority were the political police, consisting of the Corps of Gendarmes and the municipal security departments, which had wide discretion in apprehending, holding, and punishing persons believed to be dangerous to the political stability of the empire.

High in the ranks of those who held eminent positions in various phases of the autocratic administration were many members of the imperial family. Those who were children or grandchildren of a tsar bore the title of grand duke or grand duchess; and members of succeeding generations, the title of prince or princess of the imperial blood. With each of these titles went a munificent income, much of it derived from the extensive "appanage lands," held by the imperial family, collectively the richest landlord in the country. Although membership in the imperial family did not automatically confer power, members who had the inclination and a modicum of ability and who did not incur the displeasure of the tsar were likely to hold important positions. . . . These men, uncles and cousins of the Tsar, were powerful reinforcements of autocracy.

Oddly enough, in the midst of this staunchly autocratic Russia, there were two institutions alien to the prevailing system: the elected district and provincial zemstvos and the elected municipal dumas, the former administering schools, roads, and public health services in the countryside of thirty-three provinces; the latter administering similar services in the cities. It is true that their power was limited and that they functioned under the unfriendly control of the imperial bureaucracy; yet their very existence was at times a problem. Both were inheritances from the reign of the popular Alexander II (1855–81), and later tsars had endured their existence, knowing that it would be as impolitic to destroy them as unwise to encourage them.

When Nicholas II, at the time of his accession, learned that the zemstvos were hopeful of his extending their jurisdiction, he labeled their optimism a "senseless dream" and added: "Let all know that, in devoting all My strength in behalf of the welfare of My people, I shall defend the principles of autocracy as unswervingly as My deceased father." In that declaration, he was implicitly reaffirming the traditional and official doctrine of the tsarist state as embodied in the well-known phrase "autocracy, orthodoxy, and nationalism—a phrase held almost sacrosanct by the government and its supporters and used in conscious opposition to the spirit of the French revolutionary triad, "liberty, fraternity, and equality."

TSARIST VIEW OF SOCIETY

Complementing the Tsar's political principles was his interpretation of the scheme of Russian society. In his thinking, based on the traditional training he had received, the major divisions of society were the nobility, the peasantry, and the Orthodox Church. All were servants of the state in a relationship that was not overly complex. The nobility was the chief servant, providing the personnel for the higher ranks in civil and military affairs; the Church served by propagating the true faith and by encouraging morality and loyalty throughout the empire; and the peasantry discharged its duties by tilling the soil and fighting the wars. He looked upon all of these as genuinely loyal to throne and fatherland; but, knowing that the spirit falters when the body is weak, he felt that the state was under obligation to help the nobles maintain their landed estates, to keep the peasants from becoming landless laborers, and to protect the Church from losing the privileges it enjoyed as the embodiment of the established faith.

In general, official theory considered "the people" of the land to be Russian and rural. Yet there were within the country forty million or so non-Russians (for Russia counted among her subjects the inhabitants of Finland, Congress Poland, the Baltic provinces, Transcaucasia, Siberia, parts of Central Asia, and others of "foreign" origin) and about twenty million urban inhabitants. What of them? They were all subjects of the tsar, as Nicholas once reminded a governor who had excluded Jewish children from a patriotic procession, and they were required to be both loyal and useful; however, they were customarily accounted to be less worthy and less inclined to loyalty than were his rural Russian subjects. The areas inhabited by national minorities were considered sources of possible trouble involving particularly the issue of separatism, while the cities were adjudged havens of a rootless and turbulent proletariat. To thwart or redirect the inclinations of these two groups, the government had its special devices. Where tendencies toward separatism were observed among minority groups, the policy of Russification, based on intensive re-education emphasizing the Russian language and the Russian Orthodox religion, was employed. And efforts were made to anticipate the potential turbulence of the urban proletariat and to forestall it by paternalistic laws.

Such was the tsarist notion of a stable and secure Russia at the turn of the century. It not only shaped governmental policies but also defined reality for the chief officials and for the tsar. Unfortunately, the official view of reality and reality itself were never

entirely congruous. When he began his reign, Nicholas II, a sanguine monarchist, could see no reason that the state of apparent
calm he found in Russia should not continue. Ten years later,
however, even a sanguine monarchist could not overlook the fact
that Russia faced problems of a very serious nature. The critical
question, by that time, was whether or not these could be solved
without changing traditional policies. The Tsar thought that
they could be. He was mistaken, but he adhered to his interpretation of the situation as long as he was able. . . .

"SOCIETY" VERSUS "GOVERNMENT"

The expression of discontent among . . . [the peasants, the
nationalities, labor and the educated class] . . . were basically
symptoms of a condition . . . that marked one of the "two Russias," the one commonly called "society", made up of those among
the educated whose principles were irreconcilable with the regime's and who, by their own definition, were the spokesmen for
the *real* Russia. The other of the "two Russias" was, in popular
reference, "government."

The gulf between society and government had begun to appear
in the late eighteenth century, when certain men educated in
Western modes and ideas, having examined Russian life and
found it wanting, decided that the government was the actual bar
to progress. Later, in the comparatively halcyon days of the reforms of Alexander II, there was some promise of reconciliation
among the discordant conceptions of what was good for Russia,
but it had receded when Alexander III established a policy freez-
ing the existing order. And that was the policy on which the government was standing fast at the beginning of the twentieth
century. Meanwhile, among the educated, growing in number
and ambition, many had become alienated from, and increasingly
frustrated by, a government apparently incapable of governing
and unwilling to surrender a position it was unfit to occupy.

The spokesmen of society argued that Russia was culturally and
materially backward not because she lacked the capacity for
progress but because she lacked the freedom to realize her potential capacity. If government would only hearken to society or,
perhaps, capitulate to it, Russia could resume the journey toward

enlightenment and liberty that had been begun several times in the country's history (notably with the reforms of Peter the Great, Catherine II, Alexander I, and Alexander II) and then been interrupted.

The phrase "two Russias," identifying the opponents in the general political conflict of this period was a convenient one, and it has remained popular because of its brevity; but it should always be used with a consciousness of its limitations. Actually, there was not a clear-cut dichotomy in Russia—"society" on one hand and "government" on the other. Things-as-they-were did not conform to such a simple classification. Those among the educated who presumed to speak for all of Russian society were glossing over certain facts: the 74 percent of the population who were illiterate and the 19 percent who were barely literate were almost wholly unconcerned with the principal debate between conflicting factions; the clergy and the merchant class generally adhered to old traditions and had little interest in current trends; and a great part of the nobility was aligned by both heritage and interest with government. However, while the dichotomy itself was unreal, the belief in its existence was real; and that belief helped to sharpen differences between the government and the opposition by providing each with a definite image of itself and of its adversary. "Society" thought of itself as an idealistic fellowship of dedicated men and women struggling for truth and justice, and of the government as an organized group of bureaucrats who kept the country shackled by tradition and whose administration preserved unchanged the conditions of an outlived past. "Government, on the other hand, conceived of itself as the legitimate guardian of truth and justice, and of its opponents as a group of · addled chatterers.

The opposition kept the government conscious of the problems; but problems, even such as those facing Russia at the turn of the century, do not necessarily lead to revolution. Revolution must be born in the minds of men; its very essence is the rejection of the legitimacy of constituted authority by a large part of those subject to that authority, and rejection is psychological rather than physical. Before 1905, only the self-deceived could believe that most of the Russian people had consciously broken with tsarism. Visible evidence argued the contrary. The hundreds of thousands who joined in mass demonstrations of devotion and loyalty whenever the Tsar visited the Kremlin, officiated at public formalities, or traveled anywhere in his empire testified to the popular inclination to venerate him as if he were a divine figure. Their affection might be described by some as only skin deep, but there was no way of proving it either genuine or superficial except by tests such as war or rebellion—and those tests were yet to be made. There was evidence, however, that antipathy toward existing authority was growing; slowly among the peasantry, at a faster rate among workers as well as among some of the national minorities, and most vigorously among the educated.

It was the educated, and particularly that element among them known as the "intelligentsia," heirs of a long tradition of intellectual probing of Russian life, who were critical of, and intermittently in conflict with, tsarism. The position of the most radical among them was often stated in some paraphrase of the harsh words that one of their number, Dmitri Pisarev, had written in the 1860's:

"The dynasty of the Romanovs and the Petersburg bureaucracy must perish. . . . What is dead and rotten must of itself fall into the grave. All we still have to do is to give a last push and cover their stinking corpses with dirt."

The least radical believed that tsarism was legitimate and that it might be viable if it acted in time to rid itself of the bureaucracy and admit the people to a share in the government. In the preceding century, they had counselled patience, believing that it was the tsar's prerogative to initiate reforms and the subjects' obligation to carry out their duties in such a manner as to prove worthy of the reforms. But by 1904, even the hitherto patient were beginning to believe that reforms were past due, that time was running out for the regime.

ORGANIZED OPPOSITION TO
THE GOVERNMENT

As the fateful year of 1905 approached, the illegal opposition facing the government was, all told, greater than any in the previous history of Russia. It was led by, and to a large extent composed of, *intelligents* (as members of the intelligentsia were called): students enrolled in the universities and other institutions of higher learning, expelled students, and members of the professions. The "people" in whose name they spoke were at first poorly represented among them, but workers—and occasionally peasants—were beginning to recognize oppositional organizations as instruments capable of giving form to their discontent and strength to their aspirations.

The size of the opposition as it developed could not be taken as an accurate measure of its strength. It was divided into a bewildering variety of parties and groups—numerous enough to inspire the exaggeration that, for every Russian, there were two parties—and division is debilitating. The differences among some of these groups were clear only to the initiated. But all of them were aligned with one or the other of two opposition movements: the *revolutionary*, seeking to overthrow the regime by violence, replacing it with a democratic republic that at some future date would be supplanted by a socialist society; and the *liberal*, dedicated to the establishment of civil liberties and representative government by peaceful means.

Those in the revolutionary movement (mostly socialists but including a few anarchists) agreed on a common goal but were in such disagreement over tactics and doctrine that they became divided into two major parties, the Russian Social Democratic Labor Party and the Russian Socialist Revolutionary Party. The SD's were wedded to Marxism, with its emphasis on the leading role of the working class and the importance of mass revolutionary action. The SR's were affected by Marxism but eclectic in their philosophy. They gave the peasantry a place of importance in their program and believed that revolution could be effected in a number of ways. One of those methods, far removed from the mass action favored by the SD's was based on terrorizing the government by the assassination of its leading officials; to employ this method, they formed a special branch known as the Fighting Organization. Within each party there were factions, which disagreed over seemingly minor questions concerning tactics and organization: among the Social Democrats the factions were labeled *Bolshevik* (majority) and *Menshevik* (minority) at an early date, while the factions among the Socialist Revolutionaries were not sufficiently defined to merit names until the end of 1905 . . . .

The liberals, even before they were organized, were divided

into moderates and extremists. The moderates identified themselves from the beginning with the zemstvos (the municipal dumas, which might have been expected to favor the liberal opposition, stayed aloof until 1904). They were ably led during the period of their greatest influence by Dmitri Shipov, who between 1893 and 1904 occupied the most important zemstvo post in the country, that of Chairman of the Moscow Provincial Zemstvo Board. A member of the landed nobility and a monarchist by conviction, he was prominent among those who sought to convince the Tsar of the need for reform and of the advisability of expressing confidence in the people by permitting them to elect a national consultative assembly. Men of Shipov's conviction were committed to the use of legal means for achieving their ends. The zemstvos provided that means, and zemstvo leaders from various parts of the country often met to discuss common needs and aspirations. When the Ministry of Interior issued a ban on such meetings, in 1902, declaring them illegal because of their political nature, they were discontinued; but the idea of a national zemstvo organization survived in an organizational bureau, headed by Shipov, and was revitalized in 1904. National zemstvo meetings being prohibited, Shipov and other moderate liberals, including the Princes Peter and Paul Dolgorukov, formed a group of forty men called *Beseda* (Conversation) that met from time to time in Moscow to discuss zemstvo work and exerted an influence far greater than their limited number would suggest.

As early as 1901, the moderates among the liberals were being challenged by the extremists, who decried both the moderates' tactics and their aspirations as timid. One of the most prominent exponents of the extremists' position, Ivan Petrunkevich, had so repeatedly aroused official disfavor that for many years he had not been allowed the freedom necessary for leadership; yet there were plenty to help keep the group both prominent and vigorous. The majority of the extremists came from professional groups, though some came from the zemstvos. All of them, affected by the revolutionary example, wanted organization and action. Their first notable step was the founding, in 1901, of an illegal, liberal newspaper, *Liberation,* which was published in Germany and smuggled into Russia. It fulfilled its purpose as a means of organizing the liberals by helping to establish the Union of Liberation, which held its first congress in January, 1904. Although the

Union was designed as an organization for liberals of all kinds, it was dominated from the first by the extremists, a leader among whom was Paul Milyukov. The principal aim of the Union was the establishment of a constitutional government elected by means of what became popularly known as four-tail suffrage—universal, equal, secret, and direct.

The Union of Liberation spoke for the majority of liberals, but certainly not for all of the people. Yet, of the different organizations claiming to speak for all of the people, it had the greatest initial advantages: it represented a belief that was common to all in the opposition, that political freedom was the first step required in the regeneration of Russia; and its leaders, being dedicated to action, were more likely to be acceptable as coordinators of a general movement than were those who supported what many interpreted as temporizing tactics. This generally favored position of the Union of Liberation may be credited with the fact that the public's collective efforts to establish liberty and representative government came to be known as the "liberation movement."

The liberals' chances of success seemed slight, however, despite their organization and program. The use of force being denied by their own doctrine, they limited themselves to peaceful—though not always legal—persuasion, working through the zemstvos, professional associations, their own underground organizations, and whatever other means they might contrive to spread the idea of liberalism. Their activities, adequate as they were to keep up their spirit and hopes, did not seem strong enough to effect any change in the regime. But the liberals were not therefore convinced of any need for altering their course, their rationale being that, if "society" were sufficiently outspoken, "government" would in time be *frightened* into concession.

PLEHVE AND THE POLICY OF REPRESSION

At the beginning of 1904, however, the government was showing no signs of responding as predicted. The Tsar's most important minister, the vigorous Plehve, was keeping well informed, through his secret agents among the political police, of the extent of the oppositional movement; but he was not alarmed by it. He had changed his earlier attitude toward the opposition as well as his methods of handling it, and he felt—mistakenly, it was to be shown—that he now had it under control. When he had taken his post, two years earlier, replacing the assassinated minister Dmitri Sipyagin, he had been full of enthusiasm for his plans to solve the major problems and to eliminate the visible signs of unrest by liquidating the oppositional organizations. When he could make little headway at either, however, he had begun to rely on the repressive strength of the police state to maintain order: putting the affairs of more provinces under emergency "protection," using the powers of censorship more indiscriminately, and directing the political police to employ greater severity in quelling disorders and making arrests.

Measures such as these had silenced the opposition in the years following the assassination of Alexander II, in 1881, and had given Russia the superficial look of calm that Nicholas II had observed in 1894. But the opposition was no longer so easily intimidated by them. The two years of Plehve's tenure of office saw the rapid spread of illegal organizations, the serious outbreaks among the peasants of Kharkov and Poltava, the bitter—almost revolutionary—strikes in Transcaucasia and southern Russia, and continuing student disorders. Such evidences of unrest and the government's failure to alleviate the conditions producing them caused a greater number of "society" to feel that active opposition was legitimate, indeed necessary, under the circumstances. And their feelings came to be concentrated in hatred of Plehve, who, as Minister of Interior, was director of the state police and the symbol of "government." He was charged with gratuitous malevolence in the Kishinev pogrom of 1903, in which forty-five Jews were murdered in the presence of soldiers and police; and, although the charge was only partially justified, it was accepted by the opposition as wholly true and was used as an argument in proving that the government was lost to humanity. And some of his later official acts were to bring them to the conclusion that the government was lost to reason also.

It is easy, with the gift of hindsight, to review the situation in Russia at the beginning of 1904 and to conclude that she was on the verge of inevitable revolution; to support that conclusion with defensible evidence would be far from easy. To be sure, even if antigovernment activity reached a crest and subsided, as it had in the past, the country's critical problems would remain unsolved until the regime altered its course. How soon that point would have been reached under prevailing circumstances, however, no one can say. If Russia had not become involved in the war with Japan in 1904, affairs might have taken a different turn; but the war came, and with it a situation immediately favorable to revolution. . . .

THE SETTLEMENT

"The manifesto of October 17th meant the capitulation of Tsarist autocracy, victory over servitude, victory of law over arbitrary rule—that is, all that five generations of sensitive Russians both dreamt of and sacrificed for, by going to prison or into exile, by dying in penal servitude or on the gallows; and by their sacrifices they are transmitting as their legacy to future generations the obligation to transform Russia into a country of liberty, law, and European culture."

—Ivan Petrunkevich (liberal leader), *Iz Zapisok Obschestvennago Deyatelya, 1934.*

"So a constitution is granted [by the October Manifesto]. Freedom of assembly is granted, but the assemblies are surrounded by the military. Freedom of speech is granted, but censorship exists as before. Freedom of knowledge is granted, but the universities are occupied by troops. Inviolability of the person is granted, but the prisons are overflowing with the incarcerated. . . . A constitution is given, but the autocracy remains. Everything is given—and nothing is given."

—Leon Trotsky (Social Democrat, inclined toward the Mensheviks at the time), *Izvestiya Soveta Rabochikh Deputatov, 1905*

The Revolution of 1905 did not expunge the issues that had brought the "two Russias" into conflict; nor, at the end of it, could either claim unqualified victory or defeat on any one of them. "Government" had made some concessions, and "society" had achieved some of its aims. Their relative positions had been changed—but only to a limited degree. Whether or not, from the new positions, the two could work together to produce successful reform in Russia was the big problem that faced the country as the violence of revolution receded.

CHANGES IN POLITICAL STRUCTURE

The Tsar had accepted constricting limitations on his authority and had been forced to part with some of his reactionary ministers. But he was still in power; and the character of the officials to whom he would now turn for assistance in framing and administering the promised reforms would be very important to the final outcome of the revolution. Had Witte's efforts at conciliating "society" succeeded, new blood would have been introduced into officialdom and cooperation might have followed; but because of his failure, the government was still administered by a bureaucracy that had changed only slightly in recent years. Some of the bureaucrats, it is true, welcomed the October Manifesto as the beginning of much-needed change; but their influence was overridden by that of their conservative colleagues, whose position was continually strengthened by the need to keep in check the antigovernment agitation that persisted for many years after the revolution. On the whole, these bureaucrats were ill-equipped, both in training and conviction, to guide the creation of a new political order in which public opinion was to be recognized, and persons lacking any clear place in the bureaucratic order were to have a part in the scheme of government. Believers in "autocracy, orthodoxy, and nationalism," they were unlikely to make any great efforts to conciliate the public. The outlook for reform agreeable to those who made the revolution was obviously unfavorable. Changes were made, nevertheless; and they were significant ones.

The October Manifesto declared that Russia's autocratic government was to be transformed, and it was transformed in some respects. But the resulting political structure is difficult to classify. Using a Western European label, one might say, with reservations, that it was a constitutional parliamentary monarchy. Western labels, however, are not entirely adequate for a comprehensible definition of the form of government finally set up after the Revolution of 1905. That fact is illustrated by the change of the Russian entry in the *Almanach de Gotha,* the yearbook of European royalty: before 1906, Russia was classified simply as an absolute monarchy; thereafter, as a constitutional monarchy ruled by an autocrat—an ambiguous classification, to say the least.

The new political structure was, in fact, a hybrid, resulting from the efforts of the Tsar and the bureaucracy to carry out the letter of the manifesto while preserving the spirit of the autocracy. It was brought into existence by the work of three special conferences held between December, 1905 and April, 1906. The personnel of each included a number of grand dukes, certain specially designated high officials, and the incumbent ministers. Their specific task was to work out the legal basis of the new order: 1) the fundamental laws defining the structure of the state and 2) the laws specifying the methods of election, the organization, and the powers of the new legislature. The only "outsiders" admitted to any of the sessions were Alexander Guchkov and Dmitri Shipov, who were invited to present their proposals for an electoral law but not permitted to participate in, nor to hear, the discussions that followed.

Even if the special conferences had been held in a period of calm, it is doubtful that the participants would have attempted to interpret the October Manifesto in a liberal sense. But deliberating as they did, when mutinies, political strikes, and agrarian disorders were daily reminders of what many of them considered the public disregard for law and order, they were even less inclined to such interpretations. Their principal aim, as it soon became evident, was to make the throne secure against encroachment by the legislature that they were committed to establish, not to provide the country with a constitution and a parliament.

This aim would be realized satisfactorily, they felt, through the type of legislature they planned. As promised in the October Manifesto, the right to vote for deputies to the Duma was broadened to include persons from all classes, and that body's consent would be requisite to the conversion of any bill into law. But the Duma was to be adjusted to the existing regime by two definite limitations. One was the result of retaining the system of indirect election and unequal suffrage. . . . Another was the setting of a curb on the Duma's legislative power: the State Council was to be vested with legislative power equal to that of the Duma, and no bill was to become law without the approval of both bodies. Nothing in the October Manifesto had suggested that the Duma would be so limited but, in the period of disturbances following October 17, the notion had been advanced and officially approved. To that end, not only was the State Council to be transformed into a legislative body, but its members were to be so chosen as to insure its being even more conservative than the Duma. Half of them were to be appointed by the Tsar; and half were to be elected by votes of the Orthodox churchmen, the nobility, the zemstvos, the university faculties, and the associations of commercial and industrial leaders. Thus were set up the first lines of defense.

But precautions did not end there. The conferences devised four additional defenses for the autocrat. One accorded him the right of absolute veto over bills passed by both legislative bodies. Another provided that he have discretionary power in matters of finance, thus seriously circumscribing the power of the legislature: if the Duma and the State Council disagreed over budgetary matters, the Tsar was free to accept the views of either body or to employ the figures of earlier budgets. A third gave him the authority to issue emergency laws between legislative sessions, and to enforce them until such time as the legislature could meet and approve or disapprove them.

The fourth additional defense was a particularly vital one from the standpoint of an autocrat. It was that which limited the power of the legislature over the executive branch of the government. Provision was made that ministers could be interpellated by the legislature; but, aside from the use of its limited budgetary power as a means of influence, it had no further power over the executive. The Tsar remained firmly in control of the executive branch. He appointed and removed ministers. He exercised supreme command over the armed forces. He appointed administrative officials and judges. He retained the right to issue ukases. He could place areas under reinforced protection, extraordinary protection, or martial law, thus depriving persons in these areas of some or all of their civil liberties. He was still the defender of the Orthodox Church—in actuality, its ruler. He maintained exclusive control over foreign affairs, in-

cluding the right to make treaties and to declare war. And he still
had exclusive control over all administrative machinery.

The basic nature of the new political structure was made
manifest in the revised Fundamental Laws, as they were worked
out by the special conference of April, 1906 and approved by
the Tsar. And the legislature was accorded no power to change
that structure except by the Tsar's consent. In fact, it was de-
barred not only from changing the Fundamental Laws but also
from discussing them. They were to serve, in a sense, as the "constitution" of the new Russia, defining both the nature of the
legislature and certain essential features of the state. . . .

After all the work of the three special conferences, one vexa-
tious question remained to be answered: whether or not a ruler
could be an autocratic monarch and, at the same time, a constitutional monarch. Nicholas II believed that he had not granted
a constitution and that he remained an autocrat. Some of his
ministers and most of his subjects believed that he had granted
a constitution and that the term "autocrat" was simply a historical vestige of the kind that the British monarchy cherished.
Arguments could be marshaled on each side; but the decision
was to be derived from actuality, not from law or logic. Russia
had a constitution of sorts in the revised Fundamental Laws; she
had a legislature of sorts in the Duma and the State Council;
and she had civil liberties fairly broad in principle but somewhat circumscribed by law and practice. In short, she had the
beginnings of a constitutional, parliamentary system. Whether
or not this system could fulfill its limited promise was to depend
on the Tsar, the bureaucracy, the people, and the accidents of
history. . . .

THE "TWO RUSSIAS"

The Revolution of 1905 opened up the prospect of evolution
toward a state of equilibrium between the "two Russias." Before
that prospect could be realized, however, old animosities would
have to fade away, and "government" and "society" would have
to become adjusted to the art of government by consent. Like
the reforms among the peasants, these changes could be brought

about only during a prolonged period free from major crises. But the outlook for such a period was not promising; reactions on both sides indicated that the settlement would provide, at best, a breathing space. And that, only because, on the one hand, the disunity and inexperience among the elements of the revolutionary movement would impede it for the time being; and, on the other, the strength and resilience of the government would help it retain its position of superiority for the time being.

The opponents, during this period of truce, would be unlikely to move any appreciable distance from their embattled positions. The government, inexperienced in the conduct of representative processes and with little propensity for acquiring the necessary experience, would not feel the need for further change as long as it retained the strong support of the extreme right, made up of men who favored the throne but not the ideas embodied in the October Manifesto. Nor would the opposition, lacking experience in cooperation with the government and including in its ranks many who had no desire to learn, be likely to alter its position greatly.

There were many who had no intention of allowing the spirit of the revolution to die. The socialists, for instance, steeped in hatred for the old regime and accustomed to underground operations, had no thought of trying to make the settlement succeed. For them, the uprising had been an incomplete initial operation, to be followed by a future and concluding act of the "bourgeois-democratic" revolution. They treated the victories that had been won simply as new opportunities to advance their preparations for the next revolution, and studied the history of 1905 for lessons to guide them in the future. . . .

The Cadets, the chief liberal party, no longer flirted with revolution, but their program and their methods made cooperation with the government difficult, if not impossible. They insisted on the need for ministerial responsibility, the four-tail suffrage, national rights for minorities, decentralization of government, and a fairly radical agrarian reform. Since the government rejected these conditions out of hand and the Cadets refused to recognize any need for compromise, there was no position for the party to assume in the legislature but that of a bitter oppositional element.

As for the moderate liberals, who recognized the October

Manifesto as an acceptable basis for future cooperation between people and government, they had only a secondary part in post-revolutionary political life. Though they unified and organized their efforts in the Union of October 17 (or Octobrist Party), their influence was quite limited. They won only 38 of the 497 seats in the first Duma; and even when their representation was increased, after June, 1907, their gain was the result of change in the electoral system, not of any marked increase in their popular support. The negligible showing made by these proponents of moderate political views indicated the extent to which Russia was still divided between political extremes.

The Revolution of 1905 had provided the *means* for finding a middle ground between the two extremes, but it had not created an atmosphere favorable to those who sought to find it.

CHAPTER III

KEY DOCUMENTS
OF THE CONSTITUTIONAL PERIOD
OF RUSSIAN HISTORY

The following documents evoke the basic characteristics of Russian constitutionalism after 1905 and the gradual deterioration of the system. The October Manifesto marks the high tide of the revolutionary movement and the maximum concessions of the government in granting a representative and legislative Duma without the consent of which no law might go into force. Witte's report to the Emperor advances the compelling reasons why these concessions had to be made by the regime if Russia were to avoid political disintegration. The excerpts from the Fundamental Laws of 1906 illustrate how the government was already going back on its word once the tide of revolution began to ebb. In particular, the powers of the Duma were restricted, an upper house of the parliament was created, the emperor retained an absolute veto over legislation, and the authority of the autocracy was preserved in wide spheres of government activity. On the other hand, the defeat by the First Duma of Stakhovich's motion to condemn political assassinations shows the bitter feelings of the opposition movement to the repressive moves of the government. The government's reply to the address to the throne, the speeches by Nabokov and Rodichev, and the Duma's formula of passage also illustrate the unbridgeable gap between the First Duma and the government. Stolypin's statements to the Second Duma reveal the strength and determination of this statesman to implement positive policies in the face of any opposition. The June manifesto and Stolypin's declarations to the Third Duma exemplify the resurgence of conservatism, the narrowing of the representative character of the Duma, and the general political shift in Russia to the right. Guchkov's formula of passage and speeches on the

31

naval and military estimates of 1908 show how the leader of the large central party in the conservative Third Duma attempted to cooperate with the government on the basis of patriotism and essential institutional reforms. His speech in 1913, however, reveals his disillusionment at the failure of his policy and his pessimism with the government's reaction, apathy, and practical paralysis.

A. The October Manifesto

B. Most Humble Report of State Secretary Count Witte, October 1905

C. Selections from the Fundamental Laws

D. Stakhovich's Speech on Terrorism, May 4, 1906

E. The Government's Reply to the Address to the Throne of the First Duma, and the Speeches on this Reply by Vladimir Nabokov and Feodor Rodichev, May 13, 1906

F. Formula of Passage to the Next Business upon the Declaration of the Council of Ministers in the First State Duma, May 13, 1906

G. Stolypin's Government Declarations to the Second State Duma, March 6, 1907

H. The Imperial Manifesto of June 3, 1907

I. Stolypin's Government Declarations to the Third State Duma, November 16, 1907

J. Guchkov's Formula of Passage to the Next Business upon the Declaration of the Chairman of the Council of Ministers in the Third State Duma, November 16, 1907

K. Speeches on the Naval and Military Estimates of 1908 by Alexander Guchkov, May 24 and 27

L. The General Political Situation and the Octobrist Party. Speech delivered by Alexander Guchkov at the 1913 Conference of the Octobrist Party in St. Petersburg

A. FROM *The October Manifesto*

By the grace of God, We, Nicholas II, Emperor and Autocrat of All the Russias, Tsar of Poland, Grand Duke of Finland, etc., etc., etc., declare to all Our loyal subjects:

Disturbances and unrest in the capitals and in many places of Our Empire fill Our heart with a great and painful grief. The welfare of the Russian Sovereign is indissolubly bound to the welfare of the people, and their grief is His grief. Out of the present disturbances there may grow a serious popular disorder and a threat to the integrity and unity of Our Empire.

The great oath of Imperial service requires that, with all the force of Our intelligence and authority, and as quickly as possible, We bring to an end disturbances perilous to the state. Having ordered the appropriate authorities to take steps against open acts of disorder, riot, and violence, so as to protect peaceful persons who seek quietly to perform their duty, We, in order to carry out the general policies outlined by Us for quieting the life of the nation, have found it necessary to unify the activities of the central government.

We make it the duty of the government to execute Our firm will:

1) to grant the people the unshakable foundations of civic

SOURCE. Sidney Harcave, *The Russian Revolution of 1905* (New York: The Macmillan Company, 1964), pp. 195–196, 289–292.

freedom on the basis of genuine personal inviolability, freedom of conscience, speech, assembly, and association;

2) to admit immediately to participation in the State Duma, without suspending the scheduled elections and in so far as it is feasible in the brief period remaining before the convening of the Duma, those classes of the population that are now completely deprived of electoral rights, leaving the further development of the principle of universal suffrage to the new legislative order;

and 3) to establish as an inviolable rule that no law may go into force without the consent of the State Duma and that the representatives of the people must be guaranteed the opportunity of effective participation in the supervision of the legality of the actions performed by Our appointed officials.

We call on all faithful sons of Russia to remember their duty to their Fatherland, to assist in putting an end to these unprecedented disturbances, and to exert with Us all their power to restore quiet and peace to Our native land.

Issued at Peterhof on October 17th, in the year of Our Lord 1905, and in the eleventh year of Our Reign.

The original text signed in His Imperial Majesty's own hand.

Nicholas

B. FROM *Most Humble Report of State Secretary Count Witte, October 1905*

Your Imperial Majesty has been kind enough to give me Your Imperial Majesty's directives with respect to the policy that the government should follow in studying the present situation in Russia and, in this connection, to instruct me to present a most humble report.

SOURCE. Sidney Harcave, *The Russian Revolution of 1905* (New York: The Macmillan Company, 1964), pp. 195–196, 289–292.

Therefore, I have the honor of most humbly presenting the following:

The unrest that has seized the various classes of the Russian people cannot be regarded as the product of the partial imperfections of the political or social order or as the product of the activities of organized extremist parties. The roots of unrest are deeper: they are to be found in the disparity between the high-minded aspirations of Russian intellectual society and the framework within which it exists. Russia has outgrown her political framework and is striving for a legal order based on civil liberty.

Therefore, the framework of Russian political life must be changed to make it conform to the ideas that animate the moderate majority of society. The first task of the government is to fulfill the wish for the establishment of a legal order based on personal inviolability and the freedom of press, conscience, assembly, and association; and to do it immediately, without waiting for the legislative sanction of the State Duma. Normal legislative prodecure should be employed in strengthening these foundations of the political life of society, as well as in the work of making all Your Imperial Majesty's subjects equal before the law, irrespective of religion or nationality. It goes without saying that the civil liberties granted to the people must be limited by law so as to safeguard the rights of all persons and the peace and security of the state.

Another task facing the government is that of establishing those institutions and legislative principles that are in accord with the political ideals of the majority of Russian society, at the same time providing a positive guarantee that the blessings of civil liberty so granted shall not be alienated: this means the establishment of a legal order. In keeping with the aims of reestablishing peace and security in the body politic, the economic policy of the government should be directed toward the good of the masses and, at the same time, safeguarding those property and civil rights that are recognized in all civilized countries.

The aforementioned bases of governmental policy will require much legislative work and consistent administrative reorganization. It is evident that some time must elapse between the statement of a principle—even though sincerely stated—and its transformation into law, and that even more time must elapse before the new legislative standards become part of the habits of society and of the practices of governmental officials. The principles of a legal order can be activated only to the extent that the population becomes accustomed to them and acquires civic responsibility. And no government can overnight prepare a country of 135 million people, of varying origins, living under a most complex administration, and educated in various ways to recognize and adopt the principles of a legal order. The government must not only proclaim the idea of civil liberty; it must also work diligently and show unremitting firmness and consistency if it is to establish order in the land.

To accomplish its aims, the government must be uniform in its composition and unified in the pursuit of its objectives; a ministry consisting, insofar as possible, of persons having similar political convictions, should do its utmost to insure that the ideas animating its work are the ideas of all other government officials also, from the lowest to the highest. The government should, by its practices, promote the realization of civil liberty. The situation demands that the government use methods that will demonstrate its candor and sincerity; it should scrupulously refrain from interfering in the elections to the State Duma; and it should, among other things, sincerely seek to implement the measures outlined in the ukase of December 12.

With respect to the future State Duma, the government must be careful to support that body's prestige, to show confidence in its work, and to give it proper status. The government should not oppose the Duma's decisions as long as they are not basically alien to Russia's millenial grandeur—an incredible likelihood. The government should be guided by the thoughts expressed by Your Imperial Majesty in the Manifesto concerning the formation of the State Duma: that the regulations regarding that body can be altered in the future if imperfections appear or if the times pose new demands. In clarifying and settling these matters, the government should definitely be guided by the ideas of the majority of society and not by reverberations of demands, however sharply put, made by isolated groups—demands that cannot be met because they are constantly changing. But it is imperative to satisfy the wishes of the broad groups of society by means of formal enactment of civil rights and the establishment of a legal order.

It is most important to reform the State Council so as to make possible the prominent participation in it of an elected element; only in this way will it be possible to establish normal relations between this institution and the State Duma.

Without listing specific measures, which should be left to the future as circumstances change, I suggest that the state be guided at all levels by the following principles:

1. frankness and sincerity in extending the benefits of civil liberty to all walks of life and in enacting guarantees of such liberty;

2. the aim of eliminating exceptional legislation;

3. coordination of the activities of all organs of government;

4. elimination of repressive measures against activities that clearly do not threaten society and the state; and

5. counter-measures, based on law and in harmony with the ideas of the moderate majority of society, against activities that do clearly threaten society and the state.

It is evident that the abovementioned tasks can be carried out only through extensive and active cooperation with society and under conditions of calm that will permit concentration on fruitful work. We must have faith in the political sense of Russian society and believe that it does not want anarchy, with its attendant threat of the horrors of strife and political disintegration.

C. FROM *The Fundamental Laws*

---

1. The Russian state is unified and indivisible.

2. The Grand Duchy of Finland, while comprising an inseparable part of the Russian state, is governed in its internal affairs by special decrees based on special legislation.

3. The Russian language is the official state language and its use is obligatory in the Army, the Fleet, and in all state and public

SOURCE. *Imperial Russia: A Source Book, 1700–1917,* edited by Basil Dmytryshyn, pp. 317–324. Copyright © 1967 by Holt, Rinehart and Winston, Inc. Reprinted by permission of Holt, Rinehart and Winston, Inc.

institutions. The use of local languages and dialects in state and public institutions is determined by special laws.

CHAPTER I.   THE ESSENCE OF THE SUPREME AUTOCRATIC POWER

4.   The All-Russian Emperor possesses the supreme autocratic power. Not only fear and conscience, but God himself, commands obedience to his authority.

5.   The person of the Sovereign Emperor is sacred and inviolable.

6.   The same supreme autocratic power belongs to the Sovereign Empress, should the order of succession to the throne pass to a female line; her husband, however, is not considered a sovereign; except for the title, he enjoys the same honors and privileges reserved for the spouses of all other sovereigns.

7.   The Sovereign Emperor exercises the legislative authority jointly with the State Council and the State Duma.

8.   The Sovereign Emperor enjoys the legislative initiative in all legislative matters. The State Council and the State Duma may examine the Fundamental State Laws only on his initiative.

9.   The Sovereign Emperor approves laws; and without his approval no legislative measure can become law.

10.   The Sovereign Emperor possesses the administrative power in its totality throughout the entire Russian state. On the highest level of administration his authority is direct; on subordinate levels of administration, in conformity with the law, he determines the degree of authority or subordinate branches and officials who act in his name and in accordance with his orders.

11.   As supreme administrator, the Sovereign Emperor, in conformity with the existing laws, issues decrees for the organization and functioning of diverse branches of state administration as well as directives essential for the execution of the laws.

12.   The Sovereign Emperor alone is the supreme leader of all foreign relations of the Russian state with foreign countries. He also determines the direction of foreign policy of the Russian state.

13.   The Sovereign Emperor alone declares war, concludes peace, and negotiates treaties with foreign states.

14.   The Sovereign Emperor is the Commander-in-Chief of the

Russian Army and of the Fleet. He possesses supreme command over all the land and sea forces of the Russian state. He determines the organization of the Army and of the Fleet, and issues decrees and directives dealing with: the distribution or the armed forces, their transfer to a war footing, their training, the duration of service by various ranks of the Army and of the Fleet, and all other matters related to the organization of the armed forces and the defense of the Russian state. As supreme administrator, the Sovereign Emperor determines limitation on the rights of residence and the acquisition of immovable property in localities that have fortifications and defensive positions for the Army and the Fleet.

15. The Sovereign Emperor has the power to declare martial law or a state of emergency in localities.

16. The Sovereign Emperor has the right to coin money and to determine its physical appearance.

17. The Sovereign Emperor appoints and dismisses the Chairman of the Council of Ministers, Ministers, and Chief administrators of various departments, as well as other officials whose appointment or dismissal has not been determined by law.

18. As supreme administrator the Sovereign Emperor determines the scope of activity of all state officials in accordance with the needs of the state.

19. The Sovereign Emperor grants titles, medals and other state distinctions as well as property rights. He also determines conditions and procedure for gaining titles, medals, and distinctions.

20. The Sovereign Emperor directly issues decrees and instructions on matters of property that belongs to him as well as on those properties that bear his name and which have traditionally belonged to the ruling Emperor. The latter cannot be bequeathed or divided and are subject to a different form of alienation. These as well as other properties are not subject to levy or collection of taxes.

21. As head of the Imperial Household, the Sovereign Emperor, in accordance with Regulations on the Imperial Family, has the right to issue regulations affecting princely properties. He also determines the composition of the personnel of the Ministry of the Imperial Household, its organization and regulation, as well as the procedure of its administration.

22. Justice is administered in the name of the Sovereign

Emperor in courts legally constituted, and its execution is also carried out in the name of His Imperial Majesty.

23. The Sovereign Emperor has the right to pardon the accused, to mitigate the sentence, and even to completely forgive transgressions; including the right to terminate court actions against the guilty and to free them from trial and punishment. Stemming from royal mercy, he also has the right to commute the official penalty and to generally pardon all exceptional cases that are not subject to general laws, provided such actions do not infringe upon civil rights or the legally protected interests of others.

24. Decrees and commands that are issued directly or indirectly by the Sovereign Emperor as supreme administrator are implemented either by the Chairman of the Council of Ministers, or a subordinate minister, or a department head, and are published by the Governing Senate.

CHAPTER II.   THE ORDER OF SUCCESSION TO THE THRONE

25. The Imperial Throne of all the Russias is hereditary in the now happily reigning Imperial House.

26. The Thrones of the Kingdom of Poland and the Grand Duchy of Finland are indivisible with the Imperial Throne of all the Russias.

CHAPTER VIII.   RIGHTS AND OBLIGATIONS OF RUSSIAN SUBJECTS

69. Conditions for acquiring rights of Russian citizenship, as well as its loss are determined by law.

70. The defense of the Throne and of the Fatherland is a sacred obligation of every Russian subject. The male population, irrespective of social status, is subject to military service determined by law.

71. Russian subjects are obliged to pay legally instituted taxes and dues and also to perform other obligations determined by law.

72. No one shall be subjected to persecution for a violation of the law except as prescribed by the law.

73. No one can be detained for investigation otherwise than prescribed by law.

74. No one can be tried and punished other than for criminal acts considered under the existing criminal laws, in force during the perpetration of these acts, provided newly enacted laws do not exclude the perpetrated criminal acts from the list of crimes.

75. The dwelling of every individual is inviolable. Breaking into a dwelling without the consent of the owner and search and seizure are allowed only in accordance with the legally instituted procedures.

76. Every Russian subject has the right to freely select his place of dwelling and profession, to accumulate and dispose of property, and to travel abroad without any hindrance. Limits on these rights are determined by special laws.

77. Private property is inviolable. Forcible seizure of immovable property, should state or public need demand such action, is permissible only upon just and decent compensation.

78. Russian subjects have the right to organize meetings that are peaceful, unarmed, and not contrary to the law. The law determines the conditions of meetings, rules governing their termination, as well as limitations on places of meetings.

79. Within the limits determined by law everyone can express his thoughts orally or in writing, as well as distribute these thoughts through publication or other means.

80. Russian subjects have the right to organize societies and unions for purposes not contrary to the law. Conditions for organization of societies and unions, their activity, terms and rules for acquiring legal rights as well as closing of societies and unions, is determined by law.

81. Russian subjects enjoy freedom of religion. Terms to enjoy this freedom are determined by law.

82. Foreigners living in Russia enjoy the rights of Russian subjects, with limitations established by law.

83. Exceptions to the rules outlined in this chapter include localities where martial law is declared or where there exist exceptional conditions that are determined by special laws.

CHAPTER IX.   LAWS

84. The Russian Empire is governed by firmly established laws that have been properly enacted.

85. Laws are obligatory, without exception, for all Russian subjects and foreigners living within the Russian state.

86. No new law can be enacted without the approval of the State Council and the State Duma, and it shall not be legally binding without the approval of the Sovereign Emperor.

87. Should extraordinary circumstances demand, when the State Duma is not in session, and the introduction of a measure requires a properly constituted legal procedure, the Council of Ministers will submit such a measure directly to the Sovereign Emperor. Such a measure cannot, however, introduce any changes into the Fundamental Laws, or to the organization of the State Council or the State Duma, or to the rules governing elections to the Council or to the Duma. The validity of such a measure is terminated if the responsible minister or the head of a special department fails to introduce appropriate legislation in the State Duma during the first two months of its session upon reconvening, or if the State Duma or the State Council should refuse to enact it into law.

88. Laws issued especially for certain localities or segments of the population are not made void by a new law unless such a voiding is specifically intended.

89. Every law is valid for the future, except in those cases where the law itself stipulates that its force is retroactive or where it states that its intent is to reaffirm or explain the meaning of a previous law.

90. The Governing Senate is the general depository of laws. Consequently, all laws should be deposited in the Governing Senate in the original or in duly authorized lists.

91. Laws are published for general knowledge by the Governing Senate according to established rules and are not legally binding before their publication.

92. Legal decrees are not subject to publication if they were issued in accordance with the rules of the Fundamental Laws.

93. Upon publication, the law is legally binding from the time stipulated by the law itself, or, in the case that such a time is omitted, from the day on which the Senate edition containing the published law is received locally. The law itself may stipulate that telegraph or other media of communication be used to transmit it for execution before its publication.

94. The law cannot be repealed otherwise than by another

law. Consequently, until a new law repeals the existing law, the old law retains fully its force.

95. No one can be excused for ignorance of the law once it is duly published.

96. Regulations governing combat, technical, and supply branches of the Armed Forces, as well as rules and orders to institutions and authorized personnel of the military and naval establishments are, as a rule, submitted directly to the Sovereign Emperor upon review by the Military and Admiralty Councils, provided that these regulations, rules, and orders affect primarily the above mentioned establishments, do not touch on matters of general laws, and do not call for new expenditures from the treasury; or, if they call for new expenditure, are covered by expected savings by the Military or Naval Ministries. In cases where the expected saving is insufficient to cover the projected expenditure, submission of such regulations, rules, and orders for the Emperor's approval is permitted only upon first requesting, in a prescribed manner, the necessary appropriation.

97. Regulations governing military and naval courts are issued in accordance with Regulations on Military and Naval Codes.

CHAPTER X. THE STATE COUNCIL, STATE DUMA, AND THE SCOPE OF THEIR ACTIVITY

98. The Sovereign Emperor, by a decree, annually convenes the session of the State Council and the State Duma.

99. The Sovereign Emperor determines by a decree the length of the annual session of the State Council and of the State Duma, as well as the interval between the sessions.

100. The State Council is composed of members appointed by His Majesty and of elected members. The total number of appointed members of the Council called by the Emperor to deliberate in the Council's proceedings cannot exceed the total number of the elected members of the Council.

101. The State Duma consists of members elected by the population of the Russian Empire for a period of five years, on the basis of rules governing elections to the Duma.

102. The State Council examines the credentials of its members. Equally, the State Duma examines the credentials of its members.

103. The same person cannot serve simultaneously as a member of the State Council and as a member of the State Duma.

104. The Sovereign Emperor, by a decree, can replace the elected membership of the State Council with new members before its tenure expires. The same decree sets new elections of members of the State Council.

105. The Sovereign Emperor, by a decree, can dissolve the State Duma and release its members from their five-year tenure. The same decree must designate new elections to the State Duma and the time of its first session.

106. The State Council and the State Duma have equal rights in legislative matters.

107. The State Council and the State Duma enjoy the constitutional right to submit proposals to repeal or to amend the existing laws as well as to issue new laws, except the Fundamental Law whose review belongs exclusively to the Sovereign Emperor.

108. The State Council and the State Duma have a constitutional right to address questions to Ministers and heads of various departments, who legally are under the jurisdiction of the Governing Senate, on matters that stem from violations of laws by them or by their subordinates.

109. The jurisdiction of the State Council and of the State Duma includes those matters that are listed in the Rules of the Council and of the Duma.

110. Those legislative measures that are considered and approved by the State Duma are then submitted to the State Council for its approval. Those legislative measures that have been initiated by the State Council are reviewed by the Council and, upon approval, are submitted to the Duma.

111. Legislative measures that have been rejected either by the State Council or by the State Duma are considered defeated.

112. Those legislative measures that have been initiated either by the State Council or by the State Duma [and approved by both], but which have failed to gain Imperial approval, cannot be re-submitted for legislative consideration during the same session. Those legislative measures that have been initiated by either the State Council or by the State Duma and are rejected by either one of the Chambers, can be resubmitted for legislative consideration during the same session, provided the Emperor agrees to it.

113. Legislative measures that have been initiated in and approved by the State Duma and then by the State Council, equally as the legislative measures initiated and approved by the State Council and then by the State Duma, are submitted by the Chairman of the State Council to the Sovereign Emperor.

114. Deliberations on the state budget [by the State Council and/or by the State Duma] cannot exclude or reduce the set sums for the payment of state debts or other obligations assumed by the Russian state.

115. Revenues for the maintenance of the Ministry of the Imperial Household, including institutions under its jurisdiction that do not exceed the allocated sum of the state budget for 1906, are not subject to review by either the State Council or the State Duma. Equally not subject to review are such changes in specific revenues as stem from decisions based on Regulations of the Imperial Family that have resulted from internal reorganizations.

116. If the state budget is not appropriated before the appropriation deadline, the budget that had been duly approved in the preceding year will remain in force with only such changes as have resulted from those legislative measures that became laws after the budget was approved. Prior to publication of the new budget, on the decision of the Council of Ministers and rulings of Ministries and Special Departments, necessary funds will be gradually released. These funds will not exceed in their totality during any month, however, one-twelfth of the entire budgetary expenditures.

117. Extraordinary budgetary expenditures for war-time needs and for special preparations preceding a war are unveiled in all departments in accordance with existing law on the decision of highest administration.

118. State loans to cover both the estimated and non-estimated expenditures are contracted according to the system established to determine state budgetary revenues and expenditures. State loans to cover expenditures in cases foreseen in Article 74, as well as loans to cover expenditures stipulated in Article 75, are determined by the Sovereign Emperor as supreme administrator. Time and conditions to contract state loans are determined on the highest level of government.

119. If the State Duma fails to act on a proposal submitted to it reasonably in advance on the number of men needed for the

Army and the Fleet, and a law on this matter is not ready by May 1, the Sovereign Emperor has the right to issue a decree calling to military service the necessary number of men, but not more than the number called the preceding year.

CHAPTER XI. COUNCIL OF MINISTERS, MINISTERS, AND HEADS OF VARIOUS DEPARTMENTS

120. By law, the Council of Ministers is responsible for the direction and coordination of activities of Ministers and Heads of various departments on matters affecting legislation as well as the highest state administration.

121. Ministers and Heads of various departments have the right to vote in the State Council and in the State Duma only if they are members of these institutions.

122. Binding resolutions, instructions, and decisions issued by the Council of Ministers, and Ministers and Heads of various departments, as well as by other responsible individuals entitled by law, should not be contrary to existing laws.

123. The Chairman of the Council of Ministers, Ministers, and Heads of various departments, are responsible to the Sovereign Emperor for state administration. Each individual member is responsible for his actions and decisions.

124. For official misconducts in office, the Chairman of the Council of Ministers, Ministers and Heads of various departments are subject to civil and criminal punishment established by law.

D.   FROM   *Michael Stakhovich*
On Terrorism, May 4, 1906

In its answer to the Speech from the Throne, the Duma appealed to the Emperor for a complete liquidation of political offences; the concluding words were: "Sire, the Duma expects

SOURCE. *The Russian Review*, **II**, No. 3 (1913), pp. 154–161.

from you a complete political amnesty, as the first pledge of a reciprocal understanding and accord between the Tsar and the people." This amnesty was to cover all "acts coming under the criminal law, which had been prompted by religious or political motives, and also all agrarian offences." Mr. Michael Stakhovich spoke both against the form of the Address and in particular against asking for amnesty without at the same time censuring, without exception, all violent methods of political action.

Mr. Michael Stakhovich is a country gentleman of the province of Orel, and was an intimate friend of Count Leo Tolstoy; the foundation of the Tolstoy Museum in St. Petersburg was largely due to his initiative. Mr. Stakhovich was early known as a worker in the Zemstvo, an independent and liberal-minded man, and above all as a champion of religious toleration, which he advocated in a well-known speech that brought down on him official censure. During the Reform Movement of 1904–5 he was recognised as a sincere and convincing speaker, expressing the best instincts of Slavophil thought. In the first Duma, he and Count Heyden were the two most distinguished members of the small Octobrist group.

MR. STAKHOVICH:

Yesterday I was reproached by some for speaking not for myself but for Slavophils, and at the same time by others precisely for speaking for myself and not for those peasants of the province of Orel who elected me and sent me here. To my mind, whoever mounts this tribune should indeed speak of the general welfare, but for himself, that is, in the measure of his reason and his conscience. I have not ventured to speak as representing 250,000 or 25,000,000 or finally 120,000,000 persons, as did one of the speakers yesterday, on the question of the political rights of women. Such an inspiration is beyond my strength. But since such interrogations and reproaches have been addressed to me, I have asked to speak and shall speak to-day in the name of those who elected me, and I shall repeat the instructions, the wishes which they voiced. I ought to say that I live in an isolated, quiet place where, in spite of all that has been said here, they probably have not abandoned their usual life and occupations, have not ceased to plough their fields, sow their buckwheat and millet, and are not waiting with bated breath to see whether there are to be women in the Imperial Duma, whether there is to be an Imperial Council or not.[1] When we had had our elections, and I started for St. Petersburg, the peasants did indeed see me off; and they gave me a trust: "Do your best for us; secure for us the 'remaining liberty'—that is what we here call the freedoms and rights—and try to bring about a distribution of the land, as generous as possible." I consider these wishes absolutely just; we should make declaration of them here, in all conscience, and should work for them, as I shall do at the proper time. But further, they told me what was evidently not said in other provinces and to other speakers. The peasants quite definitely instructed me: "Do not annoy the Tsar, but help him to restore quiet in the country; support him."

Thus I obey these instructions, and am not annoying the Tsar. I have insisted that we should substitute for such expressions as "demand," expressions of similar meaning but more becoming to all of us, as loyal subjects, and to the one whom we address.

As I have told you, our locality is a quiet place; we have no states of extraordinary or reinforced protection and no martial law. There were arrests, as there were everywhere, but, thank God, it did not go as far as bloodshed. But we read the newspapers, and we met people and heard from them of those horrors and brutalities which have been going on all over Russia. In this vicarious way, we felt horror and sympathy. And I am therefore firmly convinced that my electors will approve when they learn that I voted here on April 27 for full amnesty.[2] And the more I reflect on this vote, the more convinced am I that the Duma, as the representative of the people, was right in expressing itself and passing such a vote, that only a majestic measure, only a sweeping gesture of confidence and love could express the feeling

[1] The Duma, in its answer, had urged that the Imperial Council should be reorganised on a more democratic basis; the debate touched on the general question of two-chamber and one-chamber legislatures.—EDITORS.

[2] This was at the very first sitting of the Duma. The first word spoken in the first Duma was the appeal for amnesty.—EDITORS.

of a great people. That beginning on April 27 was the gesture of
the Duma as the representative of all the people. But, gentlemen,
I also understand that a beginning is not yet the whole. I know
that human life grows out of those spiritual and mental roots,
such as faith, knowledge, patriotism, which nourish it. But there
are times when, in spite of the strong roots, the wheat bends
before cold day-breaks, sultry winds, before the hail which falls
instead of the expected rain. . . . Thus may human life be subjected to outside influences, however high be its feelings of
benevolence; and in spite of the roots, it may frequently stoop
to crime. I believe that life on this world does not always keep
up with our spiritual and mental growth. I have said that we
have made a beginning; but we surely know that beside a beginning, there is a responsibility for the consequences, and the
entire responsibility here rests on the Emperor. We know that if
anything happens, the whole responsibility, I repeat, falls on him.
I point this out and I consider it my duty to remind you how
great this responsibility is. I turn to those who will remember
that ten years ago, when he was crowned, as Nicholas II., in the
Cathedral of the Assumption, with the Imperial doors open, he
took an oath to God and said:

"Lord God of my fathers and King of kings, direct, teach
and guide me in this great service put upon me. May I have
that wisdom which belongs to Thy throne; send this wisdom
from Thy Holy Heavens, that I may understand what is pleasing
before Thine eyes and what is right according to Thy commands.
Let my heart be in Thine hand. Amen."

He cannot forget this solemn pledge "to act always for the
welfare of those entrusted to him and to the glory of God, in
order, at His Day of judgment, to answer to Him without shame"
(The Sacred Coronation Ceremony, Article 36, Note 2). He knows
that here he is without responsibility, as we said so assiduously
yesterday on the point of the ministers being subordinated to us;
but he remembers that, if he is without responsibility, this does
not relieve him of that responsibility there, where not we but he
alone will answer to God for every person racked in a torture
chamber and also for every one shot in a side street. Therefore I
can understand that he rejects and does not take his decisions
as precipitously as do we who are moved by simple magnanimity.
And further, I understand that he must be helped to accept this

responsibility. We must tell him that this past enmity is horrible
in its lawlessness and long bitterness, that it has brought people
to forget love, and has made the conscience forget pity. We must
say that in this internecine war, this reciprocity of bitterness—
there is the basis for a complete amnesty. But the aim of an
amnesty is different; it is peace in the future in Russia. We are
bound to say, in completion of what we have already said, that
in this the Imperial Duma shall be to its Sovereign a *surety* and
a *support*. Together with past lawlessness must disappear crime
as a weapon of struggle and combat. No one should dare any
longer to plead his cause by bloodshed. From now on let all live,
govern, and secure their rights and those of the country, not by
force, but according to *law*—according to the regenerated Russian law, which we now share in making and for which we are all
zealous, and according to the old law of God, which four thousand
years ago thundered from Sinai and said to all and for all time,
"Thou shalt not kill!"

I therefore propose as a resolution of the Duma: Recognising
a complete amnesty for political offences, committed before the
10th of May, as an act of grace for the guilty and of justice to
those who have suffered innocently, and as an act of political
wisdom, the Imperial Duma expresses the firm hope that now,
with the establishment of a constitutional order, political assassinations and other measures of violence, which the Duma con-
demns most decisively, will cease, considering them an offence to
the moral sense of the people, and to the very idea of popular
representation. The Duma declares that it will guard with firmness and vigilance the rights of the people, and defend the inviolability of all citizens, against every abuse and violence, from
whatever source it may come. (Applause.)

Mr. Stakhovich's proposal met with vigorous opposition. Mr.
Rodichev's chief argument against any such condemnation by the
Duma of political assassination was that the Duma was a legislative body and not a pulpit, that its work was to investigate the
causes of any disorder and take measures to remedy it, and not
to issue such appeals to the conscience as that suggested by Mr.
Stakhovich. Mr. Stakhovich spoke again before the vote was
taken on his proposal:—

For a long time I have had to live and think and speak so
out of harmony with others, that I have had to defend against

the majority not only what I consider right, but also what I consider common sense, and I have known for a long time that this task is a thankless one, and that it is often futile. But I believe that this is the duty of every conscientious man, no matter to which side is secured the majority, which is often deaf because of the complacent consciousness of its strength. That is why, without hoping for sympathy, but on the principles which I expressed in my first speech, I still consider myself in duty bound to speak in the name of those who elected me. Though I do not alter what I said in the first speech, I do not reject what I have heard in reply. Much of this has been quite fair, and I would have been ready to accept it myself if it had not been presented with such exaggeration and partiality. But there is one fact which I also pointed out in my first speech: all that has just been said is what we say every day in our sittings, whenever we affirm that such and such a thing must be buried, must be stopped, that it has served its time; but I say that it is not enough to bury, always concentrating on and investigating in the past. Now we must think and speak of the future, so that it should not in any way be a repetition of the past; and I believe that if none of those who speak so well mention the future and all insist only on the past, which has been condemned by us most unanimously, it means that there is nothing to be said against my demand, and that all that is necessary is the courage to voice it. . . . I can understand that the first act, the first word of the Duma related to the sufferings and interests of those thousands who are sitting in our prisons. I can understand that we—working twelve hours out of the twenty-four—should analyse and enumerate the various crying needs, the painful wounds still fresh in the popular memory—all those questions which have lately engaged the attention of public meetings, congresses, and the newspapers. We have given all these questions the precedence not at all because politics recognise only cold reason and do not wish to recognise feeling. No, representatives of the people, we should be poor legislators if we hasten to make the reservation that from our laws and from this tribune we exclude conscience and justice. . . . My respected opponent was himself the first to make appeal from this place for love and sympathy, and on this subject, with his usual talent and eloquence, he was so convincing that we could only agree with him. We evidently agree with him, if we have voted unanimously and written these important words in our Address. We speak in this Address of the public conscience and of sympathy for those who have transgressed the law. After that, I have a right to mention those who suffer because of these crimes. I have not prepared myself to sing dithyrambics to tyrants. But I only say that we should remember those of whom we have made no mention at all.

It has been said here that there have been over ninety executions. This is terrible, and we have spoken our word on the death penalty. Now I remind you that during the last three months 288 Russian citizens have been killed and 383 wounded, and that of these 671, thirteen were high officials who may perhaps have been responsible for all those horrors of which we now speak, but 658 were policemen, coachmen, and watchmen who surely were not responsible. Gentlemen, by reason of my profession I have not had occasion to test my courage, but I was for a long time at the seat of war and saw how brave men act; and I know— there are many here who were at the war, who can confirm this —that it is easier to go into the most terrible danger, into the severest firing, it is easier to go with a rush, all at once, to torture or even death when you see them before you, than to prepare for them in the ditches and wait; it is easier to attack than to await the attack; for the latter, one must be more than brave. I have seen—and I appeal to those present for confirmation—that for such deeds one's courage must be roused; the very bravest go into this danger full of the thought that they are exposing themselves to all the harm the enemy can do them, in order not to let him reach Russia, that they are screening their country, defending their fatherland, their Tsar, and their own brothers. Representatives of the people, remember what enthusiasm and strength of spirit, what a call to the sense of duty and sacrifice are now needed in the true servants of the State. Gentlemen, imagine what these 671 men lived through daily, and not for any fixed hours, but constantly, what others must live through in that future of which some of us do not wish to speak. Every policeman, when he goes to his post, must involuntarily think that what happened on that same street to another yesterday will perhaps happen to him to-day; but he goes to his post. If he goes because he has to, because of his family, he stands there and watches and guards from a feeling of duty, faithfully serving his Tsar and his country. And have I not the right to speak here of these? Should we not voice the demand that this should no longer continue? Should we not condemn crime?

No, I am convinced that, however small may be the number of those members of the Duma who here agree with me, I am convinced that the great majority of the Russian people will say that it is time to condemn political assassinations. The Russian people will say that in the future Russia has no place for the preaching of violence and murder, that she has no place for a cult which demands living victims. The Russian people will say that this is not fighting, that it is not serving them or their welfare, that it is murder, and that they do not wish it.

Mr. Stakhovich was defeated by an overwhelming majority, and his amendment was therefore not included in the Address to the Throne. The question of condemning terrorism was again raised in the second Duma, and was one of the chief occasions of its dissolution. In the third Duma all the important parties, including the Cadets, condemned terrorism.

E. FROM *The Government's Reply to the Address to the Throne of the First Duma, and Speeches on this Reply by Vladimir Nabokov and Feodor Rodichev*

The First Duma, under the direction of the Constitutional Democratic Party and acting at first with a remarkable unanimity, desired by moral pressure, supported by public opinion to secure the recognition of its authority over the Executive. For this purpose it took its first step in its answer to the Speech from the Throne. Taking up the position of an English House of Commons, it put into its Address to the

SOURCE. *The Russian Review,* II, No. 2 (1913), pp. 165–179.

Throne a carefully chosen and almost unanimously accepted expression of the very many desires put forward on behalf of the various classes of the population. This answer it sent at first direct to the Sovereign, but was instructed to communicate it through the Minister of the Imperial Household. The Prime Minister and his colleagues in the recently formed Cabinet (the Council of Ministers) attended the Duma and delivered the answer of the Ministry.

The Prime Minister, Mr. Goremykin, had taken office on the very eve of the convocation of the first Duma, succeeding Count Witte. It was an entirely new Cabinet which was formed for the work of co-operating with the new legislative institutions. Mr. Goremykin had had long experience in the higher bureaucracy, and had already held the post of Minister of the Interior (1895–1899). He was of the old school, bound to the old *regime* by long service and by tradition, and was not a man of exceptional ability or force.

Mr. Nabokov was one of the ablest members of the first Duma. He was one of the organisers of the Constitutional Democratic Party. Son of a former Minister of Justice under Alexander II. and Alexander III., he had followed an academic career and was lecturer in Public Law in the St. Petersburg School of Jurisprudence. Disfranchised after 1905 for signing the Vyborg Appeal, he has, however, been an active force in public life as one of the publishers of the Liberal organ *Rech,* and is associated with several scientific legal journals.

Mr. Rodichev is one of the most prominent of the old Zemstvo Liberals. He was one of the delegation to present the Tver Zemstvo Address to the Throne in 1895. He had been most active in the Zemstvo movement of 1904–1905, and was one of the founders of the Cadet Party. He has been a member of all four Dumas.

THE SPEECH OF MR. GOREMYKIN, PRESIDENT OF THE COUNCIL OF MINISTERS, BEFORE THE FIRST DUMA, MAY 13, 1906

The Council of Ministers has examined the Address of the Imperial Duma presented in acknowledgment of the word of welcome which His Imperial Majesty was pleased to express to the Imperial Council and the Imperial Duma. The Council has recognised that of the desires and proposals expressed in this Address, some refer to matters of legislation, while others have to do with methods of Imperial administration.

Taking for the basis of its action the observance of strict legality, and examining in the light of this principle the considerations put forward by the Imperial Duma, the Government first of all expresses its readiness to give the fullest co-operation in the settlement of those questions raised by the Imperial Duma which do not exceed the limitations of the legislative initiative that is secured to the Duma.

Such co-operation is in complete harmony with the duty of the Government to explain to the Duma its views on those questions and to defend its proposals on each of them. The Government will give such co-operation even in the question of changing the electoral law, although on its part it does not consider that this question should be taken up for discussion for the present, as the Imperial Duma is only just entering upon its legislative work, and therefore cannot have seen clearly any need of altering the method of its composition.

With particular attention does the Council of Ministers regard the suggestions of the Duma, for the immediate satisfaction of the urgent needs of the peasant population, and for the enactment of a law which will institute equal rights for peasants with persons of other classes, for satisfying the needs of the working class, for drafting a law on universal primary education, for discovering possible means of extending the burdens of taxation over the more well-to-do sections of the population, and for reforming local administration and self-government, with consideration of the peculiar conditions in border provinces.

The Council of Ministers has attached no less significance to the suggestion of the Duma, for enacting a new law which will guarantee inviolability of person, freedom of conscience, of speech and of the press, of meeting and association, in place of the present temporary regulations, for which the substitution of permanent laws, drafted in the newly instituted legislative procedure, was provided for at the time when these regulations were issued. At the same time, the Council of Ministers feels it must state that in such legislation it is essential to arm the administrative authorities with effective means whereby, under laws which presume the peaceful course of public life, the Government shall be able to prevent abuses of the liberties granted and combat encroachments which threaten the public and the State.

With regard to the solution of the peasants' land question, as suggested by the Duma—by turning over for this purpose appanage, crown, monastery and church lands, and by the compulsory expropriation of the land of private owners, including that of peasant proprietors who have redeemed their land by purchase[1]—the Council of Ministers feels it to be its duty to announce that the solution of this question on the principles proposed by the Imperial Duma, is absolutely inadmissible.

The State cannot recognise the right to property in land for some, and at the same time take away this right from others. The State cannot refuse to admit the general right of personal ownership of land without at the same time refusing to admit the right of ownership in any other kind of property. The principle that property cannot be seized, that it is inviolate, is the corner-stone of public well-being and development the world over, and at all stages of evolution in civic life. It is the basic support of social life, without which the very existence of a State is unthinkable. The conditions of the situation do not call for the proposed measures. With the extensive and far from exhausted resources which are at the disposal of the State, and with a broad application of all legal methods at hand, the land question can without doubt be satisfactorily solved without destroying the very foundation of our State interests and without undermining the vital forces of our country.

The other proposals of a legislative character included in the Address of the Imperial Duma amount to instituting the responsibility to the representatives of the people of Ministers, who are to have the confidence of the majority of the Duma, the abolition of the Imperial Council,[2] and the repeal of the limitations on the legislative powers of the Duma, as already fixed by special regulations. The Council of Ministers does not consider that it has the right to take up these proposals, for they have to do with

---

[1] A clever corollary to the Duma proposals which showed that there were peasants who might stand to lose by such legislation.—EDITORS.

[2] The Imperial Council recently reorganised by the new Fundamental Laws on a partially elective basis, acted as the Second Chamber.—EDITORS.

radical amendments to the Fundamental Laws, which, by the force of their own provisions, are not subject to revision on the initiative of the Imperial Duma.

Lastly, with regard to the anxiety of the Imperial Duma that the principles of justice and law should be strengthened in the army and navy, the Government announces that in the troops of His Imperial Majesty these principles have long since been established on firm foundations. The present solicitude of the Sovereign Leader of the armed forces of the Empire is directed, as recent measures on this subject testify, towards bettering the material conditions in all ranks of the army and navy.[3] It will be one of the main tasks of the Government authorities and of the newly established legislative institutions to find resources for putting these measures on a broader basis.

Turning to the second category of desires expressed by the Duma—on discontinuing the application of exceptional laws and on stopping the abuses of authority of individual officials, the Council of Ministers finds that these desires touch on the field of Imperial administration, and in this field the powers of the Imperial Duma are limited to the right to interpellate Ministers and Heads of Departments for illegal acts committed by them or by persons or bodies under their authority. Independently of this, the introduction, in our country, of strict legality on the principle of order and law, is one of the chief cares of the Government, which will not fail to watch vigilantly that the acts of the different organs of administration should be constantly inspired with the same aim.

The unsatisfactory character, as pointed out by the Imperial Duma, of the exceptional laws directed towards securing public order and peace in exceptional conditions, is recognised by the Government itself. The drafting of other better laws in their place is in progress in the proper department.[4] If, in spite of the unsatisfactory character of these laws, their action has nevertheless only recently been extended to several new localities, the reason lies solely in the unceasing and at present daily murders, rob-

[3] Considerable improvements had recently been introduced in the pay and upkeep of the army.—EDITORS.

[4] Both the Ministry, which has no representatives in the Duma, and the Duma itself have the recognised right of initiating legislation.—EDITORS.

beries, and acts of violence. The chief duty of the State is to protect the life and property of peaceful inhabitants. The Council of Ministers fully recognises the burden of its responsibility to the country in this matter, but declares that so long as these signs of the disorder which has seized the country do not cease, and so long as the Government shall not have, by newly enacted laws, effective means for combating lawlessness and the violation of the fundamental principles of public and personal security—so long will the Government be obliged to employ all the legal measures now in existence.

A general political amnesty, for which the Imperial Duma has made representations, involves on the one side the pardoning of those judicially sentenced, whatever be the character of the crimes they have committed. Amnesty is the prerogative of the Sovereign Authority, which decides alone and absolutely whether the Imperial pardon for persons who have fallen into crime is in accord with the general welfare. The Council of Ministers, on its part, finds that it would not be in accord with the general welfare during the present troubled times, to pardon criminals who have participated in murders, robberies, and acts of violence.

As for persons deprived of their liberty in administrative procedure, the Council of Ministers has taken steps towards the most careful examination of the administrative orders, and the liberation of all those whose release does threaten public security, which is daily being violated by criminal attacks upon it.

Apart from these considerations on the Address of the Imperial Duma, the Council of Ministers finds it necessary to indicate now, in general outline, its immediate projects in the field of legislation.[5]

The strength of the Russian State is built first of all on the strength of its agricultural population. The well-being of our country cannot be secured so long as the necessary conditions for the prosperity and development of agricultural labour, the basis of our whole economic life, are not guaranteed. Considering, therefore, the peasant question—in view of its all-embracing public significance—as the most important now brought up for

[5] It was precisely this absence of any definite Government programme, whether in the Speech from the Throne or elsewhere, that gave a footing for the exposition of a complete programme by the Duma. Mr. Stolypin recognised the mistake made in this omission.—EDITORS.

solution, the Council of Ministers thinks that the proper care and caution are necessary in seeking ways and means for solving it. Caution is here needed to avoid any sudden shock to the conditions of the peasantry which have had a historical development of their own. But in the opinion of the Council of Ministers, the recent reform of our system of government, which has given to persons elected from the peasant population a share in the work of law-making, defines in advance the main principles of the peasant reform which is before us. Under these conditions, the distinctiveness of the peasants as a class must give way to their junction with the other classes in relation to civil law and order, administration and justice. All those limitations on the rights of ownership in communal land, which were instituted to secure the punctual liquidation of the redemption debt, must also disappear.[6]

The giving to the peasant of equal civil and political rights with the other classes should not, however, deprive the State of the right[7] and obligation to show particular solicitude for the needs of the peasant agriculturists. Measures in this field should be directed toward improving the conditions of peasant land tenure within its existing limits, and toward increasing the area of land of that portion of the population which has insufficient land, at the expense of unoccupied crown lands and by obtaining possession of land of private owners through the Peasant Land Bank.

The field of work which here presents itself to the public authorities is extensive and fruitful. The improvement of conditions of agriculture, which are now at a very low level of development, will increase the measure of productiveness of the country, and thus raise the standard of general well-being. Vast expanses of land suitable for cultivation now lie unoccupied in the Asiatic possessions of the Empire. The development of migra-

[6] So far the Government had stood for the isolation and distinctiveness of the peasant class, and the Liberals were believed to oppose the communal system. The Cadets, under the influence of parties of the Left, were now prepared to maintain in principle communal ownership; and the Government was prepared to abolish it. The arrears of the redemption debt had been finally remitted in January, 1907.—EDITORS.

[7] The Government refuses to let the care for the welfare of the peasants become in any sense a monopoly of the Duma.—EDITORS.

tion will, therefore, be one of the most immediate tasks of the Council of Ministers.

Recognising the urgent need of raising the mental and moral level of the mass of the population by developing education, the Government is preparing, in accord with the wishes on this subject expressed by the Imperial Duma, projects for universal primary instruction, which will provide for an extensive participation of the public in the work of education. Solicitous also for the proper organisation of secondary and higher education, the Council of Ministers will introduce in the near future, for examination by the Imperial Duma, a plan to reform secondary schools, which will give wide scope to public and private initiative in this work, and also a project of reform for institutions of higher education, based on the principle of self-government.

Convinced that the moral regeneration of Russia, initiated by His Majesty the Emperor, cannot be realised without the introduction of true principles of legality and order, the Council of Ministers puts forward as of the first importance the question of local law courts, and their organisation on such foundations as shall bring justice close to the people, shall simplify the judicial system and make the procedure rapid and inexpensive.

Together with the drafted project of local law courts, the Council of Ministers will introduce in the Duma projects of amendment to the existing provisions for the civil and criminal responsibility of public officials. These projects start from the idea that the sense of the sacredness and inviolability of law can only take root in the population if it is linked with the assurance that the law cannot be broken with impunity, either by the people or by the representatives of authority.[8]

With the aim of securing as far as possible entire equality in the distribution of the burden of taxation, the Council of Ministers proposes to introduce for the consideration of the legislature a plan of income tax, an amendment of the death duties and document fees, and a revision of certain classes of indirect taxes.

Finally, among the legislative proposals which have been prepared, the Council of Ministers wishes to mention a project to revise the passport regulations, which abolishes the present passports and certificates of domicile.

---

[8] Almost a repetition of the famous Address of the Tver Zemstvo in 1895, for which Mr. Rodichev was expelled from St. Petersburg.—EDITORS.

In conclusion, the Council of Ministers feels called on to state that, while recognising the great importance of the measures directed toward renovating our laws on the principles of the Imperial Manifesto of October 17, 1905, the Government nevertheless is convinced that the strength of the State, its power abroad and its internal force, really rest on a strong and effective executive authority, acting according to law. The Government intends constantly to give evidence of such an authority, knowing that it carries the responsibility to the Monarch and the Russian people for the maintenance of public order. The Council of Ministers is confident that the Imperial Duma, in the conviction that the peaceful progress of the Russian Empire depends on the reasonable blending of freedom and of order, will help it, by calm and productive work, to introduce in all strata of the population that pacification which is so necessary to the country.

THE PRIME MINISTER WAS IMMEDIATELY FOLLOWED BY MR. NABOKOV

Though the newspapers in the last few days have prepared us for what we have heard to-day, nevertheless I think I am expressing the general feeling of the Duma if I say that it is one of profound disillusionment and complete dissatisfaction. When, several weeks ago, the Cabinet of Count Witte resigned, this resignation of an entire Ministry,[9] on the eve of the opening of the Imperial Duma, could have no other meaning than that from now onward the Government was resolved to take a new line, that the new Ministers would give up old watchwords and were determined to enter on a constitutional course. It seems that we were mistaken, and public opinion has shared our mistake; we do not have the beginnings of a constitutional Ministry; we have the same old bureaucratic watchwords, and at the same time the Government sets aside any hope we had that this Ministry might bring the country out of that situation in which it finds itself, and might accomplish those tasks which the representatives of the people would entrust to it. I shall not examine here the details of the declaration which has been made to you; this will probably be done better by my colleague; I dwell on a few points only,

[9] Ministers in the past had ordinarily resigned as individuals.—EDITORS.

and first of all, on that question which agitates us all and of which we spoke at the first meeting of the Imperial Duma. The President of the Council of Ministers has taken occasion to mention amnesty and to mention it in the sense of a categorical denial.

We do not know whether the President of the Council of Ministers puts the question of amnesty among questions of Imperial administration; we referred it to the prerogatives of the Sovereign Authority, and any intermediate voice between us and the Sovereign Authority on this question of amnesty we do not admit—we refuse to admit. (Loud applause.)

Further, our attention is drawn to another no less categorically imperative declaration of the President of the Council of Ministers, and in the form in which it is expressed we see a direct and definite challenge to the people's representatives. (Applause.)

When, before he has heard and become acquainted with our projects and proposals, having got to know them only from that Address which, I repeat, we made not to the executive authority, but only to the Sovereign, the representative of the executive authority tells us that the decision of questions on the principles proposed by the Imperial Duma, is absolutely inadmissible, we see here that former attitude which it is time to discontinue and abandon. We see in this attitude a challenge, and we take up this challenge; we shall introduce our legislative proposals; we consider the principle which we recognise the only admissible one; we first of all deny absolutely that these principles, as the President of the Council of Ministers has expressed himself, involve the destruction of the foundation of State interests and the undermining of the forces of the country. We believe that the whole country is with us when we say that it is the policy of half-concessions and unfinished sentences, which we have had to witness till now, that involves the destruction of the principles of State interests and has already undermined the national strength. (Applause.)

Further, we have heard, gentlemen, that those exceptional laws under which Russia is suffocating, will continue to be applied and that those persons who have undertaken the burden of administering the country, consider the revolutionary terrorism should be answered by government terrorism, that therefore the profound and grievous error which comes from the failure to understand that revolutionary terrorism is born of government terrorism, is being continued and promises for Russia new innumerable misfortunes.

I shall not examine further the statements of the President of the Council of Ministers; I shall only note and emphasise the constitutional absurdity which is created by the present state of things. The President of the Council of Ministers invites the Duma to constructive work, but at the same time starts by denouncing as inadmissible one of the main foundations of this work. He categorically refuses to support the most lawful demands of the people. Under these conditions what sort of calm, harmonious work is possible? Under these conditions what advance is possible towards that regeneration of Russia of which proclamation was made to us from the height of the Throne?

We believe that there can be only one way out of this situation; when they invite us to a conflict, when they tell us that the Government is not there to carry out the demands of the people's representatives, but to criticise and denounce them, then from the standpoint of the principle of popular representation we can only say, "let the executive submit to the legislative authority." (Prolonged applause.)

Mr. Rodichev followed.

Gentlemen, it is with a heavy heart that I mount this tribune. We still remember that hope, that faith with which the people sent us to the Duma. We came here the first day, full of readiness to believe in, of readiness to work for the regeneration of the country, and we expected that the authorities would come to meet us. We were ready to forget the past actions of those in whose hands authority remained. We were prepared not to remember that, on the threshold of a reformed Russia, authority was still in the hands of those who had worked for the oppression of the country. To-day our hopes have been shattered. We have been read a lesson, we have been told that we are undermining the vital forces of the country; we have had indicated to us the framework within which the representatives of a firm and forceful executive authority will listen to us and will show us co-operation. We have been told that the question of the responsibility of the Ministry does not enter the sphere of our jurisdiction, inasmuch as this is a question of the Fundamental Laws. This is not a question of the Fundamental Laws: it is not in any law that it need be written that a Ministry which does not enjoy the confidence of the people's representatives gives up its authority. (Prolonged applause.)

This should not be inscribed in a law, but in the conscience of those public men who are undertaking the task of regenerating the country; and if in their conscience there is not this instinct —it is fruitless to write it in the law. We have been told that in the consciences of the present members of our Government this has not been written. We take this as a declaration to the people. (Applause.)

Thus these persons, this Ministry which does not recognise its responsibility to the people's representatives, promises us that it will be a firm, effective authority, acting in conformity with law! . . . But what law? The law under which the state of rein-forced protection is maintained, the law which provides for the repeal of all existing laws, and secures to the authorities complete freedom of action. (Prolonged applause.) That is the kind of law which is necessary for those in whose consciousness there is no responsibility to the people. What they want is a free hand, and it is only with a law which allows them everything that they are able to maintain order.

It will be in place to recall to you, gentlemen, the testament of one of the greatest public men of the nineteenth century, the liberator of Italy, Cavour. He was dying in a country which was no less agitated and disturbed than is Russia at the present moment, and on his death-bed he turned to his Sovereign with the dying request of an old and faithful servant: "Only do not introduce reinforced protection, the state of siege; only do not introduce it. Remember that this is a ruinous instrument, only suitable for a government of madmen." (Applause.)

This axiom of political wisdom has at the present moment been forgotten, and we have been told that this state of lawless-ness is a state of protection. We appear before the Government with this declaration: The distress, the bloodshed in our country comes from those who have driven the country into this state of convulsion, who during a long period have been busy with oppression—from those who have denied law, have denied equal rights, who have stood for the protection of the interests of the higher and propertied classes. For this purpose they needed that very weapon with which (*turning to the Ministers*) you have undermined the well-being of the country. In the state of reinforced protection and in the practice of the old policy of repression, there are the roots of the revolution, the roots of that convulsion into which the country has now been thrown. You tell us that you will pacify the country by the old methods. We have come here in order to lay the foundation for the pacification of the country. For this, first of all, we must have the inviolable principles of law, of law obligatory for all, of a law before which the authorities first of all shall bow. From the lips of one of you (*turning to the Ministerial benches*) I heard many years ago that the request for the responsibility of the authorities before the law is worse than senseless dreams, is nonsense.[10] And now I have heard this supposed nonsense, once spoken by me, from this very tribune from the lips of the representative of authority. But when they tell us: We will observe the laws on condition of being able to break them at any given moment—I must ask you (*turning to the Ministers*): When did this readiness of yours to carry out the laws begin, and has it really begun? They tell us that just now the administrative authorities are examining the lists of persons to whom might be restored that liberty which was taken away from them illegally,[11] always provided that their release does not threaten danger. Gentlemen, the old principle— there are people who are dangerous, and there are people who are harmful—maintained, and that is the basis for a new policy of renovation! As before, Russia will be divided into persons who are agreeable and those that are not. For the disagreeable— prison, exile, ruin; for the agreeable—we know what they do among themselves. (Prolonged applause.) We have the right to demand that the authorities admit that they have been guilty of infringement of the rights of individuals. That authority which is not able to do without such repression—that authority works not for the renovation, but for the disruption of the country. (Voices: That's right.) We have been told that equal rights for peasants are the special care of the present Government, of which the individual members have till now sought to

[10] "Senseless dreams" was the official comment on the Address of the Tver Zemstvo in 1895, of which Mr. Rodichev was the spokesman.—EDITORS.

[11] That is, by administrative order.—EDITORS.

bring the peasant population closer under the authority of a guardian. At present instead of this guardianship, which was accompanied by corporal punishment, by beatings—those who did this were not held responsible, but were rewarded—instead of this guardianship, gentlemen, the Russian peasants will receive special care. (Laughter, and applause.) To those who demand land reform, who demand that the law of property be revised and secured on the firm foundations of justice, to those our future solicitous officials, till now guardians, read a lesson on the need of protecting property rights. The people's representatives know perfectly well what this right to property is, know perfectly well that the right to property should be inculcated in the consciousness of the people, and that it will be inculcated by a law which realises in its provisions the moral instincts of the people. That law which is opposed to the people's idea of law, is the greatest injustice, the greatest act of violence. Gentlemen, we have the right to demand that questions of right be decided by the people's representatives, and that the people's representatives should not receive lessons and reprimands from those persons, from that authority which is afraid of responsibility. We come to regenerate Russia, we come to pacify her; we say, the danger is great, the country is convulsed, and is waiting for the immediate cessation of the old methods of violence. These methods of violence have called forth resistance and crime as evil calls forth evil. We wish to put a stop to these crimes, but our hopes in this connection have been deceived. Instead of co-operation we meet on the part of the authorities resistance, mention of those limitations within which the country must be renovated, and within which everything must remain at the old valuation, with the old injustice. We shall not stop before our task. We see whence the challenge to the country comes, we see where the revolution is forged; we see who is ready again to throw the country into confusion, bloodshed, famine, and impoverishment. Our eyes have been opened and the eyes of the Russian people are opening; and I believe, whatever have been the views of those in authority, if they have now that public conscience which says that without the people the people can be enslaved and without the people it is possible to subject them to oppression (*addressing the Ministers*)—you have tried to do this till now, and you have ruined the country; but, gentlemen, it is possible to free the people and to regenerate the country only by a union with the country, the Ministry which regenerates the country must be in accord with the people's representatives—your conscience should show you what is to be done: Go, and give place to others. (Prolonged applause.)

Mr. Rodichev was followed by other speakers, and late in the evening the Duma adopted almost unanimously a vote of censure on the Ministry. As the Ministry did not resign, there followed a deadlock. Various negotiations took place between Government circles and the Duma, which continued to draft its own Bills, notably on the Land Question.

F. FROM *Formula of Passage to the Next Business upon the Declaration of the Council of Ministers in the First State Duma, May 13, 1906*

Chairman of the Duma: "Perceiving in the declaration of the chairman of the council of ministers that has been heard a decisive indication that the government is completely unwilling to satisfy the demands of the people and the expectations of the land, of the law, and of freedom that were set forth by the State Duma in its reply to the speech from the throne and without the satisfaction of which the tranquility of the country and the fruitful work of the people's representatives are impossible; finding that by its refusal to satisfy the demands of the people, the government is revealing an open contempt for the real interests of the people and an open disinclination to spare new shocks to the country tormented by misery, lawlessness and the continuing sway of the unpunished arbitrariness of the authorities; expressing before the face of the country a complete lack of confidence in a ministry unresponsible to the representatives of the people, and considering a necessary condition for the pacification of the

SOURCE. F. I. Kalinychev, Ed., *Gosudarstvennaia Duma v Rossii v dokumentakh i materialakh* (Moscow, 1957), pp. 271–273.

state and for the fruitful work of the people's representatives to be the immediate retirement of the present ministry and its replacement by a ministry enjoying the confidence of the State Duma, The State Duma passes to the next business."

G. FROM *Stolypin's Government Declarations to the Second State Duma, March 6, 1907*

At the basis of all of the government's bills which the cabinet is now introducing into the Duma can be found one general guiding thought, which the government will pursue also in all its forthcoming activity. This thought is to create those material norms into which must be embodied the new legal relations which spring from all the latest reforms. Our fatherland, re-organized by the will of the Monarch, must become a legal state, because so long as written law does not define the duties and does not protect the rights of individual Russian subjects, these rights and duties will find themselves dependent on the interpretation and the authority of individual persons, that is will not be firmly established.

Legal norms must also rest on exact, clearly expressed laws, because otherwise life will constantly provide conflicts between the new foundations of society and of the state which have received the approval of the Monarch, and the older institutions and laws which are either in contradiction to them or do not fully encompass the new demands of the lawgiver, and because, as well, of arbitrary interpretation of the new principles by both private and official persons. . . .

Having described to the Imperial Duma the program of the government's legislative proposals, I would not have fulfilled my task if I were not to express my conviction that only a well considered and resolute carrying into life of the new foundations

SOURCE. *Gosudarstvennaia Duma. Stenograficheskie otchety. 1907 god. Sessiia II, Chast' I* (St. Petersburg, 1907), pp. 107–121, 169.

of our state order by the legislative institutions will lead to the pacification and rebirth of our great Fatherland. In this endeavour the government is ready to apply the greatest efforts: its labour, its good will, its accumulated experience are placed at the disposal of the Imperial Duma, which will find as a collaborator a government conscious of its duty to preserve the historical traditions of Russia and to restore to her order and tranquility, that is, a government which is firm and truly Russian, such as must be and will be the government of His Majesty. . . .

Gentlemen, I had no intention of appearing a second time today before the Imperial Duma but the turn, which the debate has taken, forces me to ask you for your attention. The government would like to find a common language understandable to all of us. . . . Such a language cannot be the language of hatred and malice; I for one shall not use it. . . . The government set for itself one aim: to preserve those legacies, those principles, those cornerstones which constitute the foundation of the reforms of Emperor Nicholas II. Fighting with extraordinary means in extraordinary times the government led and brought the country to the Second Duma. I must declare, and I should like that this declaration be heard well beyond the walls of this assembly, that here by the will of the Monarch there are neither judges nor accused, and that these benches are not the benches of prisoners at the bar—they are the seats of the government. The government will welcome every open exposure of any kind of irregularity, but it must react differently to attacks aimed at creating an atmosphere propitious for an open uprising. Such attacks are intended to cause a paralysis of will and of thought in the government and the executive; they can be summed up in two words addressed to the authorities: "Hands up!" To these two words, gentlemen, the government with complete calm, confident in its uprightness, can answer with only two other words: "Not afraid!"

H.   FROM   *The Imperial Manifesto of June 3, 1907*

We declare to all of our faithful subjects:

On our command and instructions from the time of the dissolution of the First State Duma, our government has taken a consecutive series of measures to pacify the country and set right the course of state affairs.

The Second State Duma was summoned by us to cooperate, in conformity with our supreme will, in the pacification of Russia: first of all, in legislative work without which the life of the state and the perfection of its structure are impossible; then in an examination of the schedule of revenue and expenditure in order to determine the soundness of the state budget; and finally in a sensible use of the right to question the government with the aim of strengthening law and justice everywhere.

These obligations, entrusted by us to the people's delegates, imposed on them likewise a heavy responsibility and a sacred duty to use their rights in sensible work for the welfare and solidarity of the Russian state.

Such were our thought and will in bestowing on the people new principles in the life of the state.

To our grief, a significant number of the members of the Second State Duma did not justify our expectations. Many of the persons deputed to work by the people came not with sincerity, not with the wish to strengthen Russia and improve its structure but with an open desire to make more trouble and help destroy the state.

The activity of these persons in the State Duma was an insurmountable obstacle to fruitful work. In the midst of the Duma itself there was introduced a spirit of hostility that prevented an adequate number of its members who wished to work for the benefit of the homeland from joining together.

For this reason, the extensive measures worked out by our

SOURCE. F. I. Kalinychev, Ed., *Gosudarstvennaia Duma v Rossii v dokumentakh i materialakh* (Moscow, 1957), pp. 271–273.

government the State Duma either did not subject at all to examination or delayed judgment or rejected, not stopping even before the rejection of laws that inflicted a penalty on open praise of crimes and punished in particular the sowers of discord among the troops. Having refused to condemn murder and violence, the State Duma was unable to furnish moral assistance to the government, and Russia continues to experience the shame of criminally troubled times.

The tardy examination by the State Duma of the state budget made difficult the meeting in time of many urgent needs of the populace.

A significant part of the Duma turned the right to question the government into a means of conflict with the government and the arousal of distrust in it among broad strata of the population.

Finally, there occurred an act unheard of in the annals of history. A conspiracy of an entire section of the State Duma against the state and the imperial authority was uncovered by the judicial authorities. When our government demanded the temporary (until the end of the trial) expulsion of fifty-five members of the Duma accused of the crime and the taking into custody of those most involved, the State Duma did not immediately meet the lawful demand of the authorities that admitted of no delay.

All of this has caused us to dissolve the Second State Duma by a decree given to the Governing Senate on June 3 and set the date for the convocation of a new Duma on November 1, 1907.

However, believing in the love for the homeland and in the political sense of our people, we believe that the reason for the failure twice of the actions of the State Duma was that, because of the newness of the institution and the imperfection of the electoral law, this legislative assembly was filled with members who were not genuine representatives of the needs and wishes of the people.

Therefore, while leaving in force all the rights granted to our subjects by the Manifesto of October 17, 1905 and the Fundamental Laws, we have taken the decision to change only the method of summoning delegates from the people to the State Duma so that every section of the populace might have in it its representatives.

Convoked in order to strengthen the Russian state, the State Duma must be Russian also in spirit.

Our nationalities living in our state should have representatives of their needs in the State Duma, but they ought not and shall not appear in a number giving them the opportunity to be the arbiters of purely Russian questions.

In those borderlands of the state where the population has not reached an adequate level of citizenship, elections to the State Duma have to be temporarily suspended.

All of these changes in the method of elections cannot be carried out in the usual legislative way by that State Duma the composition of which we have judged to be unsatisfactory as a result of the imperfection in the manner of the election of its members.

Only the authority that granted the first electoral law, the historic authority of the Russian tsar, has the right to revoke it and replace it with a new one.

God has entrusted us with tsarist authority over our people. We are responsible before His throne for the fate of the Russian state.

Conscious of this, we derive the firm resolution to bring to a conclusion the transformation of Russia that we began, and we bestow a new electoral law which we instruct the Governing Senate to publish.

We expect from our faithful subjects unanimous and cheerful service, on the path indicated by us, to the homeland, the sons of which at all times have been a firm bulwark of its strength, greatness, and glory.

Given in Peterhof, June 3, in the year 1907 from the birth of Christ and the thirteenth year of our reign.

I. FROM *Stolypin's Government Declarations to the Third State Duma, November 16, 1907*

It has now become obvious to everyone that the destructive movement created by the extreme left parties has turned into open banditry and has brought forward all anti-social criminal elements. . . . Only force can oppose this phenomenon. . . . Up to the present, the government has followed the course of uprooting criminal acts, and it will continue on this course.

To do this, the government must have at its disposal as a weapon of authority persons tied by a feeling of duty and responsibility to the state. . . . With the existence of the State Duma, the tasks of the government in maintaining order can only be eased since in addition to ways of transforming the administration and police, the government counts on receiving the valuable support of the representative institutions in revealing illegal acts by the authorities relating to excesses by the authorities as well as their inactivity. . . . The government hopes soon to present for the consideration of the State Duma measures for self-government in certain borderlands . . . along with which the idea of the unity and solidarity of the state will be the guiding one. . . . On its side, the government will make every effort to ease the work of the legislative institutions and to implement the measures passed by the State Duma and State Council and confirmed by the Emperor. These measures will undoubtedly restore order and strengthen a lasting and just system corresponding to the Russian national conscience.

In this connection, the will of the monarch has often demonstrated how the supreme power, despite the extraordinary difficulties encountered, values the foundations of legal order that has once again been established in the country and that has de-

SOURCE. *Gosudarstvennaia Duma. Stenograficheskie otchety. 1907–1908 gg. Sessiia I, Chast' I* (St. Petersburg, 1908), pp. 307–312, 348–354.

termined the limits of the representative structure bestowed from above.

The manifestation of tsarist authority has always shown the people that the historic autocratic power and free will of the monarch are the most precious attainment of the Russian state principle just as only this authority and this power that have created the present institutions and are protecting them have been called, in times of convulsions and danger to the state, to save Russia and to turn it on the path of order and historical truth. . . . It is not necessary for me to defend the right of the sovereign to save at a time of danger the power entrusted to him by God. . . . The system in which we are living is a representative system bestowed by an autocratic monarch and consequently binding on all of his subjects. . . . Our ideal . . . is the development of the new legislative and representative system granted by the sovereign to the country which ought to add new strength and lustre to the supreme tsarist authority. The supreme authority is the guardian of the Russian state and personifies its strength and unity . . . preserving it from dissolution.

J.   FROM *Guchkov's Formula of Passage to*
the Next Business upon the Declaration of the Chairman
of the Council of Ministers in the Third State Duma,
November 16, 1907

The State Duma having heard the statement of the chairman of the council of ministers and having firmly resolved without delay to begin legislative work in order to realize changes for the state for which the time is ripe and which cannot be postponed and to oversee undeviatingly within the limits indicated by the laws the legality of the government's actions, passes to the next business.

SOURCE. *Gosudarstvennaia Duma. Stenograficheskie otchety. 1907–1908 gg. Sessiia I, Chast' I* (St. Petersburg, 1908), pp. 307–312, 348–354.

K. FROM *Alexander Guchkov.*
Speeches on the Naval and Military Estimates of 1908

Mr. Guchkov was the chief organiser of the Octobrist (Central) Party, but was not a member either of the first or of the second Duma. Under the new electoral law of 1907, which gave the predominance in the Duma to the propertied classes, Mr. Guchkov found himself the leader of the majority in the third Duma. This Duma opened with a long debate as to how far it should commit itself to the idea of Constitutionalism. Even the Octobrists were as yet very indefinite both in their ideals and in their programme. A year's work of organization marked by great parliamentary ability, enabled the Leader of the House to consolidate both his party and the Duma as a whole. Mr. Guchkov was always against revolution and was for co-operation wherever possible between the Government and the Duma. But he developed the constitutional idea on a ground which was likely to be common to all patriotic Rusians, and in these speeches which were the culmination of his year's work, he demands in the plainest language a full investigation of the causes of Russian reverses in the Japanese War. It would be difficult to do justice to the effects of these speeches. They were delivered from manuscript in a quiet voice, but when the leader of the Centre proceeded to name one after another those highly placed persons whom he asked to vacate their posts, a burst of acclamation came from all sides, and the organs of various parties were practically unanimous in the increased value which they now attributed to the Duma. King Edward VII, who was at this time at Revel, is reported on credible authority to have congratulated the Emperor that such a speech should have been possible in the National Assembly so recently created. During the following months several of the Grand Dukes resigned their posts.

SOURCE. *The Russian Review,* **II,** No. 1 (1913), pp. 111–121.

FROM THE SPEECH OF MR. A. I. GUCHKOV ON THE ESTIMATES OF THE ADMIRALTY FOR 1908, DELIVERED IN THE DUMA, MAY 24, 1908

It is curious how the position in the Far East and the relations of the naval forces of ourselves and the Japanese were estimated almost on the eve of war by that responsible director who was there the disposer of our fleet and the controller of our international Far Eastern policy. In 1903, Admiral Alexeyev reported: "With the present relations of forces of our fleet and the Japanese, the possibility of the defeat of our fleet by the Japanese is inadmissible;" and later, "that the Japanese should land at Inkow and in the Corean Gulf is unthinkable;" and in a few months, as you know, events were a cruel mockery on these assertions of the short-sighted statesman. We have paid dearly for this estimate of our forces; the preparations for war, the first steps at the time of the campaign, were based in considerable measure on this estimate of the naval forces of Russia and of the enemy. And what will you say? The man who ought to have known the real state of things, and who, I will say, so criminally misled our Government, what has happened to him? Is he punished? No, he, just like ourselves, will in a few days in our Upper Chamber settle the fate of our naval estimates, and give his vote. (Continued applause.) And from time to time this ghost, like a visitor from some other world, appears in the foreground of public opinion; and newspapers, social gossip, and some of the influential currents in our Government circles begin to suggest this man for the post of responsible director of our naval forces. And this apparition has lately taken to itself so clear an outline that, for instance, before the final vote on the question of a credit for building new ships in our Committee of Imperial Defence, I was asked to say that these rumours were at present unfounded; that there was no need to apprehend that Admiral Alexeyev would be appointed Minister of the Navy. I did so, but since then these rumours have become more and more persistent. How are we to get rid of these ghosts of the past? How are we to finish once for all with this nightmare? It is not a question simply of liquidating the grievous heritage of old disorders; we must liquidate our still more burdensome heritage in the shape of the men, the agents of the past. I think that till the Government sheds the full light of truth on the condition of our fleet, on those causes which brought it to ruin, till it names before the whole people those persons who were guilty of the catastrophe which befell our Navy, till then, these apparitions of the past will threaten the restoration of our military and naval power; till then will remain the danger that these tender blades of good intentions, which from time to time show themselves in this Ministry under the influence of the new and fresh elements which have penetrated into it, will be rudely trampled underfoot by those old phantoms, which some fine day will come and settle in and begin to keep house after the former fashion. But, for this the whole truth must be laid bare. I return to what was said by my fellow-spokesman on this subject; he urged that, in his opinion, the real step which would show that the Government desires in this matter to make a fresh start, would be an Imperial command that there should be appointed an authoritative, impartial, and inexorable investigation both of the state of our fleet before the war and of all its actions during that war. It is only by such a course that the Government will make clear to itself the true picture—only then that it will be in a position, once for all, to get quit of those persons who carry the guilt of our misfortunes. That would be a step which would at once attract the sympathies and the confidence both of the national representatives and of the whole people.

FROM THE SPEECH ON THE ESTIMATES OF THE MINISTRY OF WAR FOR 1908, DELIVERED IN THE IMPERIAL DUMA, MAY 27

But before I pass to an enumeration of those general inferences, conclusions, and criticisms for which the present estimates give ground, I ought, I think, to fix that fundamental standpoint from which we should approach the study of this question. If we are looking for certain defects in the organisation of our military forces, in the whole disposition of our imperial defence, which explain our failures in the war, we must clearly remember that the chief blame for these failures does not, of course, fall on the army. The army was not guilty—at least it was not guilty in the first degree—for our defeats, for the loss of the campaign and for the funeral of our military glory. Who, then, was to blame? Who, then, were the criminals? The criminals were the Government and the public. Some day, perhaps not soon, when the archives are opened, when the memoirs and notes of eye-witnesses have been printed, perhaps then only shall we convince ourselves that our army suffered without being to blame. The first culprit was certainly, we must say, our central Government; and it was guilty not only of allowing the war itself or even of recklessly contributing to the outbreak of this war, not only because in those long years of peace which preceded the war it took no trouble to put on a proper footing the whole work of defence; it was guilty, and most of all guilty because, when this danger appeared, the Government never recognised all the seriousness of the situation. It was assumed that this was some distant colonial war, that we had no need to meet from the outset, with the full exertion of those forces with which we were undoubtedly endowed, the threatening danger that moved on us from the East. It was thought that we might conduct this war as an episode, without in the slightest weakening ourselves on other fronts; and this poor army and its chiefs had to wage two wars—a war on a double front; one war against the Japanese, and another against St. Petersburg, against the Government, against the War Office. This last was a war of detail, of every day, of partisans; and, as we might have guessed, the Chancelleries of St. Petersburg won it. Only later, much later when already our crushing disasters had shown in what direction our further conflict with Japan was developing, only then did people here understand the large stakes that were involved. It became clear that it was a question not of Korea, not of South Manchuria; it was a question not of our Pacific provinces, it was a question of the existence of Russia, of her good name, of her military glory. And it was already late when this conviction was reached; and a belated energy could not, of course, turn back the wheels of fate. And the second fault of the Government was that at that moment when we were materially strong in the Far East, when the spirit of the army was still high and vigorous, it had lost faith in itself and in its people, and concluded that peace which has for a long time buried our international prestige and our military glory. But if the Government, even at the end of this unhappy war, understood its mistake and within the limits of its power and intelligence corrected it, the second main author of our misfortunes, the Russian public, to the very end continued in its blindness. The public, in this respect, showed not a whit more elevation or discernment than the Government. The one was as bad as the other. The unpopularity of the actual cause of war made the public shut its eyes to the enormous and vital issues which were being settled on that distant field; and the whole stream of home influence on the army—our press, the letters of relations and friends, new arrivals from Russia— only helped to take away our last remains of courage and energy, and faith in ourselves and in the possibility of success. Our public, throughout the whole war, acted as a demoralising influence on our army. (Cries from the Right: "That's true; that's right.") If the Government towards the end of the war corrected its mistake, the public only made its mistake worse; and, I repeat, when some day all these materials will be open to us, the Russian historian will pronounce a severe judgment both on the Russian Government and on the Russian public. All this does not, of course, mean that there were not in our army itself, in its organisation, very serious defects. These defects, I repeat, would not have hindered a favourable—I will not say a brilliant, but a favourable—termination of the war, if there had not been these two fatal factors which I have already mentioned. But it cannot be doubted that these defects were, all the same, very serious. The result of them was that any success could be obtained only with the greatest losses, and with the greatest risk.

That system which we call the bureaucratic, has perhaps nowhere made for itself so secure a nest as in our Ministry of War. Routine has filled everything; the system has been subordinated to the office. From the higher central military jurisdictions routine has penetrated into the local administrations, into the various sections of the army; and there it has numbed all energy, it has killed the spirit of life, it has stifled the sense of responsibility. In the army, too, it did that destructive work which had put its seal on every province of our public life. One of our capital shortcomings was always the staff of superior officers. It is characteristic that for half a century, in spite of a series of grievous lessons, we have in this respect learned nothing. Before me lies the following curious record, drawn up by a competent person. "During the last wars waged by Russia (1853–5 and 1877–8) one thing stands out with the greatest clearness—that with the growing complications of the conditions of war, our staff of commanders has in many cases proved to be unequal to the occasion. The junior officers, within the limits of their work, have been brave and energetic, but insufficiently trained; the sectional commanders, sometimes with consoling exceptions, have not been competent to make the best use of the military abilities of the forces entrusted to them. But weakest of all has been the staff of generals, whether commanding brigades, divisions, or army corps. Except for a few brilliant names, most had never been trained to handle forces of the various arm in the field; they could not hold together the different sections composing the forces entrusted to them, or keep touch with the next troops in line with them. The instinct of mutual support has not been sufficiently developed. Doing nothing at all, on the excuse, 'I had no orders,' when the neighbouring troops were being defeated, has been no rare phenomenon. Particularly has this want of intelligence been evident in the carrying out of attacks."

It is typical that all these deficiencies in the management of our forces and in their tactical training have been repeated with literal exactness in our last war. To avoid that reproach which has been made to us by one of our fellow members, who when the navy estimates were being discussed called us civilian admirals, admirals on dry land, I will here give not my own estimate, but reports whose authority even this doubting colleague of ours will not, I think, be able to doubt. The publication of the Nicholas Academy of the General Staff, *Communications on the Russo-Japanese War,* contains a whole series of very outspoken and typical reports. For instance, the account which describes the military operations before Sandepu ends with the following words: "Our leaders showed the imperfections of our military system; our methods of conducting war are founded on wrong conceptions of the handling of military forces, ideas which have no connection with the data obtained by military science. The neglect of military science in the highest branches of the army and the monopoly of its data in the hands of a very few persons, who in their turn are artificially separated from the main forces, are most unfavourable to the perfection of our military system." Another account, describing the operations of Mukden, draws the following conclusions: "In the movements of the troops themselves, we must note that they showed but little ability in manoeuvring on the field of battle, in consequence of which there was far too great a predilection for frontal attacks. Our demonstrations are carried out in the most naïvely direct manner, and no one, whether on our side or the enemy's, could possibly be misled as to their meaning. Fortresses and local obstacles are attacked from the front, so that these attacks are very expensive and a battle on our side quickly departs from any orderly form, loses any idea in its development, and becomes a series of disconnected episodes; and the senior commanders, just while the engagement is developing, allow the control of it to pass out of their hands, and confine themselves to the direction of some single section of it; often they are not on the field, or gallop along the line making display of their courage, but without entering at all into the normal conditions of present-day fighting. Our army needs before all things a radical reform, which should aim at bringing our staff of commanders into some relation with the present demands of warfare, and such training as would bring it up to the standard of modern military science. But while the troops, their equipment, and their supplies are not up-to-date and their leaders are a good fifty years behind, we are not secured from a repetition of catastrophes in the future." And the author of the account of the operations of General Mishehenko's cavalry detachment when the second army advanced in January, asks in despair, "Are we again to appear at our examination unprepared? Must we really again repeat wholesale the crudest mistakes and, in the face of experience, forget the invariable principles of the art and ethics of war, forget everything which we have learned with such difficulty and acquired with such cruel experience? I do not and will not believe it."

I shall allow myself to ask your attention for one more last extract, which is peculiarly typical, peculiarly true and emphatic. I quote from the order of the day in which the commander of the first Manchurian army at the close of the campaign took leave of his officers. Among other things, he writes as follows: "In general, among the junior and senior officers we have not

found a sufficient number of persons of strong military character, with iron nerves that disregard any surroundings and can
support undauntedly almost continuous fighting for several days.
It is manifest that neither our schools nor our life have contributed to train in our great Russia during the last forty or
fifty years strong, self-supporting characters. Otherwise there
would have been many more of them in the army. We are poor
in men of outstanding independence, energy, and initiative.
Look for them, encourage them, help them forward! Promote
the growth of these qualities so fundamental for the soldier. In
Russia men of strong character, men of independence are unfortunately in many cases not only not helped forward, but
persecuted. In time of peace, to many commanders all such men
seem troublesome; they are regarded as difficult to get on with,
and are reported on as such. As a result, such men have often
left the service. On the other hand, men without character or
convictions, but obliging, always ready to agree in everything
with the opinion of their chiefs, have been sure of promotion."
(Cries, "Quite true.") And the commander ends his farewell order of the day with words which should encourage and inspirit.
He says, "Now, by the unalterable will of our Sovereign Leader
of Russia, are granted the blessings of freedom; our people is
being released from the wardenship of bureaucracy" (cries from
the Left, "We don't yet notice it"), "and it will have the chance
of developing freely and turning all its forces to the profit of
our country. We will believe that these blessings of freedom,
with good schools, will soon show their happy effects on the
growth of the material and moral forces of the Russian people,
and will produce in every field in Russia men of action and en-
terprise with plenty of initiative, sound in soul and body; then
these forces will enrich our army too." And now, when three
years have already passed since this order of the day, we have a
right to ask: in this special sphere, in the formation of iron
characters, in the promotion of men of ability, what has been
done? And we must own that the system which minimised
strength of character, which rubbed off all contours of personality, has remained the same, that, just as before, there has continued that unnatural method of selection which has forced to
the top exactly what was useless, weak, and null, and has thrown
on one side all that was talented, all that was able, strong, and

spirited. We must own that in the higher administration of the army and in the appointment to the superior posts in it, there still prevail just the same old faults, the same nepotism, the same social or family ties, the same preference for one's intimates of bowl and bottle, and as the Deputy Markov II.[1] very well put it, the same whispers at Court.

After enumerating the special needs of the army, Mr. Guchkov concludes as follows. (He has just been saying that Germany spends about twice as much on each of her soldiers as Russia.)

I will not dwell long on this point, because those who will replace me in this tribune will, I know, develop it in further detail. I have only put it before you in order to show that from this point we must make a beginning with a quite new set of ideas on the ways in which our army can be brought to the proper level. Can we now feel convinced, gentlemen, that all these needs will be satisfied, that all the drastic reforms which have been mentioned will really be carried out by our Ministry of War? Can we expect that the turning-point to which we have come will be correctly estimated by the War Office, and that it will now take the right course? To our regret, we must own that we profoundly doubt it. As a matter of fact, if before the war the higher administration of our army was at least concentrated in the hands of the War Office, which was invested with the widest powers, or, to use the expression now in fashion, with the fulness of power, and was alone responsible both for the selection of the staff of commanders, and for the military preparedness of the army, we have since the war in this respect turned aside from what was the right way, and chosen just this moment to proceed on a wrong one. At the very time when we ought to have concentrated our full force of thought and of will in the head of the army, we have split and scattered this thought and will. In 1905, changes of the first importance were made in the superior administration of the army. By an Imperial rescript dated May 18, 1905, addressed to the Grand Duke Nikolay Nikolayevich, there was formed a permanent Council of Imperial Defence; by an Imperial order of July 8, 1905, was formed

[1] Mr. Markov is one of the chief spokesmen of the Extreme Right, the party which most leans upon Court influence.—EDITORS.

in the Ministry of War a special Chief Administration of the General Staff. It was these two institutions which divided the powers of the War Office and took from it its strength and its distinctive character. But, together with these two, was created a whole system of new institutions. Apart from the Council of Imperial Defence and the Chief of the General Staff, after the war there were also created a committee for the formation of troops and the posts of Inspector of Artillery, Inspector of Infantry, and Inspector of Engineers, with also a higher Commission of Attestation, and finally the post of Assistant Minister of War. If all the last-named posts are at least in principle subordinate to the Minister of War, the Chief of the General Staff has equal rank and rights with the Minister; and the Council of Imperial Defence, which has already been sufficiently described to you here, and will probably engage your further attention, stands actually above the Minister. Composed of very many members under the presidency of the Grand Duke Nikolay Nikolayevich, this council acts as a serious brake on the work of reform, and on any improvement in our imperial defence. (Shouts of "Bravo," applause.) In order to complete for you the picture of this organisation, or rather of this disorganisation, bordering on anarchy (cries of "Bravo; that's right") which has established itself at the head of the administration of the War Office, I ought further to say that the post of General Inspector of the Artillery is held by the Grand Duke Sergius Mikhailovich, the post of General Inspector of the Engineers by the Grand Duke Peter Nikolayevich, and that of Chief Commander of the military educational institutions by the Grand Duke Constantine Constantinovich. (Cries from the Right, "And thank Heaven for that.") If we can have no objection, if we may even think it natural and right that persons who by their position are irresponsible should serve in the ranks of the army, meeting in peace-time all the duties and in war-time all the dangers as regimental commanders, we must say that to put such persons at the head of responsible and important branches of our military system is something altogether abnormal. (Shouts, "Bravo, bravo!") Their relations with other departments of military administration which have equal rights with their own, their relations with their superior officers cannot fail to carry the stamp of their social position and of the practical irresponsibility which is connected with it. This we must say clearly, and at the same time we must admit our own impotence in dealing with this matter. But to call things by their right names is our duty. (Voices, "That's right; that's right.") The Deputy, Purishkevich,[2] was quite right when he said that we cannot allow ourselves more reverses. Really, any further defeat of Russia will not be simply a campaign lost, not simply territory ceded, not simply a money indemnity, it will be the poisoned fang that will bring our country to the grave. (Applause; cries, "That's right.") Whatever the importance of other questions which pass through this hall, we must admit that at the historical moment at which we live, questions of imperial defence and imperial security must stand higher than all others, both for their own importance and, chief of all, because they cannot be postponed. If we consider ourselves entitled and even bound to turn to the people and to the country and demand from them heavy sacrifices for this work of defence, then we are entitled to address ourselves also to those few irresponsible persons from whom we have to demand no more than the renunciation of certain terrestrial advantages, and of certain satisfactions of vainglory which are connected with those posts which they at present hold. (Continued applause from the Left, the Centre, and partly from the Right.) This sacrifice we have a right to expect of them. (A continued storm of applause from the Left, Centre, and part of the Right. Cries of "Bravo! well done!")

2 Mr. Purishkevich is another prominent spokesman of the Extreme Right. —Editors.

L.   FROM   *Speech delivered by Mr. A. I.*
Guchkov, on November 8, 1913, at the Conference
of the Octobrist Party in St. Petersburg.
The General Political Situation and the
Octobrist Party

Mr. Alexander Guchkov was the principal organiser of the
Octobrist party and led it in the third Duma. His policy was
co-operation wherever possible with the government and
more particularly with Mr. Stolypin, in order to effect as
far as possible a reconciliation between the government and
the public. The Octobrists were chiefly drawn from the
upper classes and stood for practical, moderate and detailed
reform. If the government failed to make peace with them,
it failed with the public as a whole. To Mr. Guchkov's attitude was due the comparative success of the third Duma.
At the last general meeting of his party, he, as its leader,
described the failure of this policy in the following speech.

The chief aim of our Conference is not to revise our political
credo, our programme. There is nothing in the programme for
us to renounce; and for the present, unfortunately, there is nothing to add to it. The first stage which we marked out has not yet
been traversed, and it is still early to set up further landmarks
along the same route. If our programme had been carried out,
we should now see our country completely regenerated. And here
we may note a curious feature in our history. Our programme
is for us a normal one, but at the time when it was drafted
it was condemned from the standpoint of orthodox radicalism as
heretical, as extravagantly moderate and retrograde. Now it
has penetrated into the consciousness of broader circles and has
become a minimum programme even for more radical parties.

The burning question of the hour is not one of principle, or

SOURCE. *The Russian Review,* **III,** No. 1 (1914), pp. 141–158.

of the general objects which the Octobrist Party has in view, but one of the ways and means by which these principles may be put into effect and these objects attained—in a word, the question of tactics. This question has been placed in the forefront by the course of events during the last few years, and by the general political situation at the present moment. What should the tactics of the Party be? What attitude should it take up toward the other factors in the political life of the nation, more especially toward the government and to other political parties? A practical examination of this question has already begun. A process of evolution in our tactics has already set in—a process which has perhaps not always been realised, and in any case has not been systematised and clearly formulated.

To find and verify this formula, to affirm it as the categorical imperative of further political work for all organs of our party, this is the first and most important task of our Conference. This will be at once an important act of our own political consciousness and an event of very great significance in the political life of the country at large. It is natural, accordingly, that public attention should be focussed, as it now is, on the question we are discussing, as to the further tactics of the Union, and the position it is to adopt.

Octobrism had its origin in the heart of that liberal Opposition which grew up around the Zemstvo in the struggle against the reactionary policy adopted by the government about the end of the sixties, and was maintained, with accidental and temporary digressions, until the time of disorders in the early years of the present century. This Opposition did what cultural work it could within the narrow limits and under the unfavourable conditions imposed by the general political situation, but it never lost sight of the necessity of making fundamental political reforms based on national representation as the headstone of the corner. The nucleus of Octobrists who in November, 1905, founded the Octobrist Party, was formed out of the minority in the Zemstvo Congresses. This minority joined in the general demand for broad liberal reforms in all departments of life and for a transition from the obsolete forms of unlimited autocracy to a constitutional system; but it set its face against the passion for unbridled radicalism and against socialistic experiments which threatened to bring in their train grave political and social disturbances. The men who formed the Octobrist Party from the first marked themselves off sharply from those revolutionary elements which thought to take advantage of the embarrassment of the government in order to effect a violent seizure of power. In the struggle with sedition at a moment of mortal danger for the Russian State, the Octobrists resolutely took the side of the government, which, in a series of solemn assurances emanating from the Sovereign himself, had declared itself ready for the broadest liberal reforms. A series of acts of State, from the Ukaz to the Governing Senate of December 12, 1904, to the Manifesto of October 17, 1905, contained an extensive programme of reform suited to the mature needs of the country and promising the fulfilment of hopes and dreams which the Russian public has long cherished. These acts were a triumph for Russian Liberalism; for the principles contained in them were the watchwords in the name of which Russian Liberals had been fighting for half a century.

Such was the political environment in which Octobrism came into being. In fact, it was bound to come into being. Octobrism was a tacit but solemn contract between that government, on the one hand, which was the product of the whole course of Russian history, and the Russian public on the other—a contract of loyalty, of mutual loyalty. The Manifesto of October 17 was, so it seemed, an act of confidence in the nation on the part of the Sovereign; Octobrism was the nation's answer; it was an act of faith in the Sovereign.

But the contract contained obligations for both sides; and collaboration with the government meant joint effort in the work of carrying out the broad program of reforms that had been outlined. Primarily it meant joint action for the purpose of strengthening and developing the principles of the constitutional system. Only by means of combined and friendly effort on the part of the government and of the public could this task be accomplished. A situation was created which is rare in Russian life, a situation the like of which had not been seen since the beginning of the sixties. Two forces which had been constantly, and as it seemed irreconcilably, hostile to each other—the government and the public—came together and pursued a common path. The public began to believe in the government; the government keenly realised the need of support from the public. In this act of reconciliation a prominent part was played by Mr. Stolypin, who represented a wholly exceptional combination of the qualities required at that particular moment. His charming personality, the lofty qualities of his intellect and character changed the hate and suspicion that formerly prevailed into an atmosphere of public goodwill and confidence in the government.

In the third Imperial Duma, Octobrism was able to take its place as an important factor in political life.[1] History will give a juster estimate of the significance of the third Duma than that given by contemporaries. It will give it due credit for having passed a number of important legislative measures in the spheres of finance, land reform, public instruction, and justice, for having practically laid the bases—firm bases, as it seemed—of the new constitutional system, and most of all for having by its even temper and its tranquil labours exercised a profound educative influence on the Russian public. In the gradual calming and sobering process that has been noticeable in the public temper during the last five years, the third Imperial Duma played a very important part. History will duly appreciate those difficulties, both internal and external, which the young representative assembly had to face. It seemed as though unprecedentedly favourable conditions had been established for carrying out the proposed reforms—reforms which promised regeneration in all departments of life. The severe lesson of the recent past had, it seemed, irrevocably condemned the policy which had brought Russia to disaster, almost to the verge of ruin. The revolutionary movement and the political terror that accompanied it, had been suppressed; the public sympathy in which they formerly flourished, had been withdrawn from them. With the disappearance of revolutionary excesses, the excesses of the government had lost their former justification. The government, so it seemed, had attained clearness of vision and could count in its reforming work on the support of wide and influential circles of society. In a word, a new era was opening.

But side by side with this tendency, parallel to it, but in a reverse direction, proceeded an evolution of another character.

---

[1] Entirely owing to the change made by the government in the electoral law, which threw the control of the Duma into the hands of the Octobrists.—EDITORS.

In proportion as tranquillity was restored, in proportion as the public laid down its arms and the danger of revolution receded into the distance, those elements which in former epochs and in all countries have been distinguished for the shortness of their memory, raised their heads. These were the forces that held the fate of Russia in their hands in the pre-emancipation epoch, and determined the policy which brought a great empire to unprecedented depths of humiliation. At the moment when danger threatened, before what seemed to be the inevitable hour of stern expiation of their sins and crimes, they effaced themselves, disappeared, as it were, from the surface of Russian life, abandoning their posts in mortal fear for their personal safety.[2] Now they have crawled out of their crevices—these "saviours of the country" —but where were they then? They were not to be found in the government, at any rate in the government of Stolypin's time.[3] It was among the "beings who had been men"[4] of the obsolete political system, among the Court *camarilla,* among those suspicious characters who huddled and warmed themselves around the festering sores of Russian life, among those whom the new political system mercilessly threw overboard—it was among these that the reviving reaction recruited its forces. And among these well-known and only too familiar figures—new, unexpected, strange shapes, stragglers, as it were, from some entirely different epoch of civilisation, appeared as important factors in our political life. Those irresponsible, ex-governmental, super-governmental and in the present case anti-governmental tendencies which were organically bound up with the forms of Russian absolutism quickly recovered, under the new order, their hold on the positions that had been taken from them and abandoned by them. The man who bravely fought with them and fell under their onslaught, Mr. Stolypin, made the following melancholy admission in conversation with a Russian journalist: "It is a mistake to think," he said, "that the Russian Cabinet even in its present form is the government. It is only a reflection of the government.

[2] By no means all.—EDITORS.

[3] On the contrary many remained and sturdily opposed Mr. Stolypin.— EDITORS.

[4] The title of one of Gorky's stories describing the inhabitants of a night-shelter.—EDITORS.

It is necessary to know that impact of pressure and influence under the weight of which it has to work."

It was, as you know, the right wing of the Council of the Empire and the Organisation of the United Gentry that became the official bulwarks of reaction. It would be wrong to consider these bodies as in any way faithful indicators of the temper prevailing among the Russian gentry and the higher Russian bureaucracy. Consistent, artificial selection was needed to make them what they are. The Russian gentry, who with their own hands carried out the great civilising mission of the Zemstvo, are, undoubtedly—an overwhelming majority of them at any rate— an element of progress. Moreover, the legend of the isolation of the Russian bureaucracy, of its estrangement from the public temper and public needs, is greatly exaggerated. In those rare moments of illumination when the government has entered on the path of broad creative effort, it has found among its bureaucracy not a few gifted men who gladly brought their immense political experience to the service of the great tasks opening out before them. Thus, for instance, at a happy moment in our history, the new Russian judicial system came into being as a result of the creative effort of our bureaucracy.

The third Imperial Duma, at the moment when it first met, found dominant in the Council of the Empire the so-called group of the Centre. This group was by no means homogeneous in its composition, but it was united by a common recognition of the Manifesto of October 17 and other decrees promulgated by the Sovereign during the epoch of liberation as determining bases for the forthcoming work of reform.

On this group, which constituted together with the left wing a decisive majority, the government could rely in carrying out its programme of reforms. Between this group and the Duma Centre, which was also made up of various elements and constituted a majority in the Duma, there existed, in spite of all differences of political temper, common ground, a common language, a possibility of establishing agreement by means of mutual concessions. A series of new appointments,[5] made consistently year after year in a definite direction, gradually but decisively transferred the

[5] Half of the Imperial Council is appointed in yearly nominations by the Sovereign.—EDITORS.

centre of gravity in the Council of the Empire to the right wing. The right wing was not merely mechanically or numerically strengthened. The very character of the appointments showed what political tendency was in favour at the moment. And this circumstance naturally could not fail to influence those unstable elements which had long been in the habit of adjusting their policy to prevailing tendencies.

The effect was one of painful ambiguity. On the one hand, the general position semed to be unchanged; the Manifesto had not been repealed, the promises given had not been withdrawn, the government, with the permission of the Monarch, continued to draft and to bring into the legislative bodies bills containing references to the acts of the epoch of liberation, bills bearing very definitely the stamp of that epoch. On the other hand, also with the Sovereign's permission, certain elements were consistently strengthened. These elements did not attempt to conceal their irreconcilable hostility to the new political system and to those representatives of the government who were on its side; they regarded the Manifesto of October 17 and kindred acts of the Monarch as frivolous and timid concessions wrung out either by force or deception; they made it their object to urge the Sovereign to effect a *coup d'état,* and gladly offered their services for this purpose.

The chief efforts of the reaction were directed at first not so much against the representative assembly as against the Prime Minister, who was a firm supporter of the new political system. A characteristic moment in this struggle was the memorable episode of the bill for the estimates of the Marine General Staff. This was a trial of strength. The blow was skilfully prepared and cleverly calculated. It was aimed at a vital point; the question of Imperial Defence touches every Russian statesman to the quick.

The dangerous man was beaten and broken. It was necessary to repeat the blow. And blows were showered on him. You remember the complicated intrigue that arose over the question of establishing Zemstva in the Western Provinces. You remember the fatal mistake Mr. Stolypin allowed himself to make; his ephemeral victory was turned into final defeat. The campaign conducted against this eminent statesman whose services to the Empire and the Monarchy were immense, found inspiration and support in those irresponsible, extra-governmental tendencies which rightly saw in him an irreconcilable and most dangerous opponent. The political centre of gravity moved more and more to their side. Individuals were promoted or degraded, important events occurred in the life of the State without the participation of the government and with the aid of other, secret, but more powerful factors. The government gradually lost that tinge of constitutionalism which is implied in the idea of a united cabinet. We returned to the traditions of a personal *régime* with its worst accessories.

Stolypin's struggle with these reactionary tendencies which he considered ruinous for Russia and for the Monarchy, ended in his defeat. Long before his physical death his mortal political agony had set in. And the catastrophe in Kiev evoked a feeling of joy, or, at any rate, of relief, not only in those revolutionary circles from which the shot was fired; not only in the camp of the Russian radicals was the death of this splendid fighting man regarded as a gain and as removing a dangerous opponent. It is certain that if there were some who aimed the treacherous shot there were others who did not hinder it. The senatorial revision and its results only confirmed the suspicions and surmises that arose in this connection.

Stolypin's successors naturally proved unequal to the struggle in which such a giant as he succumbed. In fact, they hardly made any attempt to continue it; the fate of their predecessor was an only too sharp and threatening warning, You must crouch and belittle yourself, was the feeling; it is dangerous to oppose, and heaven forbid that we should be the wall of defence. Only at such a price was it possible to remain in power—at the price of self-effacement. And the government effaced itself, the government capitulated all along the line.

The conditions under which the electoral campaign for the fourth Duma took place, are in the memory of all. The government drew up and carried out a vast plan for falsifying the elections. It is true that in certain respects this plan failed, and it has accordingly become the custom to regard it with indulgent irony. But it is forgotten that on the other side the failure of the plan is ascribed to the inconsistency of those charged with its execution, to digressions from the prearranged system. The electoral campaign of the government made perfectly clear the direction taken by government policy. Not infrequently the

keen edge of administrative intervention was directed specially
against the Octobrists. Accounts were settled both with the party
in general—which even when it collaborated with the government had maintained an entirely independent policy—and also
with individual members of the party, who were uncongenial to
the central or the local authorities. The government's attack
on the Octobrists during the elections to the fourth Duma was in
any case a characteristic episode in the story of one attempt of
the Russian public to co-operate with the government.

The results of the success attained by the reaction very soon
made themselves felt. Political productiveness came to an end.
The government was fast bound in a paralysis; it had neither
Imperial aims nor a broadly conceived plan, nor a common will.
Instead there were a conflict of personal intrigues and aspirations,
a continual attempt to settle personal accounts, and dissensions
between various departments. The ship of state has lost its course,
and is aimlessly tossing on the waves. Never has the authority of
the Imperial Government sunk so low. Not only has the government failed to arouse sympathy or confidence; it is incapable of
inspiring even fear. Even the harm that it does, it sometimes does
without ill-will, very often it does it unintelligently, in the way
of reflex, spasmodic movements. Only the comic element was
lacking. And this touch, too, the government has managed to
introduce, making all Russia roar with laughter, with tragic
laughter.

True, there are some Ministries which by inertia or through
the chance of favourable circumstances continue working on the
plan that was drafted under other conditions; but even these
meet at best with cool indifference on the part of the central
government, and a worst with ill-will and opposition. True,
on solemn occasions the old, familiar words are sometimes ut-
tered, but no one believes them now—neither speakers nor
hearers.

The collapse of the central government naturally finds its
reflection in a complete disorganisation of local administration.
A kind of administrative decentralisation has actually been
effected, but it is a caricature on the very idea of decentralisation.
On the strength of this peculiar type of autonomy the local authorities, confident in their impunity and guessing, so to speak,

at the views of the central government, have developed the arbitrary exercise of authority to an incredible degree, sometimes to the point of sheer ruffianism.

It is wholly natural that in such circumstances the government should find itself solitary, abandoned by all. As a matter of fact, reaction in its various forms has no roots anywhere in the country, unless we count those political organisations which have been fattened at the Treasury's expense and which try to hide under flags and banners their impotence and insignificance. The public sympathy and confidence which the government in the time of Stolypin attracted to itself at the cost of great toil and effort, receded in one moment from the government of his successors. The honeymoon is over.

But the paralysis of the government has made itself felt not only in internal collapse. Events of world-wide, immense, historical importance have occurred. Broad horizons opened up before Russia, new and unprecedentedly favourable international combinations arose. The historical traditions of Russia, her real political interests, her honour and her profit demanded of her that she, as the great Slavonic power, should play a decisive part in this world-wide crisis. Russia, a vigorous, powerful, healthy Russia, loyal to her history and confident in her future, a Russia like this would have done her duty. But that state of prostration and marasm which numbed our political organism at home, fettered our movements and paralysed our will abroad. Our timid and incapable foreign policy let slip all those advantages which opened out before Russia through no merit of our own, but through the efforts of others and by the will of a fortune that had at last turned in our favour. But it also lost even the positions won in previous reigns by incalculable sacrifices on the part of the Russian people. We must not shut our eyes to the fact that those bloodless but shameful defeats which Russia suffered during the Balkan crisis had an enormous effect on the popular temper, especially among the masses of the people and those sections of the educated classes who, like the people, regard the question of Russia's *rôle* as a Great Power as the chief article of their political faith, outweighing in importance all questions as to defects in the conduct of internal affairs.

What is to be the issue of the grave crisis through which we are now passing? What does the encroachment of reaction bring with it? Whither is the government policy, or rather lack of policy, carrying us?

Towards an inevitable and grave catastrophe! In this general forecast all are agreed; people of the most sharply opposed political views, of the most varied social groups, all agree with a rare, an unprecedented unanimity. Even representatives of the government, of that government which is the chief offender against the Russian people, are prepared to agree to this forecast, and their official and obligatory optimism ill conceals their inward alarm.

When will the catastrophe take effect? What forms will it assume? Who can foretell? Some scan the horizon with joyful anticipation, others with dread. But greatly do those err who calculate that on the ruins of the demolished system will arise that order which corresponds to their particular political and social views. In those forces that seem likely to come to the top in the approaching struggle, I do not see stable elements that would guarantee any kind of permanent political order. Are we not rather in danger of being plunged into a period of protracted, chronic anarchy which will lead to the dissolution of the Empire? Shall we not again pass through a Time of Trouble, only under new and more dangerous international conditions?

Looking back over the short but instructive political path we have traversed, we must confess that the attempt made by the Russian public as represented in our party—the attempt to get into touch with the government, to work in unison with it in carrying out in the life of Russia the principles the government itself has recognised, the attempt to effect a peaceful, painless transition from the old condemned system to a new order, has failed. We collaborated, honourably and loyally, we made no excessive claims, we had no ulterior motives. Octobrism maintained its position to the end, and was true to the contract even when the other side failed to carry out the terms. So long as we had faith in the sincerity and goodwill of the government, we could be indulgent and patient; we made concessions, we allowed respite, we could wait, for we fully appreciated the difficulty of the position; we saw the obstacles with which the government had to cope.

Yes, the attempt of the Octobrists to reconcile these two

perpetually hostile forces—the government and the public—has ended in failure. But was Octobrism an error, a historical error, for which the Russian public or, more particularly, we Octobrists are to blame? Is it our fault that under the influence of the very natural optimism which the epoch inspired in us we believed in the promises of the government, presented as they were in the form of solemn Imperial acts? Our optimism has suffered defeat. But then all the history of recent years is one long series of failures and defeats, in which we shall in vain try to discover any victors. For in that historical drama of which during the last ten years Russia has been the scene, failure has been the lot of all the actors as one after another they appeared on the political stage and disappeared, failure has been the lot of reaction and of revolution, of radicalism and of socialism, of nationalism and of liberalism. Just now reaction and possibly restoration are steadily making their way to the front. But is their success assured, and if so, is it assured for long? Now even though Octobrism has shared the sad fate of all political attempts made during the last few years, it has not been a historical error. There would have been no justification for the Russian public, if at a moment when great danger menaced the State it had refused its support to a government which, as it seemed, had conscientiously and resolutely set to work to carry out reforms long demanded by public opinion. In the history of the epoch of liberation there was bound to be a moment when the public loyally supported the policy of the government. An isolated government would inevitably have been condemned to failure in its attempts to effect reform. And thus it would have secured the best justification for a return to the older order. But if the Octobrist experiment in collaborating with the government for purposes common to both was a historical necessity and not an error, it would be a wholly unjustifiable error if the experiment were to be continued under the changed conditions of the present and with the lessons of the past before our eyes.

We are, in fact, now confronted with an entirely new political situation, one that has practically nothing in common with that which prevailed when our party was formed and our tactics were determined. The government with which we are now face to face is not the government with which we made our contract. Formerly, in spite of all defects in the reform work of the government, the country had no ground for anxiety in respect to the main acquisition of the epoch of liberation, namely, the representative assembly, with which all the future of Russia is bound up. But in the present policy of the government we cannot fail to recognise a direct menace to the constitutional system, and the beginning of a liquidation of the era of reforms. We know that the question of the system under which Russia is to be governed has been raised, if not by the government itself, at any rate in those extragovernmental circles that are stronger than the government. Functionaries of state, eager to make their career, keep officiously putting forward their plans for a *coup d'état* and offering themselves as agents for its execution. Will this be a real *coup d'état* abrupt and open, clearly indicating the future character and competency of the representative assembly? Will it take the form of a dissolution of the Duma without the convocation of a new one? Or will not a more timid, narrow, and cautious policy be adopted, that of gradually restricting the rights of the representative assembly by means of interpretations *ad hoc* on particular points, by establishing precedents as occasion arises? Perhaps the bold step of infringing the fundamental laws will not be taken for the present, and the Imperial Duma will again be convened on the basis of the existing electoral law, only that the enormous apparatus which the government has at its disposal for the purposes of a wholesale falsification of the elections would this time be applied consistently and inflexibly.

What must the Russian public do in view of this danger which menaces not particular reforms but reform itself and its vital centre, the idea of national representation? What is to be done by those political parties who have made it their object to bring about the reveval of Russia on the bases of those principles of political liberty and social justice which found expression in the decrees of the Sovereign during the epoch of liberation? What can and what should be done by the Imperial Duma, that body which has been charged by the people to guard the permanence of the political system?

True, at the price of meekness, faint-hearted concession, humiliating compacts the representative assembly might succeed in gaining a respite, on condition that it confined itself to petty, humdrum work and refrained from touching on great problems of state. And then it might be hoped that when the dark days pass and the horizon brightens, it would be found to have safely survived this gloomy time and to have held its place in the apparatus of the State and so would be able once again to occupy a commanding position in the political system and to work broadly and productively. But would the Duma really maintain its existence even at such a price? And would not this be tantamount to the political suicide of the representative assembly, the wreck of the very idea of national representation in the mind of the people? And in the meantime, in our political organism the process of dissolution would rage unchecked, mortifying the vital tissues and accumulating the elements of death and corruption.

For an Imperial Duma faithful to its duty to the Emperor and the Empire, there is only one way. If other organs of authority take refuge in timorous connivance, or it may be are themselves criminal accomplices, the Imperial Duma must take up the defence of the cause of Russian liberty and of the integrity of our political system. It must devote to this cause all the instruments of its powers, all the strength of its authority. The weapons of warfare at the disposal of the representative assembly, however limited their number may seem, have not all been made use of to the fullest extent. In the name of a long looked-for political liberty, in defence of the constitutional pinciple, in the struggle for reforms, all legal forms of parliamentary combat must be employed—parliamentary freedom of speech, the authority of the parliamentary tribune, the right of rejecting bills, and, first and foremost, the Duma's budget rights, the right of refusing votes of money.

The only government that should be able to count on the support of the representative assembly is one whose character was the guarantee that it would not become the instrument of a *coup d'état*, but would undertake the execution of that broad programme of liberal reforms which found expression in the important political acts of the epoch of liberation. These acts, in the name of the Sovereign, affirmed the principles of the constitutional system and of legal order, proclaimed the immutability of the bases of civil liberty, expressed a desire to maintain the prestige of the Imperial Duma, and to guarantee it its due importance. They maintained the true view that the government should not be an instrument for counteracting the decisions of the Duma, they recognised the importance of establishing normal relations between the Duma and the Upper House by reforming the Imperial Council through the introduction of a considerable elective element, they impressed on officials of all ranks the need for frankness and sincerity in affirming civil liberty and establishing its guarantees, and, finally, they sketched out the main lines of an economic policy aiming at securing the welfare of the masses of the people.

Compare these lofty words, which are taken in their entirety from the important government document that accompanied the Manifesto of October 17, with the present actions and policy of the government, and you will see the downward curve described by the Russian Government during this short period. To pick up the programme that its authors have dropped, "to adopt it," as indicated in the Emperor's note, "for guidance," to compel the government to carry it out—this is the most urgent task, this is the most important duty of the Imperial Duma.

And it is upon us, Octobrists, that this duty primarily lies. Once in the days of the people's madness we raised our sobering voice against the excesses of radicalism. In the days of the madness of the government it is we who should speak to the government a grave word of warning. We once believed and invited others to believe; we patiently waited. Now we must declare that our patience is exhausted, and with our patience our faith; at such a moment as this we must not leave to the professional Opposition, to the radical and socialist parties, the monopoly of opposing the government and the ruinous policy it has adopted; for in so doing we should create the dangerous illusion that the government is combating radical utopias and social experiments—whereas it is opposing the satisfaction of the most moderate and elementary demands of public opinion, demands that at one time were admitted by the government itself. Before the approaching catastrophe it is we who should make the final attempt to bring the government to reason, to open its eyes, to awaken in it the alarm that we so strongly feel. For we are the representatives of those propertied classes, all the vital interests of which are bound up with the peaceful evolution of the State, and on which in case of disaster the first blow will fall.

Who will be the allies of the Octobrists in this struggle for fundamental reforms within and without the Duma? Our political life has hardly begun; our political parties have not yet emerged from the formative stage and their boundaries are still transitory and fluctuating. Within the limits of those aims which the Octobrists now set themselves, and within the limits of those methods of combat which the Octobrists find proper, they will accept any help. But Octobrism cannot lose its independent character on account of the existence of a common danger and a common enemy, or in virtue of a similarity in technical methods adapted to the present moment. Octobrism was based on a thoroughly definite political philosophy. This philosophy was not elaborated in the study or at party meetings. It was fostered by years of experience, by definite tendencies in the Russian social organism; it grew up around the cultural work of the Russian liberal *bourgeoisie,* chiefly in the sphere of local government. The programme that formed, as it were, the deed of constitution of the Octobrist party naturally arose out of this philosophy. This programme comprises definite solutions of the main problems of Russian life which the present generation has to face; and community of tactics at the present moment cannot efface or even conceal those points of difference, those deep lines of demarcation which separate Octobrism from other tendencies in public life and give it an important and independent place in the general economy of Russian political parties.

Will our voice be heard? Will our cry of warning reach the heights where the fate of Russia is decided? Shall we succeed in communicating to the government our own alarm? Shall we awaken it from the lethargy that envelops it? We should be glad to think so. In any case, this is our last opportunity of securing a peaceful issue from the crisis. Let those in power make no mistake about the temper of the people; let them not take outward indications of prosperity as a pretext for lulling themselves into security. Never were those revolutionary organisations which aim at a violent upheaval so broken and impotent as they are now, and never were the Russian public and the Russian people so profoundly revolutionised by the actions of the government, for day by day faith in the government is steadily waning, and with it is waning faith in the possibility of a peaceful issue from the crisis.

The danger at the present moment lies, in fact, not in the revolutionary parties, not in anti-monarchical propaganda, not in anti-religious teaching, not in the dissemination of the ideas of socialism and anti-militarism, not in the agitation of anarchists against the government. The historical drama through which we are now passing lies in the fact that we are compelled to uphold the monarchy against those who are the natural defenders of the monarchical principle, we are compelled to defend the Church against the ecclesiastical hierarchy, the army against its leaders, the authority of the government against the government itself. We seemed to have sunk into a state of public despondency and apathy, a passive condition. But thence it is only one step to despair, which is an active force of tremendously destructive quality. May God avert from our country the danger that overshadows it.

CHAPTER IV

FROM   *Michael Karpovich*

Two Types of Russian Liberalism

The alternative to the revolutions of 1917 in Russia was a re-formed political structure in which a considerable role would necessarily be played by Russian liberals. In this paper, Michael Karpovich, who always opposed determinist views on the events of 1917, examines and compares the rightist and leftist wings of Russian liberalism as illustrated by the careers of two of their principal spokesmen.

The weakness of prerevolutionary Russian liberalism has become a commonplace in historical literature. Too often, it has been asserted as something self-evident, and thus not in need of further investigation. This attitude has been based largely on an a priori reasoning, the weakness of Russian liberalism being deduced from the weakness of the middle class in Russia. The latter, in turn, has been rather assumed than investigated. Moreover, another broad assumption has been involved—that of an

SOURCE. Michael Karpovich, "Two Types of Russian Liberalism," in Ernest J. Simmons, Ed., *Continuity and Change in Russian and Soviet Thought* (Cambridge, Mass.: Harvard University Press, copyright, 1955), pp. 129–43. Reprinted by permission of the publishers and the President and Fellows of Harvard College.

organic connection between liberalism and middle classes, as if it were natural and almost inevitable for a middle class to favor a middle-of-the-road policy. Coupled with this, there has been a fairly common tendency to identify the middle class with the business community, the bourgeoisie in the Marxian sense of the term.

The validity of neither of these basic asumptions can be taken for granted. The designation of a social group as a middle class merely indicates its central position in a given society, and consequently the nature of the middle class can vary from one country to another, in accordance with the country's social structure. Thus it might be argued, as it has been argued in the case of the Polish *szlachta,* that the bulk of the Russian gentry was a middle class as distinguished from the landed aristocracy. Much more important, however, is the other point—the one referring to the relationship between the middle class and liberalism. We know from historical experience that under certain conditions middle-class groups might support extremist political movements, as in the cases of Italian Fascism and German Nazism, for instance, or that at least they might retreat from their liberal positions as they did in France under the Third Empire and again in Bismarck's Germany. On the other hand, the history of European liberalism cannot be reduced to that of the "businessman's creed," as Laski attempted to do. This was only one of its component parts, and de Ruggiero convincingly demonstrated the primary importance of other elements that went into its make-up —such as religious dissent and the defense of "ancient liberties" by the privileged estates of feudal origin.

It is neither necessary nor possible for me to discuss these general questions in the present paper. The purpose of the foregoing remarks was to point out the complexity of the problem and the need for its further investigation. The history of Russian liberalism has been sadly neglected. To many, the a priori assumption of its weakness seems to have been fully justified by the course of events in Russia since the Revolution. Why should one pay much attention to a political trend which could not achieve any lasting results and which suffered such a crushing defeat? The answer to this question is twofold. In the first place, the historical process does not know any "ultimate" results—any "final" defeats or victories. And secondly, the importance of historical phenomena should be assessed as of the time when they occurred, and not only in the light of the historian's *post factum* wisdom. Certainly, *vae victis* is not a principle for historians to follow!

As elsewhere, liberalism in Russia was not a homogeneous movement. It proceeded from different social groups, and various motives induced people to join it. This lack of homogeneity was clearly refflected in the make-up of the Constitutional Democratic Party founded in October of 1905. It has been repeatedly pointed out that it came into being as the result of the merging of two forces: the zemstvo liberals, on the one hand, and the liberal-minded part of the professional class, on the other. Strictly speaking, this is an oversimplification. There were other elements in the party which by their social provenience did not belong to either of the two groups, and inside each of the latter there could be found a considerable variety of political attitudes and aspirations. By and large, however, one can accept the accuracy of this summary characterization of the two main components of the Cadet Party, and it is in the light of this division that I am going to discuss the two types of Russian liberalism as exemplified by Maklakov and Miliukov respectively.

Vasilii Alekseevich Maklakov, born in 1869, was exactly ten years younger than Pavel Nikolaevich Miliukov. If I begin my discussion with Maklakov it is because he represents some of the prevailing trends of the zemstvo liberalism which historically preceded that of the professional class. Not that he was a zemstvo worker himself, but it so happened that his political education was greatly influenced by the zemstvo liberal tradition. In his reminiscences, he speaks of his father and those around him as being imbued with the spirit of the Great Reforms of the 1860's, strongly favoring their continuation and extension, but remaining rather indifferent to politics. He also pictures them as being resolutely opposed to the terroristic activity of the *Narodnaia Volia*. Both in the secondary school and in the university, he found the Russian youth of the time on the whole sharing the attitude of their elders. According to his observations, even the student disturbances of 1887 and 1890, during the years when he himself was a student at the University of Moscow, as yet were devoid of "politics." The great majority of the students were motivated by the concern for academic freedom and their own corporate rights as well as by a feeling of "student solidarity," and they resented the attempts of some of their more radical colleagues to inject into the movement general political slogans. When in 1890 the Moscow students organized a memorial service for Chernyshevskii (d. 1889), this again was an expression of their sympathy for a man who suffered for his convictions rather than a political manifestation. In his last volume of memoirs, speaking of himself as he was at the age of twenty, Maklakov says that all his sympathies were "with those representatives [of the period] of Great Reforms who wanted to continue to improve the [Russian] state on the bases of legality, freedom, and justice, taking for their starting point that which already existed in reality . . ."

Characteristically, a trip to France that he made in 1889 served for him as a "lesson in conservatism." What impressed him was the picture of a country where "rights of the state could be reconciled with the rights of man" and where even the opposition "showed a concern for what had been created by history." The centenary of the French Revolution made him read the recent literature on the subject, and from this reading he derived a "new, historical understanding" of the Revolution—as opposed, one must assume, to the romantic and idealizing interpretation of it that was current among the Russian radicals of the time. It is not without significance that of all the revolutionary leaders Mirabeau became his favorite hero.

While in Paris, Maklakov got in touch with some leaders of the French student organizations, of a professional rather than a political nature. Their existence and the character of their work largely inspired young Maklakov in that active part which, upon his return to Russia, he took in the attempts to develop nonpolitical student organizations at the University of Moscow (mutual-aid societies and the like), within the rather narrow limits of the then existing legal possibilities. Thus he was one of the early leaders of what later became known as "academism" (a term which acquired a derogatory meaning for the opponents of this tendency from among the radical students)—in a sense, a student counterpart of that "economism" among the workers which was supported by some of the early Social Democrats and served as a target for Lenin's violent diatribes. For Maklakov, however, it was a step in the development of his liberalism, not in opposition to, but in harmony with the general program of "improving the Russian state" by starting from "that which already existed in reality."

During these years, Maklakov was greatly influenced by his association with the so-called Lubenkov circle, one of the traditional Russian discussion groups, in this case gathered around an eminent Moscow jurist and consisting of various public leaders mostly from among the zemstvo workers. A decade later, Maklakov became a recording secretary of a similar discussion group known as *Beseda* (here best translated as "Symposium") and headed by D. N. Shipov, subsequently one of the founders of the Octobrist Party. Together with some more politically minded zemstvo constitutionalists, the *Beseda* included also, besides Shipov, such other representatives of the "purer" zemstvo tradition as N. A. Khomiakov and M. A. Stakhovich. Both Lubenkov and Shipov had definite Slavophile leanings. While not accepting the original Slavophile doctrine in its entirety, and certainly not sharing its almost anarchical aberrations as exemplified, for instance, by Konstantin Aksakov's political theory, they still showed a strong affinity with Slavophilism in their somewhat diluted antistatist attitude, their emphasis on "public work" as distinguished from, if not opposed to, political activity, their relative indifference to forms of government and strictly defined constitutional formulas, as well as in their traditionalism. There can be no doubt that the influence of these men left its traces on Maklakov's brand of liberalism.

There was one point, however, where Maklakov substantially differed from the Slavophiles, and the difference can be defined by calling him a Slavophile who had learned the necessity of legal guarantees for the preservation of human rights and freedom. After several years of intense preoccupation with historical studies which led Maklakov to think of an academic career, he decided to shift to jurisprudence and to become a lawyer. The final choice was made not on the basis of either intellectual interests or practical considerations, but in response to the call of civic duty. This is what Maklakov himself has to say on the subject: "My brief life experience had shown me . . . that the main evil of Russian life was the triumph of arbitrariness that went unpunished, the helplessness of the individual in the face of administrative discretion, the lack of legal bases for his self-defense . . . The defense of the individual against lawlessness, in other words, the defense of the law itself—this was the substance of the Bar's public service." This defense of the individual, however, was not to be waged in a spirit of aggressive partisanship, and the lawyer's task was to seek for a synthesis between the rights of the state, on the one hand, and those of the individual, on the other. Here, in a nucleus, is that philosophy of compromise which became characteristic of Maklakov the politician.

The role played by Maklakov's legal career in the development of his liberal views has more than a mere biographical interest. It has a broader significance in so far as it points toward another important element in the make-up of Russian liberalism —the Russian counterpart of the German *Rechtsstaat* idea which while not necessarily connected with political liberalism eventually led many of its exponents to strive for the abolition of autocracy and the establishment of a constitutional regime. . . .

In the case of Miliukov . . . one can . . . indicate those points in which Miliukov's political upbringing seems to have differed from that of Maklakov. We knew from Miliukov himself that in his youth he was strongly influenced by both Spencer and Comte, and that as a university student he was seriously interested in Marx's writings. As the same intellectual fare was typical of the radical youth of the period, one might assume in Miliukov a somewhat greater affinity with their *Weltanschauung* than one could expect in the case of Maklakov with his mildly Slavophile leanings. While being associated with the moderate wing of the student movement, Miliukov watched with sympathy the *Narodnaia Volia's* assault upon autocracy, seeing in their terroristic activities "one of the means of political struggle." This is significantly different from that attitude of unreserved condemnation of political terror which, according to Maklakov's reminiscences, prevailed in his milieu a decade later. If the latter reflected the views of the moderate zemstvo majority, Miliukov's position agreed with that of the somewhat more radical minority among the early zemstvo liberals. One of them, I. I. Petrunkevich, who even attempted to form a kind of working alliance with the revolutionaries, later became Miliukov's chief political mentor.

In the volume of essays dedicated to Miliukov on the occasion of his seventieth anniversary, S. A. Smirnov dates Miliukov's "actively political attitude" from the famine year of 1891, while V. A. Obolenskii asserts that he already was a "convinced liberal and democrat" at the time of his graduation from the university. The fact remains, however, that in Miliukov the politician matured much more slowly than the scholar. For a number of years after graduation, he was almost completely absorbed in historical research and teaching. Within the period 1892–1903 appeared all of his most important scholarly works, beginning with the *National Economy of Russia and the Reforms of Peter the Great* and ending with the third volume of *Outlines of Russian Culture*. Miliukov's intensive scholarly activity went on even after his academic career had been brusquely terminated by his dismissal from the University of Moscow on rather flimsy charges of a political nature. One is tempted to say that Miliukov became an active politician almost in spite of himself.

Miliukov's real political activity began in the first years of the century, simultaneously with the general revival of the opposition sentiment in the country, and more particularly in connection with the formation of the Union of Liberation. From the outset, he took an active part in the Liberation movement, in contrast to Maklakov, who, according to his own admission, remained on the periphery until the establishment of the constitutional regime. The difference, of course, was not accidental. Miliukov joined the movement with an intention of forcing its zemstvo elements to adopt a more radical attitude and to ally themselves more closely with the professional intellectuals on the Left. To Maklakov, such a development was a source of serious doubts and misgivings. In retrospect, he sees the initial strength of the Liberation movement in the fact that it was primarily a zemstvo movement, organically connected with the "era of Great Reforms" and nutured in the tradition of public work performed within the framework of local self-government institutions. It was losing rather than gaining strength in allying itself with other public elements which were devoid of practical political experience. These new allies differed from the majority of the zemstvo men not only in their final aims, but, which was more important, also in the choice of means for the achievement of the immediate objectives. Under their influence, "the Liberation movement became too indifferent to that dividing line which should have separated the evolution of the state from the evils of a revolution."

Maklakov has been accused by some of his critics of evaluating past events from the vantage ground of wisdom acquired in the course of subsequent historical experience. But while to some extent this is true, there is enough evidence to permit us to believe that in a large measure his present judgment reflects the attitude he had at the time when the events he is evaluating were taking place. This attitude explains his relative aloofness from the Liberation movement. It explains also the casual way in which he joined the Cadet Party and accepted election to its central committee. He freely admits that he was not a very good Cadet, and it is on the record that on several important occasions he found himself in disagreement with the majority of the Party members and with its leaders. In its turn, the Party, while glad to make use of Maklakov's remarkable oratorical gift as well as of his legal erudition and ability, did not look upon him as a dependable Party regular.

It would be impossible, within the scope of this paper, to follow the Miliukov–Maklakov controversy through all the stages of its development. Nor is it necessary for my present purpose. What is of importance is the fundamental cleavage between these two outstanding representatives of Russian liberalism, the difference in the main premises and the general spirit of their political actions. In this case, as in that of many other Russian political trends, the Revolution of 1905 played the part of a catalyst. In Maklakov, it strengthened his fear of all and every revolution, his conviction that revolutionary methods were not only undesirable but in the long run futile. He counted on the evolutionary process in the course of which the regime was bound to change "under the pressure of life itself." In his opinion, it was preferable to try to contribute to the regime's peaceful evolution and not to aim at its complete overthrow. The "historical state power" had one decisive advantage on its side: the people were in the habit of obeying it. It was precisely this inertia of obedience that would be destroyed by a revolution, and with it would go that legal continuity which was so important for the normal growth of a nation. The results could be foreseen on the basis of historical experience: the new government issuing from the revolution either would be so weak that it could not maintain itself in power or else it would be forced to become a ruthless dictatorship.

Maklakov had no illusions as to the nature of the Russian regime of the period. But he still thought that it would be amenable to the pressure of organized public opinion had the liberals used every opportunity to reach an agreement with it, on a program of gradually introduced reforms. In this lay the historical task of Russian liberalism. Maklakov felt that the liberals were missing their chance of contributing to Russia's peaceful evolution by assuming an uncompromisingly hostile attitude toward the regime and thus allying themselves with the destructive revolutionary forces in the country. This appeal to the Acheron (the symbol of the "lower world" in Greek and Latin poetry) was bound to end in the liberals' undoing: their cause would be lost whether revolution won the victory or suffered defeat.

In the eyes of Maklakov the failure of the Russian liberals to approach their political task in a proper spirit became obvious after the proclamation of the constitutional regime. The October Manifesto of 1905 opened a real opportunity for the peaceful solution of Russia's problems, and it was up to the Cadet Party to lead the way in this undertaking. But for this a kind of psychological demobilization was necessary. Unfortunately, the Party could not get rid of its "wartime psychology," and instead of seeking a lasting peace with the government, which could be based on a compromise only, insisted on continuing to wage the struggle until the "final victory." In this connection, Maklakov cites an extemporaneous speech made by Miliukov in Moscow, upon the receipt of the news of the Manifesto's publication, in which he said "that nothing was changed, and the war still was going on."

It is on the basis of these general premises that Maklakov has severely criticized the Cadet policies of the years 1905–1907. The main points of his indictment can be summarized as follows:

The maximalism of the Party's programmatic demands, such as, in particular, the convocation of a Constituent Assembly which could not be realized unless there was a complete capitulation on the part of the imperial government;

The Party's uncompromising attitude toward both Witte and

Stolypin who, according to Maklakov, could and should be used as allies rather than abused as enemies;

The peremptory way in which the Cadet leaders rejected the idea of Cadet participation in the government advanced both by Witte and Stolypin;

The Party's tendency to use the Duma as a tribune for anti-governmental agitation rather than for constructive legislative activity;

Its dogmatic insistence on the immediate revision of the Fundamental Laws, aiming at a universal franchise, reduced powers of the upper chamber, and ministerial responsibility—matters which, in Maklakov's opinion, could be settled gradually as the constitutional regime grew stronger and took firmer roots in the Russian soil;

And finally the issuance of the Vyborg Manifesto—essentially a revolutionary measure in so far as the dissolution of the Duma and the appointment of new elections were in accordance with the constitution.

Maklakov admits that the other Cadet leaders neither wanted a revolution nor acquiesced in its eventual triumph. But he feels that, unlike himself, they were not afraid of it—some because they did not believe in the possibility of its victory, others because they thought that it could be stopped in its initial stages. Meanwhile, "as the threat of the revolution might have forced the government to make [further] concessions, they continued to play this card, not realizing that they were playing with fire." . . .

Miliukov begins his defense of the Cadet Party by a characteristically empirical reference to the actual conditions in which the Party had to formulate its program and to make its tactical decisions. The Party, he reminds Maklakov, was not living "on abstractions and armchair (*kabinetnye*) deliberations." Its position was shifting now to the right and now to the left, "together with the life of the Russian society." Elsewhere he refers to the psychology of the time—that surge of emotion which was caused by the events of 1905, and from which the rank and file of the Party did not remain immune. He points out that the Party leaders, while trying to maintain the central position, were forced to make occasional concessions to the more impatient spirit of many of their followers. He insists, however, that the Cadet program, while "radical," was not Utopian. What Miliukov means by "radical" becomes clear from his reference to "neoliberalism" as a kindred movement in Western Europe. Back in October 1905, in his opening address, at the first ("constituent") convention of the Constitutional Democratic Party, he made the same comparison in slightly different terms: ". . . our Party stands closest to those groups among the Western intellectuals who are known under the name of 'social reformers' . . . our program is undoubtedly the most Leftist of all those advanced by similar political groups in Western Europe."

In a different context, Miliukov accuses Maklakov of stressing the tactics at the expense of the program, attaching more importance to the means than to the aims. He argues that under certain conditions even a liberal might become a revolutionary, and that thus one cannot equate liberalism with a strictly legal way of political action. It is equally erroneous to confuse a defense of the rule of law with that of a given positive law, as Maklakov's reasoning tends to do. Nor should one ascribe such a decisive role to the preservation of legal continuity in the transition from one political order to the other.

If, in these last arguments, Miliukov opposes to Maklakov's traditionalism his own historical relativism, in another case, when dealing with a proper approach to political problems, he blames his opponent for an excessively relativist point of view. Miliukov sees the chief defect of Maklakov the politician in his attempt to transfer into the sphere of politics the psychology and methods of a lawyer. The latter inevitably acquires a professional habit of "seeing a share of truth on the opposite side, and a share of error on his own." A politician cannot allow himself the luxury of such an indifferent and "objective" attitude toward "the contents of truth." Here Miliukov is striking at the very heart of Maklakov's "philosophy of compromise."

Apart from this theoretical disagreement, a radically different interpretation of political events was involved in the controversy. Miliukov did not share in the least Maklakov's optimistic appraisal of Russia's chances of peaceful evolution after the proclamation of the constitutional regime. I have cited above Miliukov's admission that at the time of the publication of the October Manifesto he did not see in it any real change that would induce him to stop fighting the government. Twenty-five years later Miliukov still asserted the correctness of his original diagnosis. Referring to Nicholas II's statement that after the revision of the Fundamental Laws "autocracy remained the same as of old," he declared the Tsar to be closer to the truth than Maklakov, "even from the formal point of view." He also stoutly maintained that the Cadet leaders had been right in repelling the overtures of both Witte and Stolypin, as in neither case had there been any evidence of sincerity. By joining the government on conditions that were proposed to them, Party representatives would have walked into a trap: while being unable to exercise a decisive influence on governmental policies they would have compromised themselves in the eyes of the people.

How these considerations affected the tactical line which was followed by Miliukov in 1905–06 can be seen from the various statements made by him at that time in his capacity as party leader. Thus in his opening address at the first Party convention he expressed himself as follows: ". . . in fighting for our aim we cannot count on any agreements and compromises [with the government], and we should raise high the banner already unfurled by the Russian liberation movement as a whole, striving for the convocation of a Constituent Assembly . . ." This was said a few days before the publication of the October Manifesto. But in its closing session, which took place on the morrow of this event, the convention adopted a resolution (undoubtedly edited by Miliukov) in which it reiterated that "in so far as the state Duma cannot be recognized as an adequate [organ of] popular representation, the aim of the Constitutional Democratic Party remains the same as before—namely, [the convocation of] the Constituent Assembly." As to the Duma, "it can serve for the Party only as one of the means towards realization of the above-mentioned aim, while a permanent and close contact should be maintained with the general course of the liberation movement outside the Duma."

The last sentence obviously implied a coördination of the Cadet Party's efforts with the activities of the parties of the Left. This subject was discussed by Miliukov at the convention in the following terms:

"Between us and our allies, not adversaries, from the Left (this is how I prefer to call them) there also exists a certain dividing line, but it is of an altogether different nature from the one that we have drawn to the right of us. Together with them we stand on the same Left wing of the Russian political movement. We do not join them in their demands for a democratic republic and nationalization of means of production. To some of us these demands are generally unacceptable while others consider them as being outside [the realm of] practical politics. But so long as, in spite of different motives, it remains possible for us to march together to a common goal, both party groups will act as a single unit."

In the course of time, the difference between Miliukov and Maklakov lost a good deal of its sharpness as far as *tactical* problems were concerned. Events themselves took care of that. By the fall of 1907, the revolutionary energy was totally spent, and there were no visible prospects of its resurgence. The government had recovered its control over the country, and there was a conservative majority in the Duma. The Cadets had to adjust themselves to the new situation. "To preserve the Duma" now became the official slogan. This meant to make the best of the existing circumstances, and to take part in the legislative activity, modest as its scope might be. In this way, the Cadet Party, still led by Miliukov, was moving to the right, in Maklakov's direction. But there was also a reverse process, this time affecting the moderates of the Maklakov type and even those to the right of him. As yet it has not been studied by historians, but it surely can be traced as a slowly but steadily developing trend in the life of the last two Dumas. As the Duma was growing more sure of itself, even its conservative majority was becoming less and less inclined to acquiesce in the arbitrariness of the administration or to overlook its inefficiency. By the end of the period, the opposition spirit in the Duma was by no means limited to the Cadets and those to the left of them. Thus was prepared the ground for the formation of the Progressive Bloc in 1915 and through it for the first Provisional Government.

All this, however, does not deprive the controversy as it developed in 1905–06 of its considerable historical interest. It was then, in a period of crisis, that the two different concepts of an appropriate liberal policy found its fullest and most articulate expression. Essentially, the Russian liberals faced the same problem with which the Social Democrats were struggling at the same time: What was the nature of the transformation Russia was undergoing, and what were its possible limits? Closely linked with this problem was another question: What were the forces in the country that would be able to bring this transformation to a successful conclusion? Maklakov saw the historical need of the hour in the continuation and completion of the Great Reforms of the 1860's, in the establishment in Russia of a political order based on the rule of law and self-government, and he believed that it could and should be effected in an evolutionary way, without the destruction of the existing political and social structure. In his eyes, even a thorough democratization of the latter was not immediately feasible and could be left to the future. For the time being, lasting reforms could be achieved only under the direction of those elements in the country which were prepared for the task by their previous practical experience in the field of public or governmental work. This was why the liberals had to ally themselves with those groups to the right of them which recognized the necessity of reforms, and why they had to seek an agreement with the government whenever an opportunity presented itself. Maklakov minimized the danger of reaction for which he saw no solid base in the prevailing trends of national life. To him, the main danger was on the left and not on the right. It was the danger of uncontrollable and chaotic revolutionary outbreaks, spurred, even if not provoked, by demagogic policies and appeals.

Miliukov expected from the Russian crisis much more far-reaching results than those envisaged by Maklakov. In his concept, the introduction in Russia of a full-fledged parliamentary regime was an immediate necessity and not a program for a more or less remote future. Unlike Maklakov, he considered the country ripe for popular sovereignty, and he felt that it was the duty of the liberals to wage a battle for this aim so long as there was a chance of its attainment. A much more politically minded person than his opponent, he also wanted the constitutional guarantees to be fully spelled out at once. The extreme importance that he attached to institutional arrangements, which to his critics was a sign of his doctrinaire spirit, in reality proceeded from his firm belief in the logic of political institutions. He did not neglect the social aspects of the Russian problem either, and he emphasized the immediate necessity of a radical agrarian reform as vigorously as he fought for political democracy. I know that the Cadet agrarian project, of which Miliukov was one of the sponsors, appeared rather modest as reflected in the peculiarly slanted looking glass of the Russian political life of the time. The fact remains that it proposed compulsory alienation of private property on such a scale as would be deemed revolutionary in any one of the contemporary Western societies. Miliukov knew, of course, that his political and social program could neither win any support among the Russian moderates nor serve as a basis for an agreement with the government. Thus, in pursuing his aims, he was forced to look for allies among the Left-Wing opposition parties, much as he disliked some of their objectives and methods. If Maklakov minimized the danger of reaction, Miliukov at that time apparently minimized the danger of revolution. To him, the real enemies were on the right and not on the left.

It is not the purpose of this paper to pass judgment on the respective merits of the two political approaches I have tried to outline on the preceding pages. What I want to point out is that both stood in a direct and close relationship with the realities of prerevolutionary Russian life and both had their roots in the native tradition.

Maklakov could cite as his predecessors those public leaders and enlightened bureaucrats who throughout the nineteenth century, from Speranskii on, were concerned with the problem of introducing legality into the Russian government, the mid-century defenders of individual and civil liberty, the architects of the Great Reforms, and the moderate zemstvo liberals. Miliukov's political genealogy would include the Decembrists, Herzen in some of his phases, the more radical zemstvo constitutionalists of the Petrunkevich type, and those of the late nineteenth-century revolutionaries who were prepared to subordinate all other aims to the more immediate task of obtaining a constitutional regime for Russia.

Neither Miliukov nor Maklakov were any more "uprooted" than was the whole liberal movement in Russia, the two different aspects of which they exemplified. Too much has been made of the alleged absence of a social base for a liberal party in Russia. Strictly speaking, none of the Russian political parties had a stable and properly organized social base. If the revolutionary parties benefited from a mushroom growth in a period of national excitement, as happened both to Social Democrats and Socialist Revolutionaries in 1905, the moment the revolutionary wave receded the suddenly acquired social base began to disintegrate, and before long party organizations were reduced to their former, more than modest, proportions. After all, the liberals too had their periods of widespread popularity, first in 1904, and then again in 1906.

It might be argued that the *potential* social base of revolutionary parties was larger than that of the Constitutional Democrats. This is undoubtedly true—if one assumes the inevitability of revolutionary upheavals in imperial Russia. But from this it does not follow that the liberals had no potential base at all. Miluikov and Maklakov agree in their testimony that the Cadet Party was meeting with a mass response among the lower middle class of the cities, and that its ties with this milieu were growing. As the size of this group certainly was not smaller than that of the industrial working class, for instance, it cannot be dismissed as a *quantité négligeable*. Apparently, some of these Cadet constituencies survived even the revolutionary turmoil of 1917 as otherwise it would be difficult to account for the two million votes received by the Cadet Party in the election to the Constituent Assembly. Professor Oliver H. Radkey, in his excellent study of the election, speaks of this result as a "washout" for the Cadets. I am inclined to think that on the contrary, with practically all odds against them, the Cadets did surprisingly well.

At any rate, no conclusion can be made on the basis of the Cadet Party's defeat in the revolution as to the actual or potential strength of liberalism in prerevolutionary Russia. The Russian liberals shared the historical fate of all moderate groups caught in a revolution. There is no need of looking for some specific reasons peculiar to Russia for an explanation of this phenomenon. It is one of the concrete examples of that political polarization which we have observed of late in several Western countries, all of them with a much more numerous middle class and a far stronger liberal tradition than Russia ever possessed, and as yet not in throes of a revolution. Obviously, the assessment of the historical importance of Russian liberalism must be made on different grounds.

CHAPTER V

FROM   *Alfred Levin*
Peter Arkad'evich Stolypin: A Political Appraisal

In this penetrating assessment of the role played by Stolypin in the constitutional monarchy, Professor Levin describes Stolypin's personal strengths and weaknesses, accomplishments and failures. He emphasizes that while Stolypin accepted constitutionalism, he was responsible for serious violations of its form and spirit. He concludes, however, that Stolypin's stature must be measured by his realization of the need to adapt policy to Russia's changing social and economic structure.

The "winged words" of P. A. Stolypin delineating himself as a "constitutionalist and not a parliamentarist" became a part of the political atmosphere of the last decade of the old regime in Russia. The central theme of this study will be a political appraisal of his constitutionalism. For Stolypin's administration was the most creative, the most stable, and the longest under the auspices of the October Manifesto and the Fundamental Laws of May 6, 1906. The capacity of the premier to adapt himself and the massive operation of the bureaucracy to the spirit and the letter of the new constitutional order would serve as an indica-

SOURCE. Alfred Levin, "Peter Arkad'evich Stolypin: A Political Appraisal," *The Journal of Modern History*, **XXXVII**, No. 4 (1965), pp. 445–463. Reprinted by permission of the University of Chicago Press.

tion of whether the imperial regime could adjust itself adequately to the kaleidoscopic changes in the Russian Empire as a part of the European scene. In this perspective Stolypin's activities will be considered within the framework of the constitution he accepted as a basis for action.

More immediately, our study concerns the relation between the provincial bureaucrat in Stolypin's personality and administration and the free-wheeling statesman in the process of creating and executing policies to meet the "pressing demands" of Russian society. While he accepted a constitution, he supported concepts of prior interests and the centralized control of society. And that executive and legislative action is conditioned by his relations with, and attitudes toward, the tsar, the bureaucracy, and all elements of Russian society. These relations were bound to determine the kind of measures and actions he decided that he could and would take.

Stolypin's statements on constitutionalism were varied and contradictory. But he seems to have defined constitutionalism as adherence to a legally regulated (as opposed to an arbitrary) order determined by a fundamental law embodying civil liberties, a Prussian-type parliamentary structure (with every politically conscious element represented but weighted in favor of "dependable" strata), and a cabinet appointed by and responsible to the sovereign who regarded the constitution he granted as an emanation of his autocratic power. From this conception stemmed Stolypin's negative attitude toward parliamentarism, which he identified with a cabinet representative of the imperial Duma and responsible primarily to it. His preference was rooted in his prejudices and his criteria for the stability of the changing regime.

The very suddenness of Stolypin's emergence in the "ruling spheres" in the late stages of the 1905 revolution aroused considerable interest. And his determination to preserve order under exceptional laws and to allow only the specific measures for reform which he would present or support begot a more or less permanent controversy over his personality, program, and purposes.

A man is, at least, the measure of his physical and social environment, and the contradictions manifested in P. A. Stolypin's word and deed, in purpose and accomplishment, were determined in considerable measure by his immediate cultural heritage. In a letter of September 20, 1909, to the author of an annotated compilation of his speeches he wrote: "I do not overrate myself. I only spend capital collected by ancestors and willed to us: unbounded love and loyalty to the tsar and unbounded faith in Russia. . . . that is the treasure—inexhaustible—which cannot be squandered but which can easily be forgotten." His program was conditioned, in fact, largely by the attitudes and convictions that arose from his aristocratic, provincial, and service background and experience. We can expect of the ex-governor a certain impatience with the aspirations and the rights of the new parliamentary institutions and an inclination to react with quick repression against disturbance and even against opposition. But Stolypin's imaginative turn of mind, uninhibited by the habits and procedures of the central bureaucracy, brought an unfettered freshness to the prosecution and philosophy of reform. Furthermore, his experience and, to a certain extent, his family tradition contribute yet another basic pigment to Stolypin's political coloration, his intense nationalism.

Stolypin stemmed from a relatively illustrious *pomiestchik* (gentry) family identifiable from the sixteenth century. Among his forebears he could boast of the usual civil and military bureaucrats and here and there a strong literary tradition that may be reflected in Peter Arkad'evich's oratorical gifts. His family tradition was likewise marked for over a century by a liberal strain in economic theory and practice, and his immediate family was fascinated by constitutionalism. With his father-in-law serving in the immediate court circles, Stolypin was well within the small social stratum that provided almost all the higher officials.

More than a decade of service as marshal of the nobility in Kovno Province and as governor in Grodno molded the range of Stolypin's ideology. He developed specific convictions and programs on the reform of peasant land tenure and on the status of the minorities. In the northwestern provinces he observed the process of peasant enclosures, and as governor of Grodno he promoted that idea along with those of credit and resettlement. His contact with the Polish aristocracy, the Jewish merchants, and the Lithuanian peasants stimulated his sense of Russian national consciousness more than it broadened his attitude toward those groups, and it certainly life him no cosmopolite. He observed the subordinate social and economic position of the Russian peasantry in the borderlands and was concerned primarily with the protection and cultural salvation of those peasants.

In 1903, Stolypin's transfer to Saratov as governor brought him face to face with the entire panorama of revolution. His view of the organic relationship between peasant economy and revolt crystallized. It strengthened his conviction that the commune would have to go, and he fervently offered his arguments in reports to the crown.

Stolypin's provincial years also steeped him in the procedures and psychology of the local bureaucracy. In Saratov he acquired a reputation (which reached to the capital) for *sangfroid,* bravery, and effectiveness in suppressing rural violence at its worst. "Nervousness is pardonable to ladies," he once explained to the editor of his semi-official journal, "in politics there must be no nerves."

Finally, in the Saratov years Stolypin formulated his opinion of zemstvo intellectuals. He came to regard them suspiciously (with an element of anti-intellectualism on his part) as an essentially hostile political force, striving only for power. He averred that they had little real grasp of the traditions and interests of the country and that they even held in contempt other elements of the population. To curb their influence he would create a truly popular agrarian party, presumably to be attracted by a program of land reform.

The balance sheet of Stolypin's achievements and frustrations and the form his measures took were necessarily influenced by the attitudes of the sovereign whose will he executed and of the sovereign's immediate advisers. Most of the premier's difficulties with the crown and the court stemmed from his parliamentary policy and his relations with the imperial legislative bodies, for he regarded any effort to return to the pre-parliamentary order as "malicious provocation and the beginning of a new revolution."

Stolypin's original favor with the tsar and the bureaucracy which recommended him for high office arose from his impressive record in Saratov and probably from his vigorous support of a peasant reform which the court was beginning to consider a sensible solution of the land question. Soon he made his mark as minister of the interior and premier. His ability to establish relative quiet in a brief period, the sympathy and admiration aroused by his cool-headed reaction to the attempt on his life on August 12, 1906, and the rapidity with which he introduced and promulgated new and basic legislation generated a sense of confidence in conservative and court circles. This attitude rendered his position relatively secure for about three years. It became manifestly evident that the man was well-nigh irreplaceable. The provincial official improved his skill in bureaucratic maneuver at an astonishing rate. Honors followed in rapid succession—order, titles, and a monument on the anniversary of the attempt on his life. "I cannot tell you how much I have come to like and respect this man," Nicholas II wrote his mother on October 11, 1906.

Stolypin's strong position was translated into concrete action during the first six months of his administration—the most productive of his career. He issued his program (with its constitutional and social implications) forcefully, under Article 87 of the Fundamental Laws which allowed him to legislate when the duma was not in session. He was also able to keep the tsar's patience within bounds while he tried the Second Duma and found it wanting. At the same time he had to deal with innuendoes that he was conniving to protect the duma.

For a new man these were not inconsiderable achievements. But, while Stolypin could usually persuade the tsar to accept his views, the premier's greater breadth of view, daring, and force of character were always sources of potential irritation. Even at the acme of his power he had to tread warily. He stepped back from more liberalized positions or accepted a second-choice solution when the odds seemed insuperable. Despite his identification with field courts martial, he apparently resisted pressure to create them until after the attempt on his life in the summer of 1906. He probably regarded them as too drastic for the moment and as an unnecessary extension of the scope of extraordinary measures. In the autumn of 1906 he backed away from a bill removing irritating restrictions upon Jews when the tsar refused to confirm it because of "inner voices." In these matters a sense of proper policy prevailed over his normal inclinations and prejudices, and the retreats involved considerations of prestige and position more than heart-searching. Strategic considerations, rather than any concern about constitutional limitations of the political and ethnic opposition, led him to promulgate the Electoral Law of June 3, 1907, which weighted the vote in favor of wealthier voters and the Russian population. He concluded that resistance to insistent pressure from the throne might have more drastic consequences for himself, the Duma, and the regime than the law itself, and he wrote the manifesto introducing it. But its promulgation involved a major retreat in principle—in the name of the preservation of the principle of representation, as he persuaded himself.

Stolypin had to be alert to any infringement of the beclouded principle of autocracy, given the tsar's especial antipathy for the duma. In one of its first major steps, the Third Duma aroused the court by eliminating the term "autocratic" from its reply to the address from the throne—a step taken to emphasize the constitutional nature of the regime. And Stolypin felt impelled in his first speech on policy to refer to the "historical autocratic power," which had been Russia's salvation in moments of crisis, "returning it to the path of order and historical truth." He termed it Russia's most valued possession and noted that it had created the duma.

But Stolypin stumbled badly in April 1909, along with the entire cabinet, when he supported an admiralty budget for the projected naval general staff. This budget included a list of official titles in order to inform the duma and to render the budgetary measure more precise. Since Article 96 of the Fundamental Laws allowed only the tsar a prerogative in matters of military organization, the emperor found that he could not risk a precedent and refused to confirm the measure even though it had passed through both the duma and the imperial council. There was no question of resignation, but the premier was henceforth an open target for charges of unwonted tenderness toward the duma. And opposition to him was especially strengthened by the tsar's curt order to produce within a month legislation delimiting the duma's authority in order to avoid further violation of the law.

Stolypin's position was dangerously undermined late in his career, in April 1911, when he reacted with unusual emotion and vindictiveness to the defeat of a bill on the structure of new zemstvos in the western borderlands. The measure of his influence was at stake; he was ill, exhausted, and surfeited with petty plotting by the rightist elite. Yet his requirement, as an alternative to his resignation, that the emperor limit the terms of two members of the rightist opposition in the imperial council was not only presumptuous and offensive to the sovereign, but it also underscored the tsar's own delinquency in not curbing the aristocratic coterie and in giving it grounds for encouragement. Nicholas was not likely to forgive this bit of lese majesty. Stolypin frequently reflected a mood of despair and considered the prospect of resignation in the immediate aftermath of this traumatic experience. He realized that he was not in the inner circle during the last moments of his life.

After 1909 the "ruling spheres" developed a conviction that, with the establishment of order and the enactment or de facto operation of his reform program, there was no longer an urgent need for Stolypin as president of the council of ministers. It was felt that he might even prove too powerful for any segment of the opposition. The delicacy of his position was patent in the face of stronger opposition on high, the danger of real limitation of his power, and the anguish he suffered in getting legislative and imperial assent for even his gradualistic brand of reform.

Referring to his immediate staff in the ministry of the interior, Stolypin sadly confided to V. N. Kokovtsov: "My collaborators cannot get used to the altered conditions of legislative work." This was an essential element of the bureaucratic atmosphere that Stolypin considered a hindrance to the proper institution or achievement of the law and spirit of his efforts at reform. He could expect considerable disagreement, harassment, and opposition in the cabinet. In general, he functioned in a higher administration which seemed to be a preserve, as S. E. Kryzhanovskii termed it, "of old men who had outlived their century." Some of Stolypin's closest colleagues were basically hostile. They plotted, distrusted him, and thwarted his orders. And Stolypin, in turn, exacerbated his relations with them by riding roughshod over their bureaucratic traditions and habits. He complained ruefully to the editor of the semiofficial *Rossiia* that it was easier to violate the law in St. Petersburg than to impinge on the rights of officials.

The premier knew that in the localities, among the ambitious but less sophisticated members of officialdom, he could expect only a painfully slow adaptation to the new order. Some of his troubles stemmed from the cumbersomeness and looseness of the bureaucratic operation. Besides, Stolypin, concentrating on policy rather than administration, contributed to the chaos by leaving the departments in the ministry of the interior to their own devices and purposes. Interjurisdictional ignorance and conflicts abounded, and in the defense ministries the line of responsibility and hence of control was not clearly defined. Loose organization and control in the interior agencies, with sensitive police functions, meant continued arbitrary action under exceptional measures designed to counter oppositional and revolutionary activity. Stolypin attempted to counter bureaucratic dead weight and opposition by the appointment of younger men beholden to him and with vigor and congenial, fresh ideas. Some were selected from his entourage in Saratov, some from official St. Petersburg; they included S. P. Beletskii, A. A. Makarov, and S. E. Kryzhanovsky.

Stolypin was impressed by the relative political cohesion of the Goremykin ministry in the First Duma, and he tried to maintain at least a facade of common purpose in his cabinet. His attractive personality, evident sincerity, earnestness, and ability to idealize his purposes enlivened his reform program and generated at least temporary enthusiasm. But each minister reported to the tsar directly, and the range of their attitudes was remarkably broad. V. N. Kokovtsov, A. P. Izvolskii, A. V. Krivoshein, and V. I. Gurko had their individual patterns of thought and action which clashed at times sharply, with that of the premier. He was able to eliminate the practice of submitting contradictory measures to the tsar. But Stolypin himself grievously violated the principle of unity of action by consulting Nicholas II on the sensitive issue of the western zemstvos without first discussing it in his cabinet and by disregarding the advice of those whom he consulted.

Finally, Stolypin was not adverse to intrigue. He contrived the dissolution of the Second Duma in such a way that no other ministries were aware of the machinations of the ministry of the interior. Also, he tried to arrange for the transfer of the Peasant Land Bank from the ministry of finance to that of agriculture because of Kokovtsov's strictly financial approach to the bank's operations, particularly in connection with resettlement.

Stolypin's dealings with the local bureaucracy were more direct, but they were less successful in consistently executing the official program. He informed the British historian Bernard Pares that he intended to show the country that the government had parted company with the old order of things—even for officials with connections on high. He promised the duma that bureaucratic abuses would no longer be tolerated. And the ministry of justice submitted a bill to the Second Duma on civil and criminal responsibility of officials so that there would be no "arbitrary understanding of the new principles by private and official persons." Stolypin demanded unified action in the localities as well as at the center and asked for "officials bound by a feeling of duty and responsibility without personal views." He warned local authorities during the first days of his administration that while they were to suppress revolutionary activity they were not to violate individual rights. They were not at war with society, he observed, but with its enemies. Above all, they were to respect the letter of the law, especially on exceptional measures.

But the line was apparently too fine for governors, governors general, and city prefects, most of whom, as Stolypin himself recognized, drew no distinction between exceptional and ordinary law. Yet relatively few glaring examples of maladministration or malfeasance were punished, while the premier's frustrations multiplied after the gradual decline in his prestige following the debates on the naval general staff in 1909. He was able to gather sufficient support in his cabinet for most of his measures of empire-wide significance, but reforms involving sectional or local administrative reorganization met with obstinate, sometimes insuperable, opposition. Traditional, local interests of bureaucrat and *pomieschik* were challenged with considerably greater difficulty.

The scope of Stolypin's program and the measures he took to realize it were determined by his own horizon to a significant degree. He constantly reflected the habits, inhibitions, prejudices, and interests of the aristocratic bureaucracy relatively close to the court. This horizon largely conditioned his conceptions of constitutionalism. From this perspective he ventured rather boldly into the realm of parliamentary experience and cooperation with representatives of diverse elements of public opinion. He wanted to hear them out, give them a sense of participation in public life or stimulate hopes that they might participate in it, and, perhaps, as his opposition claimed, he wished to identify them with official policy. But this Speransky-like effort to involve popular leadership in shaping the regeneration of the country was counterbalanced by a conception of government characteristic of Russian officialdom in the statist-patriarchal tradition. Stolypin knew that the realization of the parallel tasks of repressing disorder and of effecting reform was perhaps "superhuman." He was certain that "the old police order of things" would have to be discarded if he were to introduce new people into the work of the government and regenerate the empire. But his insistence on the adoption of his own measures or of those he supported to the exclusion of competing bills, and the manner in which he enacted his proffered reforms, variously aroused wide elements of public opinion and generated a progressively broadening sense of distrust. These shortcomings in no way minimized the significance of his goals and achievements, but they limited the kind of support he could get, undermined a belief in his integrity, and laid his program and philosophy open to harassment and attack.

Many elements of Stolypin's legislative program found wide public accord. They sought not only basic economic improvement but showed an effort to strengthen constitutional guarantees and involve the population more extensively in local and central representative bodies. During a tour of the Volga region in the summer of 1909, the premier contrasted the pessimistic temper of the press in the capital with the upsurge of a "lively mood" in the provinces, "witnessing that many are being attracted to active (public) work." Efforts to attract local figures to public activity best reflected the premier's intention to consult the moods and desires of the population. He placed great emphasis on the zemstvos and city dumas in connection with vital changes in the local economy. His bill on local government not only made the zemstvos more representative but originally proposed that the central treasury bear all of their expenditures beyond regular assignments.

Stolypin's most original venture in consulting the grass roots (and revealing his seriousness in the matter) was his revival of the dormant council on the affairs of local economy. It had been created in 1904 by V. K. Pleve, but Stolypin called it for the first time. It was commissioned to work out legislative projects by exchange of opinion between representatives of central institutions and persons with a close knowledge of local conditions and needs. In his speech outlining his program to the Third Duma, Stolypin indicated that he intended to submit to the council all bills touching on local interests. He felt that this would be an effective means of ascertaining the views of the zemstvo and city duma officials and promised that this procedure would in no way retard the activities of the imperial duma. He held that, on the contrary, its committees would benefit by the work of the council and that the ministry of the interior could consider its findings for amendments to government bills.

Stolypin actually submitted the bills on the western zemstvo and Polish city administration to this council in October 1909, pleading with it for dispassionate study, politics aside. Generally heeding his advice, the council made clear, rather profusely, how deeply it appreciated the privilege of being consulted.

In some respects Stolypin's efforts to co-operate with the duma could be considered exemplary by all political elements hopeful for the development of parliamentary government. As minister of the interior in Goremykin's cabinet, he had frequently attended the duma's sessions to know its mood, leadership, and procedures. And he had been the only minister to win some respect in the raucous First Duma because of the forcefulness of his statements and the deference and tact he maintained toward it. He personally presented almost all of his reform program before the Second Duma to avoid the reproach of indifference leveled against the government by the First Duma. As a constitutionalist he publicly opposed reactionaries. He frequently called for co-operation by the duma in the enactment of legislation to regenerate Russian society and to pacify the population, and promised to put the government's experience at the disposal of the duma. He assured the deputies that no earnest opposition would be regarded as rebellious. He commended the duma for its conscientious search for abuses in the bureaucracy and promised redress and reform. In concrete terms he carefully analyzed for the imperial duma the need of naval armaments and the Amur Railway as measures of national defense. He hoped thereby to dispel doubts concerning the intentions of the administration and the adequacy of the defense agencies. The ministries of finance and war co-operated closely with the sensitive financial and defense committees of the duma.

Stolypin was always able to find leadership for a majority which supported all of his major measures—first under A. I. Guchkov and then in the nationalist coalition. As pares said in 1912, this co-operation "helped above all to give Russia her first experience in co-operation" between parliament and the administration, increased the number of Russians who received a political education, and enhanced the position of deputy to the duma.

One of Stolypin's furthest excursions into the realm of joint action with leaders of the opposition was his effort to include them in a cabinet along with more liberal bureaucrats. P. N. Miliukov's intractable insistence on a "duma ministry" and Stolypin's opposition to drastic political change brought a shift toward negotiations with moderate and liberal Octobrists. But conferences with G. E. Lvov and D. N. Shipov served only to heighten the conviction of these men that the premier needed them in his cabinet as a shield against public opinion. This impression stemmed from Stolypin's refusal to present a detailed program for their consideration and his conviction that he knew exactly what legislation was needed and acceptable. Stolypin was in no position to meet the demands of his conferees for all key posts because of his familiarity with the tsar's attitude on the matter and perhaps from considerations of political self-preservation. But they would not accept minority positions and the implied responsibility for official policy.

Shipov and Lvov may have been too suspicious. It is more likely that, given his over-all emphasis, Stolypin sought to attract men respected in public life to strengthen the "power and prestige" of the government. But the promulgation of most of his legislation under Article 87 of the Fundamental Laws and the later discussions on the formation of a coalition cabinet underscored the weakness of all of his efforts to realize his major legislation. He expected co-operation from individuals and parliament, while insisting on his own measures for reform. These measures would strengthen the kind of governmental structure he wanted. In pursuing this basic attitude he reflected again the statist tradition of the Russian aristocrat-bureaucrat which, at the very least, would restrict severely a constitutional structure by giving a heavy preponderance to traditional authority vested in the government. This structure was theoretically an autocracy and practically a monarchy limited only by whatever compromise with the legislature the administration might consider feasible. At worst, the entire structure might be disregarded, circumvented, or violated by the cabinet.

Stolypin reflected these attitudes and ideas in the whole gamut of his activities. His pronouncements on legislation indicated that the government had to retain the legislative initiative, and he placed considerable emphasis on the amendment of the government's legislative measures as a function of the duma. Also, legislation was to correspond to the Russian popular conscience —presumably as Stolypin defined it. He clearly indicated in the dissolution crisis of June 3, 1907, that he considered the protection of the state to be more important than the inviolability of the rights of deputies. When charged with following an old bureaucratic tradition by intervening in the governmental affairs of cities, he haughtily remarked that the state was a higher concept and that it alone could handle a critical situation for which the city duma had not been able to find a solution. He could not imagine why anyone in city government should take umbrage in such circumstances.

Stolypin's narrow interpretation of the duma's investigative authority was typical of the bureaucratic attitude that influenced his relations with that body. He demanded that the committee on famine relief in the Second Duma receive only information made available through the bureaucracy. The committee was to desist from efforts to gather data directly from striken areas and from experts of the zemstvos and the Free Economic Society, who were invited to attend its hearings. He also opposed a similar effort in the Third Duma to investigate the operation of state-owned railways.

Stolypin limited what might be said in the duma concerning the activities of various governmental agencies through strict interpretation of the right of interpellation. He was especially zealous in restricting the duma's actions concerned with the armed forces to budgetary items and recruitment quotas. He asserted that the army could not operate under the "poison of doubt" that it was subject to a collective will and not to that of the tsar alone.

There is no need to labor the point of a bureaucratic frame of mind or temperament revealed in the unconstitutional promulgation of the Electoral Law of 1907. The existence of the parliament may have been involved, but now Stolypin created a considerable difficulty for further co-operation with the duma. The new law provided for some representation from every element of the population in European Russia, but he knew even in 1906 that he could expect co-operation only from strata of the population who had controlled political power up to 1905, with the exception of some of the industrial middle class. Now he grievously violated the kind of constitution he was sworn to uphold. The question of adaptation, of a relapse into *proizvol* (arbitrariness)—the opposite of government by law—was involved and was bound to stiffen all of the opposition to him, liberal or conservative, obviously or subtly, and perhaps broaden it. The argument that it was the sovereign's right to change a law he had granted only underscored the violation of the sovereign's promises. Any rule might be changed henceforth in the name of the country's salvation. Kokovtsov and Stolypin's daughter inform us that the premier was excruciatingly aware of this moral lapse, and it could not but affect his uncertainty in future dealings with the opposition.

In the public mind Stolypin's application of Article 87 of the Fundamental Laws stood second only to the events of June 3, 1907 in the realm of assault on constitutional stability. The article empowered the government to promulgate legislation when the duma was not in session. Stolypin's frequent resort to this right on grounds of urgency clearly indicated that he was insisting on his own versions of reform by presenting them as practical *faits accomplis*. He argued that the duma might reject these measures, but he never allowed the Second Duma an opportunity to reach a decision on them, and the unrepresentative Third Duma never availed itself of that right. He resorted to the most drastic measures of his administration when the imperial council rejected his bill on the organization of the projected zemstvos in the western provinces. He not only applied Article 87 but put the tsar under great pressure to punish those who had opposed him in the imperial council, and he caused that august body to reverse its decision. Stolypin's procedure in enacting the zemstvo bill was, at least, a flagrant violation of the spirit of the constitution. He assumed that the rejection of his measure by one of the houses of the duma created an emergency, and he interrupted the activities of both houses in order to issue the measure under Article 87.

He stretched the sense of the law to its limits, and some of his colleagues felt that he violated it, although they did little to restrain him.

The premier's defense of his action was consistent and on a relatively high plane. He argued before both houses that scholarly studies in Germany and Austria with systems similar to Russia's supported his contention that an emergency might arise while parliament was in session as well as during a recess. He held that in the final analysis, the government, acting for the tsar, had a right to call a recess to promulgate legislation it regarded as urgent. He classified those who opposed his concepts as "parliamentarist" with considerations beyond the range of the constitution. The problem, as the government saw it, was not the limitation of the parliament's prerogative but the practical frustration of legislative action because of conflict between its two houses. He assured the council that habitual application of Article 87 was unthinkable in normal governmental operations.

Now conservative elements were faced with the kind of arbitrary action, resting on the "sovereign will," that characterized the promulgation of the Election Law of June 3, 1907. Both houses rejected Stolypin's definition of an emergency and resented his refusal to compromise. Guchkov resigned from the presidency of the duma. According to a contemporary comment of the *Times* of London, Stolypin seemed to be using his rights with a "dangerously narrow pedantry."

For the public at large there were other indications that a bureaucratic attitude of the traditional order, rather than the spirit of the new constitutional idea, conditioned some of Stolypin's actions. These were designed to repress and control opposition of an ideological or physical order. He placed student assemblies under the general law on public meetings on grounds that universities were meant for study and lecture only. This provided for supervision by the police and considerably curtailed the universities' autonomy. At the same time they were threatened with closure for the least antigovernmental expression.

While courts martial and "extraordinary protection" (under which any criminal action could be removed from judicial to administrative control) were ended in 1908, states of "reinforced protection" remained in the greater part of European Russia. Stolypin privately acknowledged that revolutionary activity was on the wane, and sentences to exile dropped significantly. Yet he continued to apply reinforced protection energetically, sometimes under pressure from powerful local figures. He recognized that reinforced protection had been extended well beyond cases involving sedition and that local officialdom was applying "obligatory ordinances" beyond their proper jurisdiction to cover non-political matters that came under regular criminal law (from billiard balls to kosher meat and non-breakable samovars, as Stolypin put it). Yet he was never powerful enough or energetic enough to halt violations of constitutional guarantees.

Stolypin's general comprehension of the nature of political parties seemed to indicate a fuzziness in differentiating the oppositional from the revolutionary. He never made a clear distinction between those who were, as a party, dedicated to a legal change in the existing order and those who would overthrow it by violence. This involved a failure to distinguish the acts of individuals from party policy and a goodly measure of guilt by association. He never forgave the Kadet party as a whole for the role played by the leading Kadets in the promulgation of the Vyborg Manifesto, despite intra-party differences. He never forgot how often the Liberals sat with the revolutionaries: at Paris in 1904 and to prepare a counterappeal on agricultural reform in the First Duma; at the Vyborg conference in 1905 and to elect the president of the Second Duma. He regarded their concept of a "duma ministry" as ruinous for Russia and generally classified them along with the revolutionaries, as those who sought power for themselves. Consequently, he would not legalize them under the law on societies of March 1906—or their allies, the Muslim party—on grounds that they pursued goals harmful to the public peace, namely, the establishment of a constitutional monarchy more limited than that provided in the Fundamental Laws. Yet he recognized the Union of the Russian People with its obvious antagonism to the Fundamental Laws.

Certainly, Stolypin's resort to secret subsidization of the extreme rightist press as a counterbalance to that of the far Left smacked of the more regressive attitudes of the upper bureaucracy. Also, his use of police agents whose irregularities in the direction of provocation he could hardly hope to control could only raise considerable question concerning the government's respect for law.

Finally, the enactment of Stolypin's most important piece of legislation, the reform of peasant land tenure on November 9, 1906, reflected some interesting "official" procedure and psychology. We have already noted its significance in the category of measures issued under Article 87. Here is perhaps the best example of Stolypin's insistence on his own legislation. He made it eminently clear to the duma that, while he might entertain other views, no other bill was likely to be adopted or feasible. He held that no political developments were able to halt the actions of the government because dissolving the commune and the consequent improvement of agricultural technology were so vital. He also called on the Third Duma to perfect and, perhaps, amend his bill. Here, too, Stolypin's primary concern with the stability of the existing order emerges from the defense of his proposal. A small peasant landowner would develop a sense of responsibility, would become "a defender of order and a support of the social structure." "I propose that, first of all, it is necessary to create a citizen, a peasant owner, a small landowner, and the problem will be solved. Citizenship will reign in Russia. First a citizen and then citizenship. Yet the potentialities of this citizenship aroused some anxieties, particularly in Siberia, where he feared that in the absence of landowners a democratic spirit would arise "that will crush us."

There is little reason to agree with many of Stolypin's liberal and revolutionary opponents that force played a major role in the separation and enclosure procedures. The procedures proved attractive enough in themselves. But in urging governors and land captains to expedite the process he invited a show of zeal by local officials who might not prove as circumspect as he desired. The law as issued in its final form on June 14, 1910, contained some elements of reinsurance that weighed it on the side of separation and enclosure. Lands of the commune which had not been redistributed among its households (as they increased or decreased in size) became the private property of these families. If individual households applied for the withdrawal of their holdings from the commune the latter might dissolve. The law also allowed families which had decreased in size to leave the commune with a disproportionate amount of land provided that they pay for holdings in excess of a reasonable norm established by the village for such families. If they could manage it, they would gladly scrape together the means to pay for their holdings in excess of the norms. Then, migration as stimulated by Stolypin, meant enclosure for new settlers. As one contemporary critic described it, enclosure was "half compulsory, half stimulated." The government could expect a better response to the enclosure program with a "little less pressure of bureaucratic authority and a little more confidence in the good sense of the population itself, a little more respect for the rights and interests of both individual land tenure and also of the communes, as a whole, and in the person of its various members." Everything, in the final analysis, depended on the establishment of a predictable legal order and the elimination of *proizvol* (arbitrariness).

Perhaps the only specific common attraction of the Octobrists and the Rightists for Stolypin arose from his concept of a "Great Russia." Like them he understood it within a relatively limited framework which had become traditional among the political slavophiles in the nineteenth century, especially among the aristocratic-bureaucratic strata. Stolypin's nationalism undoubtedly promoted some broad, positive purposes within this framework. He would consolidate the empire firmly, awaken national sentiment, and encourage the initiative of the "basic" Russian elements of the population. As he understood it, these elements included the Great Russian, Ukrainian, and Byelorussian peoples. These purposes were translated, in practice, into legislation which was significantly narrow in its interpretation of the "truly Russian" historical legacy, and which operated in a restrictive manner on the scope of the political and cultural rights of the non-Russian, non-Orthodox elements in the Empire.

Stolypin was obviously no obscurantist in this connection. Early in his ministerial career he had been frustrated by crown, court and cabinet in an effort to promote stability in the western borderlands by eliminating Jewish disabilities and he had revealed a real compassion for the plight of the Jewish townsmen. He had a sound historical perspective of the potential flexibility of the "autocracy" which could yield a parliament. And he understood thoroughly the social and economic interrelationship of the various areas of the empire. But for Stolypin "Great Russia" meant that Russian and Orthodox interests had a prior claim on his attention and out-balanced those of all other nationalities is a multinational empire. Russians alone, in his opinion, could be expected to protect their heritage won at great cost, to keep the empire one and indivisible, and to carry forward their Orthodox spiritual tradtion under the sole leadership of the sovereign power. So, he aggressively promoted the interests of the Russians to the detriment of those of major non-Russian elements of the empire. He was convinced that their concerns marked them as cultures with a centrifugal bent.

He went far, in his measures revising Finnish autonomy and introducing zemstvos and town government in western provinces, to attack the interests and sensitivities of Finns, Poles, and Jews. His Finnish constitutional law of 1910 placed the control of most Finnish affairs under the imperial ministry and under a parliament that was to include a scattering of Finnish deputies. His zemstvo measure departed from the principle of representation by class which, in the 1890 law, had established a strong position for the nobility. Now by resorting to the combination of the ethnic and property qualifications embodied in the Election Law of June 3, 1907, be guaranteed the Russian peasantry a majority over the Polish nobility of the western provinces. He assigned the population to Russian and Polish curias, and where the Russians were numerically weakest Russian officials were to sit as chairmen of the zemstvo boards.

Stolypin's arguments rested, again, on the sovereign power of the tsar and the need to defend the interests of Russia and the Russians. The emperor, as the highest authority, could regulate and change the mutual relationship between Russia and her borderlands, although at times his predecessors had been derelict in their duty, especially in the reigns of Alexander I and Alexander II. Stolypin stated a preference for the Russification policies of Nicholas I, for his "simple, honest, openly spoken policy" and his prescription to bind Poland "with other parts of the empire in a single body, in one soul." Stolypin argued that in both Finland and Poland amelioration had brought only increased hatred for Russia and things Russian, and efforts at separation. He noted that defense of Russian economic and cultural interests was perhaps more significant in the western provinces, but in Finland the cost of Finnish defense and the political position of the Russian minority were not to be overlooked. He pressed the argument that in the western provinces the wealth, the greater cultural awareness, and the more cohesive organiza-

tion of the Poles made protection of Russian interests mandatory
for the Russian state. The zemstvos were organizations for the
regulation of the economy, and he would not risk competition
between the self-interested Poles and the impoverished Russians.
The Russian state could not refuse to nurture the weak roots of
the Russian state idea, unable to develop by their own efforts.
Whenever the creative Russian forces weakened, Polish factors
developed and strengthened in the western borderlands.

Stolypin rested his case primarily on grounds of imperial
defense. He would reinforce state interests by establishing Russian control over the local economy and economic policy and by
instituting a strong, local Russian cultural consciousness tied to
the interests of the Russian Empire. The government of the
empire assembled by the Russians had to consider the ethnic,
cultural, economic, and political interests of the Russians in approaching all matters of imperial concern. He argued that no
oppression of Poland and of "little Finland" was involved, only
the guarding of the "sovereign, historical rights of Russia." But
Stolypin's political opponents from intellectual circles and the
national minorities were deeply impressed, especially in the matter of Finland, by a "disrespect for law and weakness of legal
consciousness," by a violation of the principle of equal treatment
for all regardless of nationality, and by the superfluous injection
of ethnic strife—all characteristic of the bureaucratic rather than
the constitutional order.

It is difficult for anyone who has studied Stolypin at length not
to sense the stature of the man, the sincerity of his purpose, and
his profound vexations. The negative tenor of much of the foregoing arises from the purpose of this study: to establish Stolypin's
basic position as a self-confessed and self-defined constitutionalist.
And much of his program of legislation and manner of action
shows him honoring constitutionalism, as he understood it, in
the breach. His pattern of action left the strong impression in
the opposition elements and on observers that, while he offered
an original and vital reform program, the old order still persisted
with constitutional and parliamentary trimmings. To his foes at
court and in the bureaucracy he added a growing opposition
among former conservative allies in the legislative bodies. He
clearly understood by the end of the First Duma that among those
who carried the banner of fundamental, legal change—not to

mention the social and political revolutionaries—he could not hope, nor did he desire, to gain allies. Thus, he found himself ultimately isolated on all sides. His program almost inevitably lost momentum with his death. His successors had neither the perspective, the zeal, nor the prestige to add to his program or give it vitality. The consequences for the regime were incalculable.

It is not by his constitutionalism that we measure Stolypin's stature—allocate him his proper position in the perspective of Russian civilization—but rather by his vision, his imagination which perceived the need for the adaptation of policy to a changing social and economic structure. A few perceptive souls among his contemporaries noted this capacity. The Dowager Empress characterized him in April 1911, in the midst of the crisis on the western zemstvos, as "a man whom nobody knew but who proved himself both intelligent and energetic, who succeeded in establishing order after the horrors of about six years ago; and now he is being pushed into an abyss . . . and by those very persons who insist that they love Russia and the tsar but who nevertheless endanger both him and their country." And there was a touch of greatness about the man more significant than the appeal of his oratory or even his sincerity. On February 11, 1909, finding himself in the unenviable position of rationalizing Ie. F. Azef's activities, he was moved to define his own broad purposes as the establishment of "freedom in the best meaning of the word, freedom from want, from ignorance, from lawlessness."

CHAPTER VI

FROM   *Edward Chmielewski*
The Separation of Chełm from Poland

   *One of the reforms in the structure of the Russian Empire
that was expected of the Duma was an amelioration in the treatment of the Empire's many minorities. The Polish question was
certainly one of the most critical minority questions faced by
Russia, and the handling of it by the Duma proved to be a particularly sensitive touchstone of Russian nationalism in the government and in the newly created legislature. The outcome was
that the Poles were wounded when their attempts to win moderate institutional, economic, and social concessions for the Congress Kingdom from the Duma were frustrated. The effort by
the government to separate from Russian Poland an eastern
border area with a mixed Polish-Ukrainian population and
create a new Russian province from it was regarded as a deliberate provocation by the Poles. They hoped that the bill would be
voted down by the Duma. However, the passage of the bill by
the Duma graphically illustrated the negative impact of extreme
nationalism not only on the Russian government but also on
Stolypin's Third Duma. This episode also revealed that the Russian state, supported by the nationalistically oriented Dumas
after 1907, was consciously alienating by its policies minorities
whose adherence it might need in a time of crisis.*

SOURCE. Edward Chmielewski, "The Separation of Chełm from Poland,"
The Polish Review, **XV**, No. 1 (1970), pp. 67–86.

The spirit of extreme nationalism that finally led to World War I and the collapse of the Russian Empire was reflected in the harsh and repressive treatment by the government of the racial minorities that composed about half of the population of the Empire. The Poles, in particular, as the single most important, developed, and nationally conscious minority, suffered without relief from official policies of Russification during the forty years following the failure of the 1863 uprising. It was the revolution of 1905 and the establishment in Russia of a quasi-constitutional political system with a State Duma and political parties that first revealed the possibility of new departures in the Russo-Polish relationship. The October Manifesto of 1905 promising a constitution, general elections, and a legislative assembly appeared to open a new era of freedom and reform. The existence of a Russian Parliament signified that views and policies different from the unyielding official line in Poland might be advocated and implemented.

However, the efforts of the conservative delegates of the Polish Koło (Circle) in the Duma to obtain redress of the most conspicuous Polish grievances and win moderate concessions for the Congress Kingdom in the areas of language, schools, and self-government were ultimately frustrated. These efforts were frustrated by the strong nationalist impulse that influenced a broad spectrum of opinion in Russia and touched not only the regime and officialdom but also many elements in the political opposition.

The broadest claim made by the Poles in Russia after the revolution of 1905, that of political autonomy in a kind of revival of the Congress Kingdom of 1815, was doomed by the fate of the first two Dumas with their brief and turbulent histories. Moreover, even Russian liberals, then and later, were often reticent and hesitant when rhetorical generalities had to be converted into specific reforms. Some, like P. N. Miliukov, the leader of the left-wing liberals, the Kadets, were suspicious of Polish aspiration and apprehensive of the possible consequences of a political decentralization of the Empire. With the promulgation by Prime Minister P. A. Stolypin on June 3, 1907 of a new electoral law that favored wealthier voters and the Russian over the non-Russian population and with the convocation of a conservative Third Duma, the situation worsened for the

Poles, and their representation in the legislature was radically reduced. The Koło's policy of moderation and loyalty towards the Russian state and tactical cooperation with the Duma's center brought no significant results in ultimate legislation and also aroused the displeasure of the opponents of the regime.

The Kadets favored greater social and economic radicalism than did the Poles, remained fearful of the supposed consequences of Polish nationalism, and, guided by doctrinal considerations, disapproved of the flexible tactics of the Poles who wanted positive accomplishments legislated for Poland by the Duma. To the right of the Kadets, the large Octobrist center was a loose grouping. Its position was hesitant and, in the final analysis, negative. Its theoretical program of granting Poles equal rights with Russians within the Empire was vitiated in practice by the timidity of the party's leadership and the consistent inclination of the considerable right wing to follow nationalist dictates. The nationalist course in the Third and Fourth Dumas was overtly and unrestrictedly directed by a Rightist-Nationalist combination upon which the government came increasingly to rely.

With respect to the government, Stolypin was perhaps only anti-Polish regarding the western provinces of Russia. But the Nationalist Party on which he came to count, put less of a fine point on the matter. Furthermore, Stolypin's own position was steadily undermined by rightist intrigues at court and in the State Council. Stolypin's successor as prime minister, V. N. Kokovtsov, although less of a nationalist than Stolypin, did not have the prestige and strength of character of his predecessor. He too was weakened by rightist opposition. Most significantly, the government had no carefully thought out or worked out program for the Polish question. Moreover, although the government was planning to introduce institutions of urban self-government into Poland, it also sponsored a bill that particularly wounded the Poles in their national sensibilities. In order that urban self-government should apply only to incontestably Polish-speaking areas, it was proposed to separate from Russian Poland an eastern border area with a mixed Polish-Ukrainian population and constitute it as the new Russian province of Chełm.

The decision to separate the area of Chełm from Poland in order to make of it a new Russian province was the crowning act of Stolypin's nationalist policy and had a long history behind it. The area involved, a "Polish Alsace-Lorraine," lay on the left bank of the upper Bug River and comprised the eastern parts of the Polish provinces of Siedlce and Lublin. The northern region, in the province of Siedlce, was part of eastern Podlasie and was more solidly Polish than the southern part. The latter area, between the Bug and Wieprz rivers, contained a mixed Polish-Ukrainian population and had been colonized simultaneously from east to west. The intermingling of the Poles and Ukrainians had been facilitated by the Union of Brest in 1595–1596 and the establishment of the Uniate Church. Indeed, after the forcible reunion of the Uniates in western Russia with the official church in 1839, Chełm became the last remaining outpost of the Uniate church in the Empire. However, in 1875, after the impetus given by the Polish rising in 1863, the Union of Brest was formally dissolved and the Uniates in the provinces of Siedlce and Lublin were obliged to accept Orthodoxy. For the next thirty years, the policy of maintaining the enforced conversion of the Uniates to Orthodoxy was pursued by St. Petersburg where its strongest proponent was Konstantin P. Pobedonostev, the procurator of the Holy Synod.

After the proclamation of the edict on religious tolerance in April 1905, anywhere from 100,000 to 200,000 inhabitants of the two Polish provinces gave up Orthodoxy and became Roman Catholics of the Latin rite. The problem of nationality was complicated by the fact that not all the Poles were Catholics and not all the Ukrainians were Orthodox or Uniate. According to the official Russian statistics of 1906, the Orthodox population of the future province was thirty-eight percent. Polish statistics, based on the official figures, numbered the Orthodox at twenty-seven percent, while Henryk Wierciénski, the Polish expert, arrived at twenty-five percent for the Orthodox population and fifty-seven percent for the Catholics. In any case, only in the district of Hrubieszów did the Orthodox population surpass the Catholics in number.

During the pre-constitutional era, the question of the separation of Chełm was actually raised eight times but was rejected by the government. The first plans were made in 1864 when the division of the Kingdom into provinces was being discussed. Nicholas A. Miliutin's assistant, Prince V. A. Cherkasskii, proposed that the creation of a province of Chełm would have a decisive effect on the "revival" of the oppressed Russian nationality that would otherwise be impossible so long as the area remained connected with the Polish centers of Siedlce and Lublin. But Miliutin opposed the scheme for financial reasons and also because out of a total population of 421,798 only 138,000 were Orthodox. He argued that as long as the Uniates were still subject to Rome, a new province would simply strengthen papal influence. Furthermore, the Russian population ought to enjoy full rights whatever the administrative divisions of the Empire, while the creation of the province might suggest that Poland still retained a special position. The question was dropped until the Uniate Church in the area was brutally liquidated in 1875, but another proposal in 1878 to separate the Bug region from Poland was disallowed. In 1882, the governor of Siedlce, supported by Pobedonostsev, suggested the separation of Chełm so that the governor of the province might concentrate on the problem of religious conversion, in 1889, the Orthodox bishop of the newly created diocese of Warsaw-Chełm, Leontius, in concert with Pobedonostsev, asked for the introduction of the Julian calendar into Poland and again raised the question of Chełm. These proposals were opposed by Governor General I. V. Gurko who wished to keep the Uniates under his surveillance. He also preferred to preserve Chełm as a part of Poland in connection with the campaign of Russification, and he objected to the separation as a measure that would complicate military administration and strategy in view of the fact that the governors general were also commanders of the Warsaw Military District.

The Holy Synod constantly returned to the thought of separating the former Uniates from Poland, and Gurko's successor, Count P. A. Shuvalov, agreed to the idea of a separate province. However, he wanted it to remain under the jurisdiction of the governor general in Warsaw. On the other hand, his successor in 1897, Prince A. D. Imeretinskii, disagreed and I. L. Goremykin, the minister of the interior, was also opposed. Imeretinskii, who moved freely in Polish aristocratic circles, wished to avoid unnecessary dissatisfaction and friction. The governor of Lublin, Tkhorzhevskii, twice raised the issue of separation and, although backed by Pobedonostsev, was overruled by Imeretinskii and the latter's successor, M. I. Chertkov. In 1901, Chertkov stated that a clear national division was impossible in the provinces of Lublin and Siedlce, that other motives were "conjectural," and that financial support would be required for Russian institutions. The creation of a new province would be meaningless unless the government undertook a policy of Russification as thoroughgoing as in its northwestern and southwestern provinces. Consequently, he argued, it was enough to protect the Russian element from the Poles and Catholicism.

In 1902, D. S. Sipiagin, the crude and reactionary minister of the interior, summoned a special commission to discuss the question of Chełm, but the group remained divided. Pobedonostsev pointed out that, despite the church reunion imposed in 1875, the mass of the population refused to attend Orthodox religious services. The creation of a new province was indispensable in order to protect and strengthen Orthodoxy and remove the population from the influence of Catholic Lublin and Siedlce. N. V. Muraviev, the minister of justice, emphasized in opposition that Chełm was part of the legal system of the governor generalship. Witte, the minister of finance, doubted the usefulness of a new administrative division since in all of Poland, as in Russia, the administration was in the hands of Russians anyhow and another division would not affect the lives of the inhabitants. Funds would be better expended in attaining more durable aims by subsidizing the Orthodox Church and religious institutions.

Sipiagin drew a distinction between the aims of Russian policy in Poland and in the western provinces. In the former, the aim was to protect Russians and former Uniates from Polish and Catholic influences. In the latter, the government desired complete Russification and the fusion of the region with Russia. The latter policy should also be extended to the area beyond the Bug River because of the "Russian" origin of its population. Furthermore, in order that the formal creation of a new province should be meaningful, the act must be accompanied by a series of measures designed to Russify the region. Poles should be forbidden to acquire property and Catholicism had to be repressed. "Perhaps" the Poles could be forcibly transferred to Poland in exchange for the Russian population remaining in the Kingdom. However, A. N. Kuropatkin, the minister of war, was hostile to an increase in the number of provincial administrative centers in border areas of the Empire as militarily inadvisable since plans for mobilization would have to be altered. Also, the economic dislocation and the effect on Polish opinion would make military administration even more complicated. Governor General Chertkov supported Kuropatkin because of the "complications" involved and added that it was essential to end all the rumors concerning the creation of a new province of Chełm. The special commission concluded that a simple formal separation would be inadequate without actual measures of Russification which were not possible under existing circumstances since unprovoked and harsh actions would lead to "an undesirable confusion of minds among the Polish population." Only in the course of years, after the population had been convinced that it belonged to the Russian people and the Orthodox Church, would the moment arrive to crown this process by separating Chełm from Poland. The Emperor concurred in this conclusion.

The situation was radically affected by the revolution of 1905. The prerevolutionary autocracy had reacted hesitatingly to suggestions, even from the powerful Pobedonostsev, for changes in the administrative machinery of the Empire. It had not been a particularly pressing concern whether or not Chełm was a part of the Kingdom since the Poles remained oppressed and no concessions to them were being considered. The government had considered itself strong enough not to be obliged to have recourse to debatable administrative changes in order to maintain its authority. Therefore, it had accepted the views and arguments of the local authorities. But with the grant of certain civil liberties and the establishment of a constitutional system, whatever its limitations and drawbacks, the possibility presented itself that, sooner or later, Poland might wring a larger degree of self-government from St. Petersburg. Under these circumstances, the problem of Chełm acquired a greater urgency and Russian nationalists were concerned to limit as much as possible the area in which the Poles might assert themselves.

Specifically, after the grant of the edict on religious tolerance in April 1905, the Orthodox clergy of Chełm, led by the vigorous Bishop Eulogius of the newly established and separate diocese of Chełm, were alarmed by the conversion to Catholicism of large numbers of former Uniates. In June 1905, Eulogius re-

ported to the minister of the interior the extraordinary growth
of Catholicism, and, in November, he led a delegation to the
capital to warn of the danger of Catholic propaganda. The minister, P. N. Durnovo, raised the possibility of attaching some
districts of the Bug area to the neighboring Russian provinces
of Grodno and Volhynia. While N. A. Sukhomlinov, the commander of the Kiev Military District, agreed to the proposal, K.
F. Krzhivitskii, the commander of the Vilno Military District,
preferred the creation of a new province.

In March 1906, Durnovo presented to the Council of Ministers
Eulogius' statements and those of the governors. He questioned
the value of separating Chełm in order to preserve Orthodoxy,
cast doubt on the possibility of Russification in border areas,
and suggested that the economic dependence of the Russians on
the Poles should first be ended. The governor general of Poland,
G. A. Skalon, like his predecessors, argued against the idea of a
new province as involving administrative and strategic complications that would outweigh any possible religious advantages,
especially since the Orthodox population did not form a com-
pact mass.

Finally, a special conference was held at the end of 1906 under the assistant minister of the interior, S. E. Kryzhanovskii.
Among the participants was Bishop Eulogius, who was able "to
interest" the Emperor in the question. It was proposed to create
a new province by utilizing Article 87 of the Fundamental Laws
but, as a gesture to Skalon, to leave it under the authority of the
Warsaw governor general in military matters. The province was
to preserve the existing legal system and tax structure but was
to be subordinated administratively to the governor general and
Court of Appeals in Kiev. However, in the light of social unrest, official unwillingness to arouse the Poles and undermine the
loyalty of the moderates, and possible repercussions in the forthcoming Second Duma, the Council of Ministers decided, in December 1906, to postpone action in order to prepare a project
that might be elaborated in connection with the proposal to introduce urban self-government that would make the separation
of Chełm less bitter for the Poles to accept.

The issue was taken up again by the Council of Ministers in
1907, and finally decided, with the consent of the Emperor, to
have the necessary legislation drawn up. The task was entrusted

to Kryzhanovskii and took two years to complete. According to Kryzhanovskii, while the bill was being prepared, it was proposed that, as a certain compensation for the parts of the provinces of Siedlce and Lublin that were to be separated from Poland, there be joined to Poland some adjacent sections of the province of Grodno that were inhabited by Poles; specifically, a few localities in the districts of Bielsk and Białystok. But Stolypin would not agree to this proposal out of the fear of being subject to "attacks on the part of nationalist circles which would have considered inadmissible the cession to Poland of lands officially not belonging to it."

The new province was to comprise six districts from the provinces of Lublin and Siedlce. The latter was to be abolished and its remaining western territory was to be incorporated into Lublin. No attempt was made to alienate private property or introduce agrarian reforms, so that the existing social structure remained inviolate; that is, 536 estates would continue to own 500,000 *desiatiny*, while 750,000 peasants owned 594,500 *desiatiny*. Existing legislation, the Napoleonic Civil Code, and the non-class communal (*gmina*) structure were to be retained. The new province was to be judicially and educationally subordinate to the Kievan court and school districts but militarily subject to the governor general of Warsaw. State lands and properties were to be administered from Zhitomir, the capital of the neighboring province of Volhynia. The bill discriminated against Poles in various ways. The use of Polish was forbidden in private as well as public schools, in the courts, and in official correspondence. The Julian calendar was to be introduced. Poles from the Kingdom might not settle in the new province, and land might be purchased by Poles or Jews only from Poles. It was officially estimated that 304,600 inhabitants, or thirty-eight percent of a population of 758,000 in the new province, would be of the Orthodox faith. On the basis of nationality, there would be 406,000 "Russians" (the official designation for the Ukrainian natives) and 209,000 Poles. The bill was approved by the Council of Ministers and submitted to the Duma in May 1909.

After a short general debate caused by a protest declaration of the Koło, the bill was sent to a specially created sub-committee presided over by the Nationalist D. N. Chikhachev that worked on it for more than two years, so that the general Duma debates did not begin until November 1911. In the subcommittee, Kryzhanovskii explained the government's motives for introducing a bill to create a new province of Chełm. He stated that the thought had arisen in 1865 but had not been implemented because of financial reasons and because the city of Chełm still had a small population of 4000, while the urban center of Zamość was Polish in character. Furthermore, there had not appeared to be any urgency since it had seemed possible to safeguard the interests of the "Russian" nationality through general administrative measures. The reunion of the Uniates in 1875 with the official church had had a "formal" character, "had not penetrated the national consciousness" enough to wipe out the influence of the Union, and had also been opposed by Catholic influences. Kryzhanovskii conceded that the October Manifesto and the edict on religious tolerance of April 1905 had brought an "intensification of Latin-Polish propaganda" as well as "the abandonment of Orthodoxy by quite a significant segment of the Russian population and its conversion to Catholicism." Consequently, the idea of separation had come up again among the Orthodox population "in order to protect themselves against gradual engulfment by the advancing Latin-Polish element." Petitions had come from Chełm expressing the fear that, with the introduction of local self-government in Poland, the Poles would completely destroy the national self-consciousness of the Russian part of the population and subject it to the influence of the Polish proprietary class and Catholicism.

Kryzhanovskii admitted that the creation of a new province would not in itself guarantee "Russian national interests." A "permanent fusion" with the central provinces of the Empire would result only from a radical administrative, legal, and structural transformation of Chełm requiring many years. But the action of separation would encourage the Russian natives and check the Poles and Catholicism. Leaving matters as they were would mean "new successes" for Polonization. By contrast, after the separation, the Russian population would gain "new strength" to resist the "militant" Catholic clergy and the Polish gentry. Besides, since a large-scale administrative reorganization of local government throughout the Empire was being contemplated, it would be premature to consider drastic changes in Chełm until the reforms in the central provinces had assumed their final form. The separation would also facilitate reforms in Poland by eliminating the need for special measures to safeguard Russian interests.

The minister pointed out that, while the ancient historical boundaries of Chełm included almost half of Lublin and Siedlce, the new frontier should be moved east to include any areas "with a predominantly Russian population that has preserved the Orthodox faith and Russian language." His statistics indicated that the new province would have an Orthodox population of 304,885 and a Catholic one of 310,677. However, since the latter were in part Russian, having become Catholic "almost only since yesterday," the corresponding figures on the basis of nationality might be fixed at about 406,000 Russians and 209,000 Poles. Kryzhanovskii's conclusion was that the new province would be "undoubtedly a Russian province." Finally, referring to the need for a "stronger local authority" and for an end to "religious and racial conflict," he urged that the province be placed under the governor general of Kiev. It might also be included in the Catholic diocese of Volhynia, the clergy of which "has relative moderation and less national fanaticism" than the diocese of Vilno with its "extreme Polonism and excessive religious intolerance." Kryzhanovskii refused to give the sub-committee the opinions of the five governors general in Warsaw regarding the separation of Chełm since four of them—Gurko, Imeretinskii, Chertkov, and Skalon—had opposed the project and only one, Shuvalov, had favored it. But this information was revealed by Ludomir Dymsza of the Koło, and its authenticity was not denied by the minister who was present.

In its report, the sub-committee noted that, in 1902, S. Iu. Witte, then minister of finance, had been against the creation of a new province because in Poland, as in the western provinces, the administration was in Russian hands. However, the official view had changed in the meanwhile. In a meeting of the Council of Ministers in October 1909, Prime Minister Stolypin had stated that

"if in the western region the ministry sought to create a zemstvo with a Russian complexion, then, in the cities of the provinces of the Kingdom of Poland, we expect to see Polish self-government subordinate only to the Russian state idea."

Therefore, because of the threat to the Russian population, the sub-committee agreed with the government that the separation of Chełm from Poland was essential. On the other hand, the government's bill "was subject to strong criticism by the representatives of the Nationalist Party who predominated in the committee" and insisted that the boundaries of the province be extended. Kryzhanovskii was present in the committee as the representative of the government, "but since Stolypin's orders were not to oppose the wishes of the Nationalists, I had to keep silent."

The Nationalists and Rightists in the sub-committee contended that the government's bill did not succeed in giving the Orthodox population of Chełm a majority. They also argued that religion was not a clear or exact criterion of nationality in the area because of the extensive conversions to Catholicism after 1905, the economic dependence of the peasantry upon the gentry, and the fact that the profession of Catholicism did not necessarily mean Polish nationality. Consequently, it was proposed to include in the new province all places "with a significant Russian population," both Catholic and Orthodox, as well as Orthodox religious centers and areas with "cherished historical memories" for Russia. Also, smaller administrative units of district and commune should not be divided. A final desideratum was that the province should have a "convenient figure." The boundaries recommended by the committee were averred to have an advantage over those proposed by the government in that the configuration of Chełm would be "more rounded and less broken." The effect of this recommendation was to increase the population of the province from 758,000 to 898,000. This would mean 463,900 "Russians" and 268,000 Poles; 327,300 Orthodox and 404,600 Catholics. These statistics were challenged by the Poles on the committee but were accepted by the Nationalist-Rightist bloc.

The Duma's sub-committee introduced other modifications into the government's bill. The preservation of the governor generalship of Kiev was termed "extremely undesirable." It no longer served a purpose since the southwestern provinces, acquired by Russia after the partitions of Poland in the eighteenth century, no longer differed essentially from the neighboring ones. They, like the province of Chełm, should be directly subject to the ministry of the interior. Chełm might preserve the Siedlce court system, which the government bill had abolished, the existing civil and commercial laws based on the Napoleonic Code, and most criminal laws. However, the new province was to be subordinate to the Educational District and Court of Appeals of Kiev.

The government's bill was liberalized by the sub-committee only in matters of property and language. The motivation was obviously to guarantee Octobrist support. The Octobrists on the committee were willing to accept the bill as a measure designed to restrain the Polonization of Chełm but were anxious to pay some regard to the principles of the October Manifesto by toning down several of the manifestly anti-Polish aspects of the bill. The committee rejected the government's proposal to extend to Chełm the law of May 1, 1905 for the nine western provinces of Russia that followed Poles to acquire land from Poles but not from Russians. Since Russian land ownership in Chełm was slight, the committee concluded that the proposal had little practical significance, was "pointless," and would arouse "dissatisfaction" in moderate Polish circles. On the other hand, Polish immigration into the new provinces from Poland would be allowed only with the permission of the governor in order "to preserve the province from the excessive influx of people who might prove undesirable in view of the goals being pursued by the establishment of the new province."

The committee also did not agree to exclude the Polish language completely from the courts. A limited use was allowed before justices of the peace and in communal courts—in order not to discourage possible conversions to Orthodoxy. Also, as against the government bill, the committee allowed the teaching of Polish in those intermediate schools that had a majority of Poles, because these students were usually in the largely Polish towns where there was no need to safeguard the Russian nationality. The prohibition of such instruction would be regarded, in addition, by the population as an "aggressive attack on the Polish nationality." On the other hand, apart from this concession, the laws and regulations allowing the teaching of and instruction in Polish that applied to Poland and the western provinces were not to obtain in the new province where the rules for the central Russian provinces were to be introduced.

The plenary discussion of the bill by the Duma began on November 25, 1911 with the committee report delivered by D. N. Chikhachev. He emphasized the contention of the Nationalists that in Chełm the ethnographic data did not correspond with those of religion and that "the Russian population speaking the Little Russian dialect" was the predominant element. He drew a connection between the separation of Chełm and the bestowal of local self-government on Poland, since "the sole way of facilitating the introduction of urban and rural self-government is to separate the Russian part of the Kingdom of Poland." He stated that the sub-committee had rejected the governmental proposal on the limitation of Polish land ownership "out of considerations of exclusively practical expediency." Chikhachev also referred to the charge that the bureaucrats of the old preconstitutional order had rejected the proposal to separate Chełm as harmful and pointless. He deplored their satisfaction with half-measures and their inability to see the question of Chełm as one of national significance. By contrast, the Duma, as a representative institution, was able to pursue a "consistent and systematic national policy."

Chikhachev's address was supported by A. A. Makarov, the arrogant minister of the interior, who pointed out that, despite the historical arguments, the matter was not one of an international territorial disagreement, that, "Poland is not a state but part of the Russian Empire," and that the essence of the issue was the necessity of preserving the national consciousness of the Russians in Chełm and their feelings of loyalty to the Russian state. Makarov also spoke in favor of restrictions on the right of Poles and Jews to acquire land as a necessary measure "in defense of the Russian people living there."

The principal speaker, and the initiator of the bill, was Bishop Eulogius, who was actively supported by the Nationalist stalwart, V. A. Bobrinskii. Eulogius took up Makarov's argument. "We fully believe that in the entire expanse of our great state, from Kalisz to Vladivostok, there is no Kingdom of Poland, but only a single Russian state." Indeed, the term, "Kingdom of

Poland," was "an archaism" without any "real significance."
Bobrinskii attacked the policy of Alexander I and of the bureaucrats in the second half of the nineteenth century as one that
had preserved the dependence of the Russian peasant upon his
Polish lord with the result that more Russians had been Polon-
ized in the past hundred years than during three hundred years
of Polish rule. Both speakers emphasized that the economic sub-
ordination of the peasantry of Chełm was more significant than
administrative reforms and that the next step must be one of
organized assistance by the state. Representatives of the Rightists, like N. E. Markov and F. F. Timoshkin, criticized the bill
in the committee version as too moderate. They charged that its
terms and reservations and its concessions to the Poles fostered
the illusion that a Kingdom of Poland existed as a separate en-
tity, while the bill gave no protection to the Russian peasantry
from the oppression of the Polish gentry. They advocated forcible population transfers and the adoption of a program of systematic and thorough Russification.

No other issue discussed by the Duma aroused more activity
on the part of the Koło than the Chełm bill. The Poles, like
their opponents, had recourse to prolonged historical disquisi-
tions in order to demonstrate the ancient ties that bound Chełm
to Poland. The pointed to the long and successful activities of
the Roman Catholic Church in the area. They criticized the
historical material and fabricated statistics used by the government. They insisted on the impossibility of drawing a boundary
in such a racially and religiously mixed area. They spoke of
the organic links between Chełm and Poland and warned of the
administrative, economic, and cultural chaos that would result
from the passage of the bill. They deprecated the inflammation
of nationalist passions. The tactics of the Poles were essentially
defensive and aimed at the preservation of the status quo in
Chełm.

In line with the Polish parliamentary program of self-restraint
and moderation, the Koło maintained the hope that by coop-
erating with the Duma center, avoiding conflicts with the government, and opposing radical schemes of social reform, the
loyalty of the Poles would be rewarded by modest concessions
that might, in the course of time and with the further liberalization of Russia, be broadened in scope. This hope was brought

out in Władysław Grabski's remarks, which also referred to the
anti-Russian demonstrations that were occurring in Galicia. He
declared that, unlike the revolutions of 1830 and 1863, the revolution of 1905 in Poland had been not a national but a "social
revolution." Also, after 1905, anti-Russian sentiments were on
the wane. The Poles accepted Russia's new structure of government, and the German danger was coming to be regarded as the
main challenge to the Polish cause. However, the current nationalist policy of the Duma as represented by the bill on Chełm
was cutting the ground from under the feet of the Polish deputies in the Duma who accepted the Russian state.

On the question of Chełm, as on all questions of nationalism,
the Octobrists were split. During the plenary discussion, G. V.
Skoropadskii and V. A. Potulov spoke in favor of the separation.
The former insisted that "the moral support" which the Russian peasant would receive from the passage of the bill would
have "vast significance." The latter added that, although it was
asserted that the separation would arouse the hatred of the
Poles, the last four years of the Duma had proved "that Polish
hearts burn with hatred of everything Russian." Although the
right wing of the Octobrist party intended to vote for the bill,
the initiative for its passage remained in the hands of the Rightists and the Nationalists. On the other hand, the Progressives
and the Kadets clearly expressed their negative reactions to the
government's bill. Speaking for the former, A. A. Uvarov, the
erstwhile Octobrist, brushed aside the official statistics as ten-
dentious compilations. He rejected the project as one of no
value either to the administration or to the local population but
as one that would simply affront the "sensitive nationalism" of
the Poles. He pointed out the transparent inadequacy of the city
of Chełm as a provincial capital. He emphasized the administrative confusion that would ensue with educational and judicial control in Kiev and the administration of state lands and
properties in Zhitomir. The law code was to remain Polish,
while appeals had to be made to Kiev which was unfamiliar with
the code. Warnings of the supposed danger of Polonization were
sheer pharisaism, and Orthodoxy could easily be protected
within the existing provincial structure.

The Kadet F. I. Rodichev stated that the formula "Russia for
the Russians" merely meant places and privileges for Russian

bureaucrats. "Polish nationalism is that of the oppressed; your nationalism, that of the oppressors." I. V. Luchitskii noted that the separation of Chełm would signify no change that might benefit the Ukrainian peasantry, and he was seconded by the Social Democrat N. S. Chkhedize who termed the life of the Ukraine "one continuous tragedy" and who asked, "In what way is Russification better than Polonization?" The Kadet V. A. Maklakov accused the bill of being "without content" and charged that it would only create "an exclusive patrimony (*votchina*) for the ministry of the interior." He also warned that the narrowly conceived nationalism of the government would strengthen German influence among the Slavs.

On January 20, 1912, when the vote was to be taken for a second reading of the bill, V. K. Von Anrep spoke for himself and those Octobrists who agreed with him, including Nicholas A. Khomiakov, the liberal former president of the Duma. He opposed the bill and concurred with Maklakov that it was without content. "Introducing nothing positive, it introduces a good deal that is negative." At the same time, he cautioned that it would give "completely unfounded hopes to the Poles," namely, the opening of broad perspectives of eventual Polish autonomy. The separation of Chełm would leave the Congress Kingdom ethnically homogeneous and might lead the Poles to expect excessive concessions as compensation. Although Von Anrep was shouted down by the Right, he was able to state that, despite all kinds of promises that were being given by the rightist parties to the Poles concerning the reforms that the Kingdom would be granted after the separation of Chełm, he was certain that the Duma would "very much have to think carefully before implementing such promises as are being given here at random."

The second reading of the bill by articles was accompanied by the same stormy debates as had been the opening discussion. A proposal by Rodichev to include in the province only localities having an Orthodox population of no less than forty percent was rejected. A later proposal of his, at the third reading, to adopt the boundary recommended in the original government bill was also voted down. The Duma also rejected an amendment by the Progressive N. N. Lvov to draw the provincial boundary on the basis of religious statistics since statistics on nationality were prejudiced and unreliable. A furor was created by Article 10 of the bill "to separate the newly formed province of Chełm from the provinces of the Kingdom of Poland and subordinate it in general administration to the ministry of the interior." This article was twice voted down, possibly because enough Octobrists felt that the wording was an unnecessary affront to the Poles. In any case, Articles 11 and 12 that dealt with the process of separation were passed and, at the third reading, Article 10 was voted with the phrase "to remove the province of Chełm from the administration of the governor general in Warsaw."

F. F. von Taube, the assistant minister of education, addressed the Duma on the matter of restricting the use of Polish in the schools and urged that it was "logically necessary" for Chełm to be included within the general school system of the Empire. But the Duma accepted an Octobrist motion to preserve the school laws operative in Poland, and the school language restrictions of the bill were rejected. The assistant minister of justice, A. N. Verevkin, protested the provisions of the bill allowing the limited use of Polish in the proceedings of justices of the peace and communal courts since "the entire purpose" of the bill was "the gradual fusion of the province of Chełm with central Russia and the protection of the local population against denationalization." The Duma, however, agreed to the use of Polish in the lower courts and also accepted the provision that the Poles be allowed to acquire land. On the other hand, it voted the article allowing Polish migration only with the permission of the governor.

At the end of the third reading, the bill was passed by the Duma in essentially the committee version on April 26, 1912 by a vote of 156 to 108. The Rightists G. A. Shechkov and S. V. Voeikov expressed indignation that only the eastern parts of Siedlce and Lublin were being separated, rather than the entire provinces, thus leaving the Russian population of the western districts "under the yoke" of the Poles. They also protested the right of Poles to acquire land and deplored the fact that the bill did not free the Russian population of Chełm from dependence upon the Polish gentry. Speaking for the Kadets, "the genuinely elected representatives of the Russian people," Rodichev dismissed the bill as a measure of national and religious oppression.

Von Anrep regretted that the bill was simply an irritant that provided no benefits to the native Russian population.

The bill was sent to the upper house of the legislature, the State Council, where it was passed with a rapidity totally uncharacteristic of that chamber, from June 11 to June 14, 1912, so that the measure might become law by the summer of that year. The pressure, urgency, and impatience with opponents of the bill were such that several members of the committee, chaired by P. P. Kobylinskii, refused to consider the project within the narrow limits prescribed by the chairman and left the committee. M. G. Akimov, the president of the State Council, also refused to allow the chamber to discuss Kobylinskii's actions. The reporter of the committee was the reactionary D. I. Pikhno. He declared that Chełm was "without any doubt" Russian, that the boundaries were drawn "carefully and conscientiously," and that there were no "substantial inconveniences" in the creation of the new province. Makarov addressed the upper house and attributed all the uproar over the bill to "Polish chauvinism." He referred to the "state significance" of the measure and indicated that it was merely the first step in bringing Chełm close to "Russian principles." The Pole Ignacy Szebeko complained of the statements being made "loudly and bombastically" about a united and indivisible Russia. Aleksander Meysztowicz expressed the hope that the geographical shape of "a boot" presented by the new province would be avoided if certain localities with a Polish population in the majority were excluded, but this proposal was voted down. The Council also rejected a motion by the Polish industrialist Stanisław Rotwand that Chełm remain subject to the Warsaw Court of Appeals rather than come under that of Kiev because of the retention of the Napoleonic Code. An attempt to eliminate the article allowing Polish immigration only with the consent of the governor was likewise defeated. The bill was passed on June 14.

The passage of the bill to separate Chełm from Poland was the crowning action of the Third State Duma in its handling of the Polish question. It demonstrated clearly that whenever any issue involved nationalist sentiments, whatever the facts, merits, or statistics of the case, the Duma would have a conservative majority. While the smaller left wing of the Octobrists might be restrained by conscience or principle, the center and right wing of the party would vote with the Nationalists and the Rightists. This was illustrated by a remark made by the Octobrist leader A. I. Guchkov in a newspaper interview: "The question of Chełm is a question of honor for the Poles and for Eulogius. Please do not be surprised that the honor of Bishop Eulogius is dearer to us." Octobrist ambiguities were also revealed in an exchange between S. I. Shidlovskii and Miliukov during a debate over the budget of the ministry of the interior on March 16, 1912. The Octobrist stated that nationalism would be a formula uniting all citizens of the Empire and establishing honorable conditions of existence for all of them. The unity of the state has to be preserved, but internal relations ought to be based on justice or there would never be domestic peace. The Polish question, in particular, had to be approached "with some circumspection" because of the Poles' culture and traditions, "and there is no reason whatsoever to attack these traditions for nothing and unnecessarily." Miliukov replied that the Chełm bill was hardly an example of "circumspection," and he feared that the hopes placed by the Poles in the Octobrists would be deceived.

Indeed, the outcome of the matter was a severe blow to the Poles and to their belief that a spirit of loyalty and cooperation would help them to win modest concessions from the Duma or at least, as in the question of Chełm, would guarantee maintenance of the status quo. The Koło opposed the bill persistently and fiercely but from a carefully defined position of loyalty to the Russian state and hostility to the idea of a revolution, whether national or social. Its members expressed regret at being obliged to go into opposition and even dissociated themselves from the anti-Russian demonstrations being staged in Galicia. However, their expectations were disappointed. While the final version of the bill did preserve in Chełm many existing institutions, the social structure, and certain rights for the Poles, it was to be expected that in the future a policy of Russification would be pursued so that the new province would be incorporated into the central provinces in more than a formal administrative fashion. Furthermore, if the Kingdom of Poland were to be granted rights of self-government, the territory of their ap-

plication would be much reduced, and the ties between Chełm
and the other areas of Poland would become further attenuated.

It should be added that, despite a new head of the Council of
Ministers after the assassination of Stolypin, the attitude of the
government during the prolonged Chełm affair remained consistent. Although the bill had originated during the prime min-
istership of Stolypin, the debates on it began in the Duma in
November 1911, two months after Stolypin's assassination in
Kiev. The new prime minister, Kokovtsov, was not at heart an
advocate of the official nationalist course. At Stolypin's grave,
he spoke the words, "Enough of nationalist rhetoric; now conciliation is necessary." He also took action to forestall any po-
groms against the Jews. In Kiev, he was visited by a delegation
of Nationalists from the Duma headed by P. N. Balashov and
D. N. Chikhachev. They referred to Stolypin's close connection
with the party and sympathy for its ideals. However, they added
that the party did not have confidence in Kokovtsov because it
feared that his policy would be "completely different, alien to
clear national ideals, permeated by excessive sympathy towards
the West, and, consequently, towards foreign elements. . . ." The
Nationalists stated that they could not support him unless he
assured them that he would carry on Stolypin's policy.

Kokovtsov reacted with some heat to this demand, whereupon
the Nationalists said that they would support him if he would
give not necessarily "assurance" but merely "hope" that he would
adhere to Stolypin's policies. After pointing out that Stolypin's
influence had been on the wane after the zemstvo crisis and that
"no amount of support" by the Nationalists could have saved
his political career, Kokovtsov declared that he would never be
the "plaything" of any party, but that if the Nationalists' motto
really was the greatness of Russia, then agreement between them
and the government was simple.

"But I do not share, and cannot serve, your policy of oppressing
foreigners. This policy is harmful and dangerous. . . . To persecute today a Jew . . . then a Pole, a Finn, and to see in all of
them enemies of Russia who it is necessary to curb in every way,
with this I do not sympathize and will not go along with you."

However, although Kokovtsov was honorable and intelligent,

he lacked the command, drive, and forceful personality of his predecessor. From the beginning, his position was weaker than Stolypin's had been at court, within the cabinet, and in the Duma. Kokovtsov's first appearance before the Duma was to defend a governmental project dealing with factory medical funds, but in his second appearance he defended Stolypin's nationalist Finnish bills and stated the principle of the "continuity" of cabinets. In a speech for which he received an ovation from the right and center, including the Nationalists, as well as a telegram of congratulations from the Emperor, Kokovtsov referred to the "expectation" that every successor had to be in opposition to, or at least in disagreement with his predecessor. But in questions affecting

"the vital interests . . . the integrity and unity of the state, its glory and power, in all the fundamental questions of the satisfaction of the vital needs of the Russian people, there must not be hesitations and disagreements on the part of the successor. . . ."

Kokovtsov stated that, as Stolypin's successor, he had to defend "with the same conviction" the nationalist projects that had been introduced in the legislature by Stolypin. "Russian legislation" ought to embody a "just appreciation" of the Russian nationality. Thus, the fears of the Nationalists proved to be unfounded, and Kokovtsov followed Stolypin's nationalist course by pursuing to its enactment the bill on Chełm. And, as an ironical conclusion to the Chełm question, the measure that was designed to appease the Poles for the separation of Chełm, urban self-government in the Congress Kingdom, was vetoed by the State Council in 1914.

CHAPTER VII

FROM *Out of My Past:*
The Memoirs of Count Kokovtsov

*V. N. Kokovtsov was Russian minister of finance from 1904 to
1914 and chairman of the council of ministers from the assassination of Stolypin in 1911 until the beginning of 1914. These
excerpts from his memoirs, one of the principal sources of
information on the period, reveal in the most graphic and ex-
plicit way the decay of the tsarist regime in the years immediately
preceding the outbreak of World War I. Although rather narrow,
conservative, and bureaucratic, Kokovtsov was also honest, able,
and principled. His account shows the internal divisions and
vacillations within the Russian government, the lack of purpose
and coordinated policy, the weaknesses of the Duma, and, finally,
the right-wing intrigues against him that finally led to his dismissal by the weak and inconstant tsar. The excerpts here begin
with the assassination of Stolypin in Kiev in September 1911
and Kokovtsov's nomination as the new chairman of the council
of ministers.*

These were trying days for me. I had little time to sleep, and

SOURCE. Excerpted from, *Out of My Past: The Memoirs of Count Kokovtsov*, Harold H. Fisher, Ed., (Stanford University Press, 1935), pp. 274–275,
282–284, 295–300, 328, 336–343, 349–352, 359–362, 364–366, 379–380, 399–400,
415–416, 418–420, 439, 447, 454–455. Reprinted with the permission of the
publishers, Stanford University Press. Copyright 1935 by the Board of Trust-
ees of the Leland Stanford Junior University.

my nerves were under a great strain. In the midst of it all a deputation of Nationalists of the southwestern region came to see me—P. N. Balashev, D. N. Chikhachev, Potocki, and Professor Chernov. Balashev acted as spokesman. He referred to Stolypin's close connection with the Nationalist Party and to his sympathy with its ideals. This party, however, did not look with favor upon my possible appointment as Stolypin's successor: they considered me too much under the influences of Western Europe and international finance. "We cannot support you," Balashev concluded, "unless we are assured that as Stolypin's successor you will carry on his policy."

I reminded Balashev that I had not yet been appointed to succeed Stolypin, nor had I even been approached on the subject, and I confessed that it would be a great relief to me if the Nationalist Party would take steps to see that I was not appointed to such a responsible position.

Evidently I spoke with some heat, for Chernov hastened to say that the Nationalist Party recognized only too well the necessity of co-operating with the government, but that it could co-operate only with a government for which it had respect. The Nationalists, however, would openly range themselves on my side if I would give them not necessarily assurance but merely hope that I would adhere to Stolypin's policies.

In reply, I told my visitors that they attributed more authority to the Chairman of the Ministers' Council than he actually possessed. Absolute power belonged to the Tsar alone. In times of emergency exceptional powers were given to some ministers, it was true, but only till the crises had passed. Moreover, it often happened that a minister's exercise of these special powers led to his sudden fall, regardless of whether or not he was supported by any one party. As a case in point, I mentioned Stolypin's loss of influence after he had sponsored the introduction of the zemstvos into the southwestern regions. In conclusion, I said that should I be obliged to become Chairman of the Ministers' Council there was one principle which I should follow unfailingly: I would never lie to my Emperor, I would never be the tool of any political party, and I would discharge my duties to the best of my ability as long as I felt I was in the right. As for the Nationalist Party, if its motto was the greatness of Russia and her liberation from any domination, then we could effect an understanding.

But if its policy was to suppress the non-Russian population, I would oppose it as being dangerous and harmful; for to persecute a Jew today, a Pole tomorrow, and a Finlander the next day was to create enemies of Russia within the Empire itself and thereby to undermine the very greatness so eagerly sought.

This ended the interview. . . .

[T]he Empress, who found it painful to stand for any length of time, sat down in an armchair and called me to her side. We talked for more than an hour in a very informal way on all sorts of subjects. But a part of this conversation impressed itself upon my memory because it contained a sharp thrust at myself and showed me the peculiar, mystic nature of this woman who was called to play such an extraordinary part in the history of Russia.

Speaking of events at St. Petersburg, and of the manner in which my appointment had been received by a coterie which was never pleased with anything, the Empress said, "We hope that you will never range yourself with those horrible political parties which only hope to be able to seize power or to subjugate the government."

I answered that even before my appointment I had tried to keep free from allegiance to any party, to stand for the views of the government, and to be as independent as possible. It was my opinion that co-operation with the Duma was an essential factor of our new state life. I could not deny, however, that my position was more difficult than that of Stolypin. He had his parties, first the Octobrists and later the Nationalists, who, although weaker, knew how to ally themselves with the Octobrists or with the Right. As for myself, on the other hand, I could not submit to the dictates of any group, even though in this way I might deprive myself of support. Besides, the position of all parties in the Duma was more difficult than it had been under Stolypin. They had broken up into smaller fractions; they were afraid to stand too close to the government lest they hurt their chances for success in the elections of 1912; and, finally, there was now no united conservative majority in the Duma which would support my views and which had been so advantageous after the sharply defined revolutionary attitude of the first two Dumas.

Then suddenly the Empress interrupted: "I notice that you keep on making comparisons between yourself and Stolypin. You seem to do much honor to his memory and ascribe too much importance to his activities and his personality. Believe me, one must not feel so sorry for those who are no more. I am sure that everybody does only one's duty and fulfills one's destiny, and when one dies that means that his rôle is ended and that he was bound to go, since his destiny has been fulfilled. Life continually assumes new forms, and you must not try to follow blindly the work of your predecessor. Remain yourself; do not look for support in political parties; they are of so little consequence in Russia. Find your support in the confidence of the Tsar—the Lord will help you. I am sure that Stolypin died to make room for you, and this is all for the good of Russia." . . .

When I returned to St. Petersburg on October 8 [1911] the members of both chambers were beginning to assemble. Many of them visited me, exploring the ground for a possible exercise of influence; and from these visits I became aware that the parties were absolutely without unity, and that no one of the conservative political groups had any real influence upon the Duma. Each of them gossiped about the others and tried to undermine my confidence in its rivals.

Among the Octobrists there were clearly defined symptoms of decomposition, since, with the removal of Guchkov from the leadership of this heterogeneous party, numerous internal frictions arose. The Nationalists, under the leadership of Balashev, regarded their importance as much greater than it actually was. Besides, the loss of Stolypin was all too fresh in their memory and the expression of lack of confidence in me which they had made at Kiev was still too well remembered to permit the establishment of cordial relations between us, even if I had been so inclined, which I was not. The unfavorable impression they had made on me at Kiev was intensified by their efforts to discover what attitude I should adopt toward the subsidies which their party had received from Stolypin.

As early as 1910, during the beginning of the campaign for the Duma election of 1912, serious disagreements had arisen between Stolypin and me. Stolypin had pointed out that in no country was the government indifferent toward elections· to legislative institutions, and that in Russia, despite the law of July 3, 1907, an indifferent attitude on the part of the government was bound to increase the opposition parties in the Duma, especially the Cadet Party. Therefore, he had demanded—and received, despite my objections—large sums to prepare for the elections. He had wanted to obtain immediately from my department a lump sum of four million rubles; all I could do was to break the payment up into installments and to argue him into accepting a little over three million, the payments to be extended over the period 1910–1912 and distributed through agencies at my command.

Despite all my protests Stolypin had been adamant in his conviction that all these expenditures would not be futile. I had argued that the sums would simply be distributed among the most trifling and useless organizations and provincial publications which no one read, that they would merely constitute tempting means of financing those near to governors and the Department of Police, and that those who got nothing would only bear resentment against the government. But my arguments had been to no avail. . . .

Then, on February 12, [1912] I was invited to an audience with the Empress Marie Fedorovna for the next morning. For an hour and a half we discussed Rasputin. I answered her questions as directly and honestly as I was able. She wept bitterly and promised to speak to the Tsar, but added: "My poor daughter-in-law does not perceive that she is ruining both the dynasty and herself. She sincerely believes in the holiness of an adventurer, and we are powerless to ward off the misfortune which is sure to come."

On that same day I was amazed to receive a letter from Rasputin. "I am thinking of leaving forever," he wrote, "and would like to see you so as to exchange some ideas; people talk much of me nowadays. Say when. The address is 12 Kirochnaia, at Sazonov's." Of course, I have not retained his peculiar spelling. My first impulse was not to answer, but after some deliberation I decided to receive Rasputin because my position obliged me not to avoid a man who had perturbed all Russia and also because when I next spoke to the Tsar I wanted to be able to give my personal impression of the *starets*. Also I was afraid I might incur the Tsar's displeasure for refusing to see a man who had requested an interview. Finally, I hoped to be able to show Rasputin that he was digging a grave for the Tsar and his authority.

Having resolved to go through with this interview I asked Mamontov to be present as a witness who could testify, in case of need, what actually took place. I fixed on Wednesday evening, February 15. When Rasputin entered my study I was shocked by the repulsive expression of his eyes, deep-set and close to each other, small, gray in color. Rasputin kept them fixed on me for some time, as if he intended to hypnotize me or as if he were studying me on seeing me for the first time. Next he threw his head sharply back and studied the ceiling; then he lowered his head and stared at the floor; all this in silence. As I had no idea how long this would continue, I said, "You wanted to tell me something?"

My words had no effect. Rasputin grinned a silly grin and muttered: "Nothing, nothing, never mind, I was merely seeing how high the ceiling is." And he continued to stare at the ceiling until Mamontov arrived. Mamontov greeted Rasputin and began to ask him whether or not he really wanted to go away. By way of answer Rasputin again fixed his cold, piercing little eyes on me and asked quietly: "Well, shall I go? Life has been hard for me here; people make up stories about me."

"Indeed, you will do well to go away," I replied. "Whether people tell lies or the purest truth about you, you must recognize that this is no place for you; you do harm to the Tsar by appearing at the palace and especially by telling everybody about your nearness to the Imperial family."

"What do I tell? To whom? It is all lies, calumnies! I do not insist on going to the palace—they summon me," Rasputin almost screamed.

Mamontov stopped him quietly: "What is the use of denying, Grigorii Efimovich, that you are the first one to spread tales. But the point is, this is no place for you, and it certainly is not seemly for you to say that you appoint and dismiss ministers. Think carefully and tell me truthfully why generals and high officials have been so nice to you: is it not because you undertake to solicit in their favor? Did you not tell me that you had had Sabler appointed Chief Procurator and did you not offer to speak to the Tsar in order to secure a better position for me? I tell you if you do not leave the palace alone it will be worse not only for yourself but also for the Tsar."

Rasputin listened to this with his eyes closed and his head lowered, and did not answer a word.

"Well," I said, "what are you going to do?"

"All right," he replied, "I shall go. But mind, let them take care not to call me back, since I am so bad that I harm the Tsar."

Such was my first meeting with Rasputin. In my estimation he was a typical Siberian tramp, a clever man who had trained himself for the rôle of a simpleton and a madman and who played his part according to a set formula. He did not believe in his tricks himself, but had trained himself to certain mannerisms of conduct in order to deceive those who sincerely believed in all his oddities. Others, of course, merely pretended to admire him, hoping to obtain privileges through him which could not be obtained in any other way.

The next day we had a musical soirée at our house. In a favorable moment Mamontov told me that Rasputin had already reported at Tsarskoe Selo that he had seen me and that I had urged him to go to Pokrovskoe. He told me, too, that according to Rasputin the latter's friends at the court were very angry. I determined, therefore, to report to the Tsar on the very next morning and give my version of the interview which I had not sought. This I did. I attempted to persuade the Tsar that only calamity could result if Rasputin were permitted to carry on as he had been doing. His Majesty then asked me if it were true I had told Rasputin that I would deport him if he refused to leave the capital. I denied having made any such statement. His Majesty then said that he was glad to hear this, as he had been informed that Makarov [the minister of the interior] and I had decided to remove Rasputin on our own authority. When asked for my impression of the "little peasant" I held back nothing. I added, however, that while I condemned Rasputin for his disreputable behavior, I condemned still more those who sought his protection and assistance. This practically concluded the audience. It was obvious that the whole business was distasteful to the Tsar, for he had spent most of the time looking out of the window. I believed it my duty, however, to say what I did. When I mentioned this to the Tsar he expressed his appreciation of my sincere loyalty and devotion to duty.

At about four o'clock that afternoon Mamontov telephoned to say that the substance of my morning's conversation with the Tsar was already known to Rasputin. When I expressed surprise at the quickness with which the latter had obtained the information, Mamontov assured me that the Tsar had had plenty of time to recount at lunch what I had said to him that morning. Madame Vyrubova would thus become informed; telephone communication with Rasputin was then a simple matter.

Rasputin actually did leave St. Petersburg the following week.

The press seized upon the news, and *Rech* even published an article approving the orders to deport the man, which I was alleged to have given but which I had not. I was eager to see what influence these events would have upon the Tsar. But during my next report he did not once mention them; he was kind and gracious as usual. Those attached to the court, however, were excited about them.

A few days later I found myself obliged to take part in another extremely delicate incident concerned with the copies of the letters of the Empress Alexandra Fedorovna and the Grand Duchesses to Rasputin hectographed by Guchkov. I never saw the original letters and did not know how Guchkov came into possession of them. Passages of the letters of the Empress could, of course, have been interpreted most objectionably if one were to read them apart from their context, but everybody who knew the Empress knew well that the true meaning of the letters was altogether different. They showed all her love for her sick son and her striving to find in her faith in miracles a means to save his life. They showed the exaltation and religious mysticism of this deeply unhappy woman, who paid such a terrible price for all her errors. . . .

Makarov feared that the appearance of photographic reproductions of these letters might create a still greater scandal than the typed copies, and he asked me for help. He agreed that he should try to persuade the holder of the letters not to permit their circulation, and in case this did not work should try to buy them, for which purpose I agreed to allow a certain credit. In case this, too, failed, we were resolved to find other means.

In a few days Makarov phoned me to say that he had the letters and had had no trouble getting them because the man who had them not only was quite a decent fellow but also was afraid that the possession of the letters might get him into trouble with Rasputin and his crowd. Makarov gave me the letters to read. There were six of them: One long one from the Empress, which had been quite correctly reproduced in Guchkov's copy. One from each of the four Grand Duchesses, the contents of which were perfectly innocent—apparently the Grand Duchesses had written at their mother's insistence; they said merely that they had been to church and that they had looked for Rasputin but could not find him in his usual place. And one, a small sheet of note paper, with a carefully scribbled "A" from the little Tsarevich.

Makarov and I did not know what to do with the letters. His first impulse was to hide them in order to prevent them from falling into anyone's hands, but I firmly advised him not to do so, as he might be suspected of some evil intent. I also opposed his suggestion to give them to the Tsar; this would have placed the Tsar in a very awkward position and would have antagonized the Empress. I advised him to request an audience with the Empress and to offer her the letters, explaining frankly how they had fallen into his hands.

Makarov promised to follow this advice, but did not do so. During his very first report, having the letters handy and seeing that the Tsar was in splendid humor, Makarov told him the story of the letters and placed in his hands the envelope containing them. The Tsar turned pale, nervously took the letters from the envelope, and, glancing at the Empress's handwriting, said: "Yes, this is not a counterfeit letter." Then opened a drawer of his desk and threw the letters inside, with a sharp gesture quite unusual with him.

I had nothing to say to this but to remark to Makarov, "Why did you ask me for advice only to act in the opposite way? Now your dismissal is certain." My prophecy was soon fulfilled. . . .

The summer of 1912 was spent chiefly in preparing for the election. One of my main worries was with the many insistences that came to me regarding subsidies for the election campaign. The Octobrists and the Nationalists vied with each other in protesting their unity; given the least financial support, their success in the coming election was assured. The organizations of the Right, however, proved to be the real virtuosos in such protestations: they presented a carefully drawn estimate of the money (964,000 rubles) they needed for campaign purposes and hinted that their attitude toward me would depend upon whether or not this sum was forthcoming. I should like to say just here that Makarov, despite our other differences, supported me in maintaining the needlessness of the campaign expenses for the control of the press. My own opinion on this matter was the chief cause of the hostility of the Right toward me and this had its influence on my dismissal two years later. . . .

That autumn, instead of going to the Crimea, the Tsar went

hunting first at Belovezh and later at Spala, where the Tsarevich fell dangerously ill and nearly died. Until the middle of October the entire country lived under the shadow of a possible catastrophe, and it was not until the second week in October that the reassuring news came that the Tsarevich was out of immediate danger. Only then did I go to Spala to report. A great many pressing matters were awaiting decision, the most important of which concerned the elections to the Duma, which were at that time drawing to a close. The majority of the elected members held moderate views, but they were not united by common convictions, nor were they under any definite general direction.

In this connection I should like to digress to recount an episode in which the differences between Makarov and me were put aside for the moment, and to show what startling methods were then being practiced by some prominent administrators.

Early in September a number of governors assembled in St. Petersburg to receive instructions from the Minister of the Interior regarding the methods to be emloyed by different local election committees. I learned from conversations with the governors that the committees had no general election policy but each acted according to its own ideas.

At my request Makarov granted me permission to have a discussion with the assembled governors in his presence. The majority of them reported that the election was going on rather colorlessly; that the extreme Left organizations were under cover, being careful not to show their cards, but that it was certain that they would not win many votes; and that the Cadets, the Octobrists, and the Nationalists of the Balashev type would get most of the votes, since the extreme Right was not very active, although it could be expected to retain its former strength.

In all of the governors' reports, however, one note sounded quite distinctly: the chiefs of gubernias had at their command very small means with which to influence the course of the elections. The only organized social group accessible to influence was the rural and the city clergy. The diocesan authorities cared only for the opinion of the Holy Synod, and its Chief Procurator and had little to do with the governors. But even in this group not all bishops were in sympathy with the too moderate instructions of the Synod. They regarded as unsound its instruction to support all conservative parties, beginning with the Octobrists, and to make no distinction between the parties of the Right. The bishops would have preferred to receive more definite instructions for the support of some particular party. Some of the governors implied that many bishops did not quite trust even the sincerity of the Synod's instructions, believing that they were merely the result of pressure exercised upon the Chief Procurator by the Minister of the Interior and the Chairman of the Ministers' Council. Many bishops believed that, personally, V. K. Sabler was in sympathy with only one party—the extreme Right. All the governors were agreed that the *zemskie nachalniki*[1] exercised hardly any influence upon the peasants in the elections, and that no hopes should be built upon this element.

I received an almost unanimous reply also to my question as to the influence exercised upon public opinion and the course of the elections by the local conservative press, which had been generously supported by the government in certain gubernias. This influence, the governors said, was nil, since no one read these publications. Several governors said frankly that it was common knowledge that these papers were published at the government's expense, and since the editors of these papers were generally unfit for their work, and the content was of poor quality for want of well-trained and able collaborators, even those who received the publications free of charge refused to read them. . . .

I should also like to relate at this point the circumstances which led to differences between me and the extreme Right and to its campaign against me, beginning with the convocation of the Fourth Duma. I had often argued with Stolypin against subsidizing the local conservative press as a means of combating the influence of the opposition, but I argued in vain. He had felt a little resentfully that I was trying to interfere in his official affairs. Nor did the Tsar support me against Stolypin. I often saw the paper *Zemshchina* on His Majesty's desk and always made bold to point out that the subsidy of this paper—180,000 rubles a year—was utter waste, for the paper was not generally read and many people wondered why it was continued, since it frequently attacked government officials, myself in particular. . . .

Immediately after the dissolution of the Third Duma, some of

[1] Land captains—an office created in 1889 giving appointees from the nobility administrative and judicial power in the local affairs of the peasantry.

its members—Markov II, Novitsky, and Purishkevich—visited me and insisted on the necessity of placing at their disposal for use in the coming elections large sums in addition to the usual subsidies. When I suggested that they present their demands to Makarov, they assured me that he was one with them but felt bound by his promise not to increase election expenses. Therefore, they had come to me, for they regarded my unwillingness to appropriate this additional sum as the barrier to be overcome. They had even prepared an estimate of their needs—960,000 rubles. I asked Markov why they had not asked for the round figure of a million, to which he replied, "We well know that you like exact figures and so we have excluded all superfluous matters." There were only a few items, the largest of which called for more than 500,000 rubles to be used in conducting "agitation" in the form of provincial conventions, lectures, pamphlets, the press, traveling expenses, and, of course, some "secret" expenses.

I refused these demands. My visitors were very angry, and Markov II rose from his chair and hotly declared: "When Petr Arkad'evich was alive, things were different; he would have made you give us what we want; now you will be left to reap the fruit of our failure, since you will get a Duma very different from the one you could have had from us for the paltry sum of 900,000 rubles." He never forgave me for this refusal, and a year later, May 27, 1913, he sought to settle his account with me by his speech in the Duma. . . .

His Majesty was especially interested in the election returns, which showed that in nearly all gubernias a majority of moderates had been returned. St. Petersburg, it is true, had returned mostly Cadets, but any disappointment the Tsar might have felt at this result was more than offset by the fact that Guchkov had been defeated there. His Majesty earnestly hoped that Guchkov would also be defeated in Moscow, where he was running as a gubernial candidate. His hope was gratified.

As we went to lunch, the Tsar mentioned a matter which I should like to record here. . . . Senator Trussevich had been appointed to investigate the responsibility for Stolypin's assassination. This investigation had revealed the negligence of four persons: Assistant Minister of the Interior Kurlov, Chief of the Kiev Secret Service Kuliabko, Assistant Director of the Police Department Verigin, and Kurlov's assistant, Lieutenant Colonel Spiridovich. Makarov had accepted these findings without comment. The Minister of Justice, Shcheglovitov, had favored bringing these men to trial. The First Department of the State Council had asked them to explain their negligence, had found their explanations unsatisfactory, and had decided to request the Tsar for permission to arraign them before a criminal court. His Majesty, however, had not confirmed the decision of the State Council's First Department, although he must surely have understood that such an arraignment could not finally establish the guilt of the accused, since they could appeal for a retrial before the Senate and it might reach an entirely different verdict. Moreover, whatever the verdict, it had to be confirmed by the Tsar.

It was not until we went to lunch that I knew the Tsar's decision in this matter, and when I learned it I must confess I was a bit staggered. In order to signalize his son's recovery by some generous act, he had decided to dismiss the case. In fact, he had already sent the Imperial Secretary a memorandum to that effect, and had informed Spiridovich of his decision. "I see him," said the Tsar, "at every turn; he follows me about like a shadow and I simply cannot see this man so crushed with grief; surely he did not want to do any harm and is guilty of nothing except his failure to take every measure of precaution." It was beyond my power to alter the decision, but I felt in duty bound to speak my mind. I pointed out that such negligence as these men had displayed was unpardonable. Bogrov might just as easily have turned his Browning on the occupants of the Imperial Box as on Stolypin. No loyal Russian could ever become reconciled to a decision which permitted men guilty of such a crime to go unpunished while petty government officials were tried and punished every day for much less serious offenses. "Your generous impulse, Sire, will not be understood. Moreover, your decision precludes the possibility of completely clearing up this 'dark' affair by a final Senate investigation, which, incidentally, might reveal something more serious than criminal negligence, at least as far as General Kurlov was concerned."

The Tsar admitted the force and validity of my arguments, but did not offer to make any change in his decision. . . .

Soon afterward the Tsar and his entire family returned to Tsarskoe Selo. A few days later, on October 28, and quite unexpectedly for the entire Council, the Minister of War gave me something of a surprise. Without a word of warning, he presented me with a special request for a supplementary credit of sixty-three million rubles to be used to increase our defenses on the Austrian frontier. He considered this necessary because of conditions in the Balkans. He based his request upon an old law which had been repealed when the new budget regulations were published, and announced that he was acting on the orders of the Tsar, who had unconditionally approved his request. I was not so much amazed at the incongruous demand—I had long been used to such—as at the fact that only a day previously I had discussed matters of a military nature with the Tsar at some length and he had not said a word about General Sukhomlinov's new demand. . . .

I convoked the Ministers' Council on October 30, and wrote a letter to the Tsar saying that I had no right to comply with this new demand, since, according to law, only the Ministers' Council, and not an individual Minister, was authorized to present to the Tsar a resolution for an appropriation of credits, which had subsequently to be confirmed by the Duma.

My letter was returned to me with a note in the Tsar's hand: "This is not the time to consider such formalities. In any event, I expect the Council's memorandum not later than November 1. The money must be appropriated." . . .

These discussions in the Council always made me unhappy. They demonstrated my isolation and helplessness. By public opinion I was regarded as the head of the government and responsible for its policies. Actually, my power to formulate and direct such policies was undermined by a split within the Cabinet. Moreover, my opponents in the government had the support of the Tsar, who lent a ready ear to their nationalistic schemes and professions. He liked to think with them that Germany would not dare to engage Russia in war and that the might of the Russian people was great enough to put Germany in her place at any time. My policy of caution was represented to him as a proof of my personal cowardice and as the professional ruse of a Minister of Finance to ensure at all costs the financial well-being of his country. Frequently, I suggested that harmony in the government might be increased by ministerial changes, but these were never made. Apparently the Tsar had paid heed to Meshchersky's hints that it was contrary to the spirit of the Russian régime and suggestive of parliamentarism to make ministerial changes on the advice of the Chairman of the Council. At any rate he would not consider parting with such men as Kasso, an advocate of "firm government," or Rukhlov, a self-made minister risen from the bottom of the Russian peasantry; or Shcheglovitov, a guardian of the law who was always ready to subordinate justice to politics; or Krivoshein, a consummate politician who at that time enjoyed the favor of the Tsar, the Duma, the zemstvos, and the press. I often considered requesting His Majesty to accept my resignation, but refrained from doing so because I felt I had a duty to perform in moderating both our domestic and our foreign policy and because I was absolutely unwilling to force upon my gracious and considerate Sovereign the unhappy task of choosing between the other ministers and me. Nor have I ever regretted withholding this request.

The Fourth Duma convened on November 1, 1912, and the remainder of the year was devoted to its business. For some time it was unable to organize and to begin its work. This was due to the fact that although the elections had returned a majority of moderates, there was no common will or settled purpose among their several factions. I was personally acquainted with many of the Duma members, several of whom had been in the Third Duma. These called on me frequently, though furtively, on the pretext of securing some sort of information, and from the hints they dropped I could clearly see that there was chaos among the Duma parties.

My relations with the several parties varied, but in the main they were not happy. I learned from the Moscow deputy Shubinsky that his friend Rodzianko avoided me lest he compromise his chances of being elected President of the new Duma. The opposition parties, of course, had nothing to do with me. The Cadets did not know to what tune they should dance. The Nationalists, through their leader Petr Nikolaevich Balashev, gave me to understand that they were expecting me to work in close contact with them, but that because of their great number, I must take the first step—Mohammed was to go to the mountain. I was even informed that Balashev coveted the presidency of the Duma and was waiting for me to inaugurate his campaign.

In all this, I fear I was not sufficiently pliant. At any rate, I was later assured that I was not clever enough to handle the Duma as the late Stolypin had done. Nevertheless, I tried to steer a straight course. I solicited favor from no one, shunned all intrigue, and bided my time till the Duma made some order out of its party chaos.

This, I believe, was the wise course to follow, for there was no one in the Duma upon whom to rely; all the groups sought power, influence, and government support; but none had any definite policy. The Left group was out of the question. Side by side with the Cadets there were the Progressists, headed by Efremov and Konovalov, both of whom considered it beneath their dignity to have any but purely official relations with the government. The Octobrists feared the predominance of the Nationalists and resented the loss of Guchkov, Kamensky, Glebov, and others. The Nationalists assumed a hostile attitude toward me from the start; they were greatly influenced by the Kiev deputy, Savenko, and his friend, Demchenko—the more level-headed and business-like of the two. The Nationalists immediately established close contact with Rukhlov and Krivoshein and said openly in the Duma lobbies—as I learned immediately —that they would begin a campaign against me. . . . As for the Rights, they simply forgot the path to me. Their leaders, Markov II and Purishkevich, could not forgive me for refusing to grant them a subsidy of one million rubles for the election campaign. They found a powerful supporter in the person of the former Nizhni Novgorod Governor, Khvostov, who knew perfectly well that I had been responsible for preventing his appointment as Minister of the Interior in September 1911, after Stolypin's death.

Thus my relations with the Fourth Duma were very cool and formal and often hostile, though outwardly most cordial and correct. This was definitely demonstrated in the debates on the so-called government declaration. I had sepnt much careful effort in its preparation, and it had been difficult to secure agreement in the Council and to manage the Tsar, who thought that the declaration smacked too much of Western-European parliaments.

The tone of the declaration was moderate. I avoided acute problems and pleaded for peace both at home and abroad. I stressed Russia's sincere interest and effort in liquidating the trouble in the Balkans, and made a bid for the co-operation of the people's representatives in all government work.

In general, the press of Western Europe received the declaration sympathetically. Many political leaders sent me messages of congratulation. The Russian press, however, was either indifferent or openly hostile. *Novoe Vremia* made it an occasion to attack me personally.

In the Duma, the Left was unexpectedly reserved. The Octobrists and the Right applauded me. Outwardly it seemed that I had been successful—as one may also judge from the stenographic report of my speech. But when the debates started, it was another story. The Nationalists accused me of not supporting nationalistic policies, and of disregarding the legacy of Stolypin. The Rights also attacked me, seeking to complicate my position. But most astonishing was the fact that half of the ministers—Rukhlov, Krivoshein, Shcheglovitov, and Maklakov, the recently appointed Minister of the Interior—sided with my adversaries. These ministers were reliably reported as being in close contact with my opponents in the Duma.

I felt obliged to point out to the Tsar the anomaly of this situation in which ministers of the Council openly opposed the Council's Chairman. Once more I suggested that I be permitted to resign, or that I be permitted to find colleagues upon whose support I could depend, so that harmony in the Council might be restored. But again the Tsar would not hear of such changes; he thought I attached too great importance to the back-stage activities of my fellow ministers. In complying with his wishes, I may once more have exhibited unpardonable weakness, but I could not find it in my heart to disobey my Monarch. If in his estimation Russia needed my services, it was not for me to shirk my duty. Nor did I wish to abandon my beloved work. . . .

During these months, the events in the Balkans occupied the center of interest. As these events became more complicated, Sazonov came to me more and more for advice. He found in me an ardent advocate of peace. I perceived only too well our unpreparedness for war, the weakness of our military organization, and the consequences of a war for Russia. Therefore, I always championed a policy of moderation and conciliation. The Tsar, however, did not approve of the Chairman of the Ministers' Council being so directly concerned with foreign policy. He considered them his own private concern and was displeased to see that the Minister of Foreign Affairs discussed them with me privately and in the Ministers' Council. His Majesty did not once mention to me directly that I was meddling with affairs not of my concern, but he could not understand why it was that the foreign ambassadors addressed themselves to me and not exclusively to the Minister of Foreign Affairs. He made it plain by well directed hints that neither the Ministers' Council nor its Chairman had anything to do with foreign policy. I felt obliged to carry on, however; but I was careful not to cause any complication, especially since *Grazhdanin* was hinting that the Chairman of the Council was beginning to "usurp the prerogatives of the Supreme Power which alone is supposed to handle foreign affairs. . . ."

The turn of the year was largely taken up with preparations for the festivities celebrating the 300th anniversary of the House of Romanov's accession to the Russian throne. Late in March I was informed by the Chief Court Marshal, Count Benckendorf, that the Tsar wished to be accompanied on these festive journeys only by Maklakov, Rukhlov, and myself—the other ministers were to go directly to Moscow. But even though we three were to accompany the Tsar, we were to provide our own transportation and accommodation, a matter in which I was greatly aided by Rukhlov, who, as Minister of Ways and Communications, had means at his disposal. This, of course, is no reflection on His Majesty, who would gladly have provided for us; it is simply an indication of the regard in which ministers of the government were held by the managers of the Imperial Court.

Evidently the Tsar's journey was to be in the nature of a family celebration. The concepts of state and government were to be pushed into the background and the personality of the Tsar was to dominate the scene. The current attitude seemed to suggest that the government was a barrier between the people and their Tsar, whom they regarded with blind devotion as anointed by God. This attitude of the people was due, I believe, not to any lack of prestige on the part of government leaders but to the results of the seven years of peace and prosperity that had followed the disturbances of 1905–1906. The Tsar's closest friends at the court became persuaded that the Sovereign could do anything by relying upon the unbounded love and utter loyalty of the people. The ministers of the government, on the other hand, did not hold to this sort of autocracy; nor did the Duma, which steadily sought control of the executive power. Both were of the opinion that the Sovereign should recognize that conditions had changed since the day the Romanovs became Tsars of Moscow and lords of the Russian domain.

Despite the solemnity which pervaded the Romanov celebrations they were rather colorless. Our first stop on the journey was at Vladimir, then, in order, Nizhni Novgorod, Kostroma, Yaroslavl, Suzdal, and Rostov. Everywhere I was impressed by the lack of enthusiasm and the smallness of the crowds. At Nizhni Novgorod, Rukhlov gave voice to this same impression: there was nothing in the feeling of the crowd but shallow curiosity. Down the Volga from Nizhni there was a biting cold wind, and the Tsar did not once show himself where stop-overs had been arranged. There were handsomely ornamented descents from the shore to the water where small groups of peasants were gathered apparently waiting to see their Tsar; but in vain, for the steamship went steadily on till it reached Kostroma, where it stopped for the night. Here alone was there anything approaching enthusiasm at the sight of the Tsar and his family. It seemed that the return of warm weather had thawed out the crowd.

Then there was Moscow with all its splendor. But even in this historic city a smaller crowd than usual thronged the Krasnaia Ploshchad.[2] The Tsarevich was carried along in the arms of a Cossack of the bodyguard, and as the procession paused opposite the Minin and Pozharsky monument I clearly heard exclamations of sorrow at the sight of this poor, helpless child, the heir to the throne of the Romanovs. As the days of celebration flew by I felt only the lifelessness and emptiness of what was supposed to be a festive anniversary. There was brilliance and a motley throng but complete unawareness of the dangers which beset Russia both at home and abroad. . . .

My budget speech for 1913 was in every sense of the word my Swan song, for when the time for the debates on the budget for 1914 arrived I was no longer Minister of Finance. The budget was presented by my successor, Bark, who limited himself to very brief remarks mainly devoted to praise of the Chairman of the Budget Committee.

The preliminary work of the Budget Committee was especially

[2] Red Square.

protracted in 1913, and the debates did not begin till May 10. In my speech, I pointed out that the budget had been balanced by recourse to ordinary revenues only, despite the fact that there had been many extraordinary expenditures. I did my best to avoid any statements that might give rise to the "polemics" which so frequently characterized these debates. As can be seen from the stenographic report, my speech was well received, especially by the Center and the left wing of the Right group. . . .

The main opposition, however, came from the Right, the Nationalist Savenko, and from the extreme Right represented by Markov II. . . .

Two weeks later Markov II answered me in my absence by shouting to the Duma, "And I shall tell the Minister of Finance simply this: 'One should not steal.' " What he meant, no one knows. Such an implicit accusation of the head of the government, however, was unpardonable. The acting president of the Duma, Prince Volkonsky, ought to have reprimanded Markov II, but did nothing. Nor did any member of the Duma raise his voice against the innuendo.

Later Prince Volkonsky apologized for his fault and offered to tender his resignation. When I suggested that the place to make an apology was from the Duma tribune, Volkonsky agreed but said that Rodzianko and the Council of Elders opposed such a course. Rodzianko himself came to see me about the incident to learn what I proposed to do. I explained that it would all depend how the Tsar reacted to this unrebuked insult to his Chairman of the Council. I suggested that he publicly forbid such conduct in the future.

I brought the matter before the ministers. They decided not to ignore it but to request the Tsar's permission to stay away from Duma sessions until amends had been made and assurance given that the offense would not be repeated. In the meantime they would be represented by their assistants. Shcheglovitov and Maklakov would even have gone so far as to recommend the dissolution of the Duma.

The Tsar confirmed the Council's decision, which was soon known in the city. Rodzianko visited me to inform me that the Council of Elders was opposed to his making a statement to the Duma. Shubinsky and N. N. Lvov also called on me; the former favored the government's point of view, as did the latter, although he was a member of the opposition and had had practically no dealings with me. Lvov said that Rodzianko had distorted the truth, saying that the Duma would be dissolved if an apology was not forthcoming. This, of course, was not so and when Lvov had learned the actual truth he was quite ready to endorse the government's decision.

The press, however, was adverse in its criticism. Both *Rech* and *Novoe Vremia* suggested that the government ought not to follow a policy of obstruction; these papers failed to understand that it was the Duma and not the government that refused to effect a reconciliation. The incident was not liquidated till the autumn, in the beginning of a new session. Then Rodzianko did what I had advised him to do in May, and received congratulations for having ended this unfortunate affair. . . .

I digress briefly at this point to relate an incident which occurred while I was at Yalta. I had been sent a copy of the *Grazhdanin* from St. Petersburg, a column of which, the "Diary," was written by Meshchersky himself. This column was entirely devoted to me and my proposed trip abroad. He boldly accused the government of "parliamentarism"; he attacked the ministers, especially the Chairman of the Ministers' Council, for lowering the prestige of the Imperial authority; and, finally, airing his pet theory, he expounded the necessity of doing away with this "Western-European innovation," of abolishing the Ministers' Council, and of returning to the former Ministers' Committee headed by a dignitary as worthy and as loyal to his Tsar as were, for example, I. L. Goremykin and A. S. Taneev. Because of my personal antipathy toward "the young and talented Minister of the Interior," the Diary continued, I was continually opposing him in his efforts to carry out the will of the Monarch. Maklakov, it said, had a detailed plan for curbing the "unbridled" freedom of the press, but as I needed "the plaudits of the Duma" his plans were doomed to defeat. It was high time the Tsar learned who was his servant and who was the servant of "the Rodziankos and the Guchkovs."

The "Diary" was read immediately at Yalta. Count Frederichs[3] was deeply indignant and asked me if I did not intend to show

---

[3] The Minister of the Imperial Court, Baron Frederichs, was raised to the rank of Count during the Romanov celebrations.

it to the Tsar and request him to put a stop to this baiting, which only served to undermine the prestige of the government. Meshchersky was boasting everywhere, but with absolutely no grounds, that he enjoyed the Tsar's special favor. It could be argued, therefore, that such a campaign against the Chairman of the Ministers' Council was intended to undermine his position at a time when he needed all his prestige for the purposes of his trip. In answering, I told Count Frederichs that the Tsar had probably read the "Diary," as he was in the habit of reading everything Meshchersky wrote. I knew from experience that it would do no good to mention the matter to the Tsar. I expressed my conviction that there was a campaign against me, and after my return I intended to repeat my request for permission to resign. This the Count begged me not to do—especially at a time when Russia needed me so badly and since the Tsar was well-disposed toward me.

To prove he was correct in estimating the Tsar's opinion of me, he volunteered to drop a hint to His Majesty regarding some court title for me. Such a title would add to my prestige abroad. I told Count Frederichs that I was not anxious to have any title; the only purpose it could serve would be to reveal the Tsar's attitude toward me. I advised him not to broach the subject.

At the same time I decided to write Maklakov and call his attention to the questionable conduct of his protector Meshchersky and to the impression the latter's attacks produced upon the Tsar's entourage. I said I should never bring myself to ask the Tsar to arbitrate any differences between us, but that since he was on very intimate terms with Meshchersky he was bound to assume full moral responsibility for the inevitable consequences of the writer's personal grudge against me. Three weeks later, in Florence, I received Maklakov's answer. He said that he was not very intimate with Prince Meshchersky, nor did he believe himself justified in engaging in private discussions with him regarding his articles, but if I desired the administration to punish the *Grazhdanin* he was ready to report to His Majesty, the Tsar, to this effect. Knowing His Majesty's attitude toward the editor of this paper, however, he could not take it upon himself to apply such punishment on his own authority. I replied immediately that I was most sorry he had not had time to read my letter, as I had said plainly that I considered it out of the question to involve the Tsar in a matter pertaining to myself personally; I also informed him that I was instructing my Assistant, P. A. Kharitonov, who was acting in my stead in the Ministers' Council, not to permit the presentation of such a report to the Tsar when it was quite within the power of the Minister of the Interior to act on his own authority.

Naturally, there was no report of any sort. My correspondence with Maklakov fell into the hands of Meshchersky through Maklakov himself, and our relations became even more strained. Hostile articles in the *Grazhdanin* became an everyday occurrence, and after my return to St. Petersburg they became so violent that I could plainly see that my fate had been decided, since it was Prince Meshchersky's policy to trample in the mud only those whose days had already been numbered.

I reminded His Majesty . . . of Meshchersky's continual repetition of the theme that the Chairman of the Ministers Council was gradually usurping the Tsar's authority and becoming a veritable Grand Vizier. This, I suggested, encouraged the ministers to intrigue against their Chairman, thus weakening the government. Already the different factions of the Duma were becoming embroiled in the feud. I had two other previous issues of the same paper in which I was portrayed as "not a Tsar's Minister" but a "Duma bootlicker" who schemed night and day to dim the halo surrounding the Sovereign and to exalt the representatives of the people. It was recommended that I be replaced by such a loyal Tsar's minister as Goremykin or Tancev, who would restore the Tsar's authority to its rightful state. I told His Majesty that I had asked Maklakov to use his influence to prevent Meshchersky from continuing these attacks, which really undermined the Tsar's authority, but Maklakov had replied that he had no influence with the Prince.

The Tsar listened patiently, but he was not impressed. He considered that I attached too much importance to these newspaper articles—much more than they deserved. He contended that the influence of newspapers, of *Grazhdanin* especially, was much less than I thought.

There was no more to say. I hinted that someone else might be better able to preserve unity among the ministers, but the Tsar would not hear of any such suggestion. We completed the remaining routine work, His Majesty expressing particular satisfaction with the budget, especially with the fact that I had been able to meet the demands of the Ministry of War; and then I left. We parted on good terms. . . .

Monday, January 27, [1914] I spent at home receiving callers. . . .

Then my wife and I went to dine at Maklakov's house. We started out with an unpleasant feeling, for since November I had not been on good terms with him and I knew that he was one of the links in the chain of the intrigue surrounding me. . . .

After dinner Count Frederichs asked me to tell him the meaning of the rumors regarding my retirement. "Last Saturday," he said, "when in accordance with Trepov's request I spoke to the Tsar, he spoke of you in the most gracious terms and I assure you that you enjoy his entire confidence. I know that you are in an unfortunate situation, that people intrigue about you and against you, and as a friend I advise you to talk frankly and sincerely with His Majesty, explain to him that your situation has become insufferable, and ask him to dismiss the ministers with whom you can work no longer. I assure you, you will be successful providing you are firm."

I thanked Frederichs and said I should like nothing better than to have such a talk with His Majesty. I reminded him, however, that I was no Witte and could not force my will upon the Tsar. Nevertheless, I promised to speak out during my next report—even though I felt sure my official days were numbered.

Leaving Frederichs I approached another group of guests, among whom was Count A. A. Bobrinsky. He told me that the Tsar had confirmed the order to make photographic reproductions of the archaeological finds for Emperor William. I answered that I should probably not be in office to receive the completed pictures, as rumor predicted my dismissal. "What of it?" he said. "It will be but a short vacation which you so badly need." These words of a man who never spoke to the wind and who, moreover, belonged to the extreme Right and had reliable sources of information were the first definite confirmation I had had that it had been decided to remove me. . . .

The morning of January 29, following a night endless and sleepless because of painful and persistent thoughts, I spent in familiar occupations. My wife went for her usual morning walk, and I occupied myself in my study with my routine work. At exactly eleven o'clock a messenger brought me a short letter written in the Tsar's hand and addressed to the "Chairman of the Ministers' Council," a letter which I still have. Before I opened it I knew that it brought my dismissal. It read as follows:

"Tsarskoe Selo, January 29, 1914

"Vladimir Nikolaevich:

"It is not a feeling of displeasure but a long-standing and deep realization of a state need that now forces me to tell you that we have to part.

"I am doing this in writing, for it is easier to select the right words when putting them on paper than during an unsettling conversation.

"The happenings of the past eight years have persuaded me definitely that the idea of combining in one person the duties of Chairman of the Ministers' Council and those of Minister of Finance or of the Interior is both awkward and wrong in a country such as Russia.

"Moreover, the swift tempo of our domestic life and the striking development of the economic forces of our country both demand the undertaking of most definite and serious measures, a task which should be best entrusted to a man fresh for the work.

"During the last two years, unfortunately, I have not always approved of the policy of the Ministry of Finance, and I perceive that this can go no farther.

"I appreciate highly your devotion to me and the great service you have performed in achieving remarkable improvements in Russia's state credit; I am grateful to you for this from the bottom of my heart. Believe me, I am sorry to part with you who have been my assistant for ten years. Believe also, that I shall not forget to take suitable care of you and your family. I expect you with your last report on Friday, at 11:00 A.M. as always, and ever as a friend.

"With sincere regards,

"Nicholas"

Then as now I could see clearly that the Tsar had written the letter under the influence of that pressure which had been brought to bear upon him for the purpose of removing me. Evidently the Tsar did not trust himself during a conversation with me, fearing that I might advance arguments which would force him to change his mind; on the other hand, the persons enjoying his confidence persisted in their purpose, and therefore he had decided to take a step which made his decision with respect to me irrevocable.

The conviction that the letter was written under the influence of my enemies is supported by evidence within the letter itself. During the past eight years he said he had noted the harmfulness of combining in Russia the duties of Chairman of the Ministers' Council and those of the Minister of Finance or the Interior. Three years previously, after the assassination of Stolypin, when he had deliberately appointed me chairman, he had said: "It goes without saying that I wish you to remain Minister of Finance." Since then, moreover, not only had I never heard from him any remarks on the awkwardness of such a combination but I had on many occasions heard him say that during my term of office there had been much less friction in the Council than ever before.

The letter also mentioned Russia's tremendous economic growth, which created a series of new demands which needed new men for their fulfillment. Now who had been responsible for this tremendous economic progress? Whose work had it been to preserve Russian finances during the Russo-Japanese War and during the period of domestic strife, thus paving the way for Russia's economic progress? Why was it that this same person was now found inadequate to face the new economic problems? And why had he not been informed as to what these problems were? Still more strange, and, I dislike to say it, still less intelligible, was the statement to the effect that during the last two years the Tsar had not been altogether pleased with the policy of the Ministry of Finance and that this could not go on. At no time during the entire ten years of my administration had I heard any expression of disapproval, nor had I received, either orally or in writing, any implied criticism of my policies and accomplishments in the Ministry of Finance. Always my reports had been received with definite expressions of favor and pleasure. In October 1912, in discussing the project of appointing me ambassador to Berlin, the Tsar had asked me to suggest someone to succeed me as Minister of Finance, and added, "providing, of course, that he will carry on as you have done, for I cannot consider that any change should be made in your splendid policies."

The last words of the letter made a peculiar impression upon me. Instructing me that on Friday next I was to appear with my last report at my usual time, the Tsar seemed to warn me not to try to make him change his decision, as it was irrevocable. As if during these last ten years the Tsar had not learned to know that I should never ask to be left at my post against his will! . . .

The day after my dismissal Goremykin called on me. I took advantage of the opportunity to wish him success. "What success can I hope for?" he said. "I am like an old fur coat. For many months I have been packed away in camphor. I am being taken out now merely for the occasion; when it is passed I shall be packed away again till I am wanted the next time.". . .

I must add one name . . .

Empress Alexandra Fedorovina. Remembering her fate at the hands of the Bolsheviks, it was my resolve for many years not to mention in my memoirs the important part she played in my dismissal and in Russian affairs. I considered it unfair to attempt to justify my own actions when those persons whose names would necessarily be involved were no longer here to speak in their own defense. Yet in all the years since 1917 none of the Russian émigrés has undertaken to explain the personality of the Empress.

In the absence of such accounts from exiled Russians, we have been obliged to depend on the writings of non-Russians, most of whom have been ill informed and most of whose work is characterized by anecdote or calumny or both. Thus the personality of the last Empress of Russia has either remained unrevealed or has been distorted. . . . In view of these facts, I have decided that it would be best for me to say my word, hoping that it will be a contribution to this delicate subject. . . .

At first I enjoyed Her Majesty's favor; in fact I was appointed Chairman of the Ministers' Council with her knowledge and consent. Hence, when the Duma and the press began a violent campaign against Rasputin, the details of which I have already related, she expected me to put a stop to it. Yet it was not my opposition to the Tsar's proposal to take measures against the press that won me her disfavor; it was my report to His Majesty about Rasputin after the *starets* had visited me. From that time on, although the Tsar continued to show me his favor for another two years, my dismissal was assured. This changed attitude of Her Majesty is not hard to understand if one bears in mind the traits of her character outlined above. In her mind, Rasputin was

closely associated with the health of her son and the welfare of
the Monarchy. To attack him was to attack the protector of what
she held most dear. Moreover, like any righteous person, she was
offended to think that the sanctity of her home had been questioned in the press and in the Duma. She thought that I, as head
of the government, was responsible for permitting these attacks,
and could not understand why I could not stop them simply by
giving orders in the name of the Tsar. She considered me, therefore, not a servant of the Tsar but a tool of the enemies of the
state and as such deserving dismissal.

CHAPTER VIII

FROM   *George F. Kennan*
The Breakdown of the Tsarist Autocracy

In this essay, the renowned authority on Russia and the Soviet Union, George F. Kennan, finds himself revising his earlier view that, had World War I not intervened, the chances were good for the gradual evolution of the autocracy into a constitutional monarchy. He acknowledges that the final years of tsardom before 1914 witnessed impressive efforts in the social, economic, and cultural modernization of Russia. However, he points to four major causes for the downfall of tsarism: (1) "the failure of the autocracy to supplement the political system in good time with some sort of a parliamentary institution," (2) the irresponsible policy of Great Russian nationalism, (3) the personality of the last Russian tsar himself, and (4) the revolutionary movement. He concludes that the disintegration of the Russian political system was far advanced even as war broke out.

The discussion that follows proceeds from the premise that what occurred in Russia in February–March 1917 was, precisely, a *breakdown* of the autocracy under a fortuitous combination of

SOURCE. George F. Kennan, "The Breakdown of the Tsarist Autocracy," in Richard Pipes, Ed., *Revolutionary Russia*, pp. 1–15 (Cambridge, Mass.: Harvard University Press. Copyright 1968, by Richard Pipes. Reprinted by permission of the publishers).

momentary strains—not the overthrow of the existing order by revolutionary forces. In essence, the regime may be said to have collapsed because it was not able to muster sufficient support to enable it to withstand this sudden combination of strains. In quarters whose support would have been essential to enable it to do this, there was either distrust, indifference, outright hostility, or, in the particular case of the bureaucracy and the army, a mixture of disorientation, demoralization, and ineptness. The central question involved is therefore the question as to which of the regime's policies—that is, what elements of its behavior, what errors of commission or omission, or possibly what circumstances outside its control—were decisive or outstandingly important in bringing it to the helpless and fatal predicament in which it found itself at the beginning of 1917.

Such an inquiry presents special difficulty in view of the bewildering interaction of long-term and short-term causes. One is compelled to ask not just what were the long-term weaknesses that rendered the regime susceptible to the danger of collapse under relatively trivial pressures in the first place, but also what it was that caused the collapse to come at this particular moment.

I should like to begin with an examination of some of the long-term weaknesses and failures of the regime and then conclude with some brief reflections about the developments of the final wartime period just preceding its fall.

LONG-TERM WEAKNESSES AND FAILURES OF THE REGIME

When one looks for those more basic mistakes and failings that undermined the tsarist autocracy and caused it to lose what the Chinese would call the "mandate of Heaven," one is obliged first to deal with certain broadly held misimpressions on this score—misimpressions that Soviet historians, in particular, have been at no pains to dispel. One of these is that the autocracy lost the confidence and respect of the people because it failed to bring a proper degree of modernization to Russian society in the economic, technological, and educational fields—that it made no adequate effort to overcome Russia's backwardness. Another is that the regime was intolerably cruel and despotic in its treatment of the populace generally; and that a revolution was required to correct this situation. In each of these impressions there are, of course, elements of truth; but both represent dangerous, and in general misleading, oversimplifications. That this is true is so well known to experts in the field that it needs, I think, no great elaboration here. But I shall just mention briefly, to avoid unclarity, my own impressions of the situation.

Let us take first the subject of industrialization. Here, it seems to me, we have one of those fields in which the tsar's regime had least to be apologetic about from the standpoint of responsibility for the modernizing of the country. The rates of industrial growth achieved in Russia in the final decades of tsardom would appear to compare not at all unfavorably with those achieved in Western countries at comparable stages of development. The 8 percent growth rate that I understand to have been achieved in the 1890's, and the comparable 6 percent figure for the period from 1906 to 1914, are respectable figures, to say the least. One must doubt that the pace of industrialization could have been pushed much further without producing adverse social consequences out of all proportion in seriousness to the gains involved. Nor does there seem to be any reason to suppose that if revolution had not intervened, and if the dynamics of growth observable in the final decades of tsardom had been projected into mid-century, the results achieved would have been significantly inferior to those that have actually been achieved under Soviet power. This is, of course, only another way of saying that if industrialization was the main concern then no revolution was needed at all: there were easier and no less promising ways of doing it.

It has often been pointed out by way of reproach to the tsar's regime—both at the time and since—that this growth was achieved only by an excessive acceptance of investment and equity participation by foreigners in Russian industry, as well as by excessive state borrowing from other governments. Certainly, the proportion of foreign equity participation in Russian industrial concerns was very high, particularly in mining and metallurgy; and it is perfectly true that the Russian government was the most heavily indebted, externally, of any government in the world at the time. But I am not sure how well these charges stand up as reproaches to the policies of the tsar's government.

Whether the high rate of foreign industrial investment was a bad thing depends on whether one accepts the Marxist thesis that any important degree of such external financing represented a form of enslavement to the foreign investors. The experience of the United States, where foreign capital also played a prominent part in nineteenth century industrial development, would not suggest that this is the case. And as for the government borrowing: much of this, of course, found its way, directly or indirectly, into the process of industrialization, and particularly into the building of railways. But the main stimulus to such borrowing was not the need for industrial capital but rather the effort by the government to maintain a military posture, and to engage in military ventures, that were far beyond its means. These practices, and the heavy indebtedness to which they led, were indeed among the significant weaknesses of the regime; but they do not constitute a proper source of reproach to the regime in connection with its program of industrialization. Had the foreign borrowings of the government been restricted to what it required in order to do its share in the stimulation of the growth of industry, the resulting burden of debt would surely have been well within its means.

Another reproach often leveled at the tsar's government in this connection was that industrialization was given precedence over agriculture and that it was partially financed by the exploitation of the peasantry through such devices as high indirect taxation, rigged prices for agricultural products, forced exportation of grain, and so on. Certainly there is much substance in these charges. The program of rapid industrialization was indeed put in hand long before any attack of comparable vigor was made on the problems of the peasantry, and the peasant was made to contribute heavily to its costs. But these circumstances seem to me to be illustrative less of any error or unfeeling quality on the part of tsarist statesmen than of the cruelty of the dilemmas with which they were faced. Without at least a certain prior development of industry, and particularly without the construction of railway network, no modernization of Russian agriculture would have been conceivable at all. And while somewhat more might perhaps have been extracted from the upper classes through ruthless taxation, there is no reason to suppose that this could have changed basically the logic of the situation, which was that the cost of industrialization, to the extent it was not covered by foreign borrowing, had to be covered by limitations on consumption by the great mass of the Russian people—which meant, in fact, the peasantry. To have tried, through the device of heavy taxation, to switch this entire burden to the relatively well-to-do or property-owning classes would merely have tended to destroy existing possibilities for the accumulation of private industrial capital; but such private accumulation was precisely what the government was concerned, and for very respectable reasons, to stimulate and promote.

The truth is that the tsar's government, if it wished to get on in a serious way with the industrial development of the country, had no alternatives other than foreign borrowing and an extensive taxation of the peasantry. The claim that it should have avoided one or the other of these devices is thus equivalent to the allegation that it moved not too slowly but much too fast in the whole field of industrialization. For this there might be much to be said. But this is not the way the reproach is usually heard.

In the case of agriculture, the pattern is obviously more complex. Certainly, the reform of the 1860's left much to be desired: it was not properly followed through; the burdens resting on the peasantry down to 1905 were inordinate; the economic situation of large portions of the peasant population remained miserable. In all this there were just grounds for reproach to the regime; and I have no desire to minimize its significance. It seems reasonable to suppose that the additional burden of bitterness that accumulated in peasant minds in the final decades of the nineteenth century contributed importantly both to the peasant disorders of the first years of the new century, and to that spirit of sullen contempt for the dynasty, and indifference to its fate, that manifested itself at the time of the revolution.

Against these reflections must be set, however, two compensatory considerations. One has, first, the fact that the most important single factor involved in producing the land hunger and economic misery of the central-Russian village in these decades was nothing having to do with governmental policy but simply the enormous increase in the rural population that occurred at that time—a doubling, and more, just in the years between the emancipation and the outbreak of the world war. Second, there is the fact that after 1906 the government did finally address itself vigorously, intelligently, and in general quite effectively to the problems of the Russian countryside. The fact that this effort came late—too late to be successful in the political and psychological sense—should not blind us to its imposing dimensions. What was achieved in those final years from 1907 to 1914 in a whole series of fields affecting the peasant's situation—in the purchase of land by small peasant holders; in the break-up of the peasant commune and the facilitating of the transition for communal to hereditary tenure; in the consolidation of strip holdings, with all the enormous labor of surveying and adjudication this involved; in resettlement and in colonization of outlying regions of the empire; in the development of the cooperative movement in the countryside—strikes me as impressive in the extreme.

One can truthfully say that the tsar's government deserved reproach for its failures in relation to the peasant throughout most of the nineteenth century. And there can be no doubt that the price of these failures figured prominently in the reckoning the autocracy had to face in 1917. No one would deny, in particular, the importance of the impact that the spectacle of all this rural misery and degradation had on the growth of the Russian revolutionary movement in the nineteenth century. And one can well say that such efforts as were made to improve the situation of the peasantry came much too late in the game. What one cannot say is that they did not come at all or that revolution was necessary because the tsar's government, as of 1917, had still done nothing effective about agriculture. The fact is that the revolution came precisely at the moment when the prospects for the development of Russian agriculture, the war aside, had never looked more hopeful.

Similar conclusions could be drawn, I should think, with relation to education. That Russia was slow in coming to popular education no one would deny. But that the progress made in this field in the final years of tsardom was rapid and impressive seems to me equally undeniable. If, as I understand to be the case, enrollments in primary schools throughout the empire more than doubled in the final two decades before 1914; if in this same period enrollments in institutions of higher learning more than tripled and those in secondary schools nearly quadrupled; or if, for example, the incidence of literacy among military recruits increased from 38 percent in 1894 to 73 percent in 1913—then it may be argued, I think, that all this might have been done earlier; but it cannot be said that nothing consequential was being done at all. The official goal, as adopted five or six years before the outbreak of the world war, was the achievement of universal, compulsory primary school education. The tsarist authorities hoped to achieve this goal by 1922. The rate of progress made prior to the war suggests that it would probably have been achieved at the latest by the mid-1920's had not war and revolution intervened. This is certainly no later than the date at which it was finally achieved by the Soviet regime. Again, one simply cannot accept the thesis that the old regime kept the Russian people in darkness to the end and that a revolution was necessary in 1917 to correct this situation.

In all these fields of modernization, the pattern is in fact much the same: initial backwardness, long sluggishness and delay, then a veritable burst of activity in the final years. If it was in these fields that one was to look for the decisive failures of the autocracy and the reasons for revolution, then it would have to be said that there was much less reason for an overthrow of the regime in 1917 than there was in 1905. Had the 1905 Revolution succeeded, one might well have concluded that the tsar's regime had been overthrown because it failed to bring the Russian people into the modern age. To account for an overthrow coming in 1917, one has to look for other and deeper causes.

The first and most decisive of these causes seems to me to have been, unquestionably, the failure of the autocracy to supplement the political system in good time with some sort of a parliamentary institution—the failure, in other words, to meet the needs of the land-owning nobility and then, increasingly, of the new intelligentsia from all classes for some sort of institutional framework that would associate them with the undertakings of the regime, give them a sense of participation in the governmental process, and provide a forum through which they, or their representatives, could air their views and make their suggestions with regard to governmental policy. In the absence of any such institution, literally hundreds of thousands of people—student youth, commoners (*raznochintsy*), sons of priests, members of the national minorities, members of the gentry, even members of the land-owning nobility itself—people bursting with energies and of the love of life in all its forms; people vibrating with intellectual excitement under the flood of impressions that swept over Russian society as its contacts with the West developed during the nineteenth and early twentieth centuries; People passionately concerned with public affairs, intensively aware of Russia's backwardness, and possessed by no more consuming passion than the desire to contribute to its correction—all these people found themselves, insofar as they did not become associated with the armed forces or the administrative bureaucracy, repelled by the regime, held at a distance from its doings and responsibilities, condemned either to a passive submissiveness in public affairs that did violence to their consciences as well as their energies or to the development of forms of association and political activity that could not, in the circumstances, appear to the regime as other than subversive. What was required, initially, was not a widely popular assembly. There was much to be said for the view that the Russian people at large were not yet ready for this. At any time in the nineteenth century, even a central assembly of the local government boards (*zemstva*) would have constituted an important safety valve, and in fact a very suitable one, insofar as it would have enlisted as collaborators in the tasks of government at the central level not mere theorists devoid of practical experience but people who had had the best sort of preparation: namely, experience at the local, provincial level in the fields of administration intimately connected with the lives and interests of common people. To attempt, with relation to so great and complex a process as that of the loss of public confidence by the Russian autocracy, to identify any single error as a crucial one is, of course, always to commit an act of oversimplification; but if one were to inquire what, by way of example, might appear as outstanding historical errors of the regime, I should think one would have to name such things as the flat repulsion by Alexander II in 1862 of the initiative taken by the gentry of Tver, under the leadership of Unkovskii, in favor of a central *zemstvo* organ; or the rebuff administered by Nicholas II to the representatives of the *zemstva* and the nobility who called on him in 1895 to urge—if only in the mildest of language—the recognition of the need for a more representative system of government. In the entire record of the last decades of tsarist power, I can think of no mistakes more calamitous than these.

There was, of course, eventually, the Duma; and it was, as an institution, not really so bad as it has often been portrayed. Its initial members could, as Vasilii Maklakov pointed out, have made much better use of it than they actually did. The franchise was indeed a limited one, but it was not so severely limited as to prevent both First and Second Dumas from being violently oppositional, and even extensively revolutionary, in spirit. Nor can I develop any lively sympathy for the great unhappiness manifested by the Kadets over the fact that the Duma was not given the right to appoint and control the government. For an American, in particular, it is hard to regard a fusing of the legislative and executive powers as absolutely essential to a sound political system. But leaving aside the adequacy of the arrangements governing the constitution and functioning of the Duma, it is obvious that the granting of it by Nicholas II came far too late and in precisely the wrong way—under pressure, that is, and with obvious reluctance and suspicion on his part. Given the situation that existed at that particular moment, it was natural enough for him to do so. There could have been no more than a minority of the members of the First Duma whose political aspirations, if satisfied, would not have ended in the violent destruction of the autocracy; and the tsar understood this very well. And yet it was Nicholas himself, his father, and his grandfather who were responsible for the fact that this was the way things were. Had they acted earlier—and the 1860's would not have been too soon—they might have had a different, more respectful, and less menacing sort of a parliamentary body before them. And the difference would, I think, have been decisive. The conservative and liberal intelligentsia, from which the dynasty really had something to hope, might have rallied to its side and the radical revolutionary movement, from which it could expect nothing good, would have been split. The effect of waiting forty years and establishing the Duma in 1906 instead of in the 1860's was just the opposite: it unified the radical-revolutionary movement against the regime and split the conservative and liberal intelligentsia, whose united support was essential if the dynasty was to survive.

It was true, of course, that to grant a parliamentary institution would have involved at any time on the tsar's part a readiness to share the power which the dynasty had previously exercised absolutely. But in the mid-nineteenth century, there were still people on the other side who would have been willing to content themselves with this sharing of supreme power. By 1906 there was practically no one left, not only in the revolutionary movement but among the liberals as well, who did not insist, by implication at least, on destroying the tsar's powers entirely rather than just sharing in them. It was the destruction of the autocracy as such, not really its limitation, that was implicit in the demands of the First Duma for a responsible government, for control in effect of the police, and above all for a general amnesty.

In the 1860's the dynasty might still have had before it, in a parliamentary institution, people who were anxious to see it succeed in its tasks and willing to help it do so. By 1906 it was confronted, in every political party to the left of the Octobrists and even party in the ranks of that grouping, not by people who constituted a loyal opposition, not by people who really wanted the dynasty to succeed with the tasks of modernization to which I referred earlier on, not by people who wished to have a share in the dynasty's power, but by rivals for the exercise of that power, by people whose chief grievance against the regime was not that it was dilatory or incompetent but that it stood in their own path, whose complaint was not really that the autocracy misruled Russia, but that it prevented *them* from ruling—or misruling, as history would probably have revealed—in its place.

With Unkovskii and his associates in 1862, Alexander II might, it seems to me, have come to some sort of political terms. With Miliukov and his associates, decorous and mild-mannered as they outwardly were, this same possibility no longer existed. It had become by that time a case of *kto kogo* (who whom)—either the tsar or they. Yet without their help, as February 1917 revealed, the dynasty itself could not be defended.

In the mid-nineteenth century, in other words, the autocracy could still have opted for the status of a limited monarchy. In 1906 this option no longer remained open to it. And the failure to accept it when it *had been* open left only one possibility, which was its final and total destruction.

This great deficiency—namely the denial of political expression —must be clearly distinguished from the question of physical cruelty and oppression in the treatment of the population. It was suggested, at the outset of this discussion, that it was a misimpression that the regime was intolerably cruel and despotic in this respect. This is, of course, a controversial statement; and I do not wish to make it unnecessarily so. I am well aware of the fact that the tsarist police and prison authorities, as well as the military courts, were guilty of many acts of stupidity, injustice, and cruelty. I am not unmindful of the observations of my distinguished namesake, the elder George Kennan, on the exile system in Siberia. But the standards of the present age are different from those of the latter—unfortunately so. The tsarist autocracy did not engage in the sort of prophylactic terror—the punishment of great numbers of the innocent as a means of frightening the potentially guilty—of which we have seen so much in our age. Its treatment of many individual revolutionaries, including incidentally Chernyshevskii, seems to have been, if anything, on the lenient side. The censorship was irritating and often silly, but it was not sufficiently severe to prevent the appearance in Russia of a great critical literature. Most important of all, one has to distinguish, when one speaks of police terrorism, between that element of it that is spontaneous and the element that is provoked. That the Russian revolutionaries behaved provocatively, and deliberately so, on countless occasions is something that few, I think, would deny. Now, it is a habit of political regimes to resist their own violent overthrow; it is something to be expected of them. Stolypin used harsh measures—yes—in suppressing the disorders of the period following the war with Japan, but measures no more harsh than the situation required from the standpoint of the regime. Had there been a time in the history of the United States when political assassinations—assassinations of public officials—were running at the rate of more than one and a half thousand per annum, as was the case in Russia in 1906, I rather shudder to think what would have been the reaction of the official establishment here. In situations of this nature, where there is a constant interaction between the strivings of revolutionaries and the defensive efforts of a political regime, the question of responsibility for violence becomes a matter of the chicken and the egg. If one abstracts from the behavior of the regime in the administration of justice and in the imposition of political discipline that element that was provided by provocation from the revolutionary side, then the use of police terror cannot be regarded as more than a minor determinant of the alienation of great sectors of society that underlay the breakdown of 1917.

So much for the denial of parliamentary government and political liberty. A second crucial deficiency of the autocracy was one that it shared with a large part of upper-class Russian society, and with a portion of the lower classes as well, and that was for this reason not only much more difficult to recognize at the time but has been more difficult of recognition even in the light of history. This was extreme nationalism—that romantic, linguistic nationalism that was the disease of the age.

The spirit of modern nationalism was pernicious for the Russian autocracy for two reasons: first, because it reflected itself unfortunately on the treatment by the tsar's government of the national minorities; but second, because it led to an adventurous foreign policy, far beyond what the capacities of the Russian state at that time could support.

In an empire of which nearly half, or something more than one half (depending on where the Ukrainians were ranked) of the population was made up of national minorities, an absolute monarchy was confronted, in the age of nationalism, with a basic choice. It could make political concessions to the Great-Russian plurality and thus at least keep the strongest single national element firmly associated with it in an effort to hold down the minorities; or, if it did not wish to do this, it could employ a light touch with the minorities, do everything possible to reconcile them to the Russian state, and play them off against the potentially rebellious central Great-Russian group. The tsar's government did neither. Operating against the background of a sullen Russian peasantry, a frustrated Russian upper class, and a lower-class Russian intelligentsia veritably seething with sedition, it set about to treat the national minorities in the name of Russian nationalism with an utterly senseless provocation of their national cultures and feelings and a rigid repression of all their efforts to establish a separate national political identity. This was a policy calculated to make sure that if there were anyone among the minority elements who was not already alienated from the autocracy by virtue of its general social and political policies, he would sooner or later be brought into the opposition by the offense to his national feelings. Among the manifestations of this stupidity none was more serious than the anti-Semitism that set in after the murder of Alexander II—an aberration of policy that was at first simply clumsy and reaction-

ary in an old-fashioned religious sense but then assumed, under
Nicholas II, forms that were truly disgraceful and bespoke a
profound perversion of political and philosophic understanding.
This tendency was particularly unfortunate because it came at
a period when, for the first time, a great many young Jews would
have been prepared, given half a chance, to forget the specific
circumstances of their religious and cultural origin and to become essentially russified. And this anti-Semitism was of course
only a part of nationalistic policies that affected in some way and
at some time practically every one of the minorities that lined
the periphery of the empire. The revenge for this extraordinary
blindness became apparent, quite naturally, in the form of the
high percentage of members of the national minorities to be
found in the revolutionary movement. It is impossible to say
what 1917 would have been like without the Chkheidzes and
Martovs, the Trotskys, Dzerzhinskiis, Radeks, Sverdlovs, Stalins,
and Ordzhonikidzes; but certainly the non-Great-Russian component in the revolutionary opposition to tsardom was a great
one, particularly after 1881, and it must be assumed to have
added greatly to the difficulty of the predicament of the autocracy at that final moment.

The second manner in which the disease of extreme nationalism manifested itself in tsarist policy was, as already noted, in
the field of foreign affairs. Particularly was this true under Nicholas II. The origins of the war with Japan were, from the Russian side, disreputable and inexcusable. There was no need for
this involvement; it could easily have been avoided; the attendant military effort was clearly beyond the physical resources of
the country at that moment of rapid economic and social transition; and the folly of the venture from the domestic-political
standpoint was at once apparent in the events of the Revolution
of 1905. And as though this war were not folly enough in itself,
it had the further effect of making it more difficult than ever for
Russia to resist involvement in the much greater and even more
dangerous European war that was shortly to come. The financial
distress in which the tsar's government finished the war with
Japan left it more dependent than ever on the financial bounty
of the French government and the French bankers and more
helpless than ever before the French demands that Russia become in effect an instrument of French policy against Germany.

Whether this added element of financial dependence was decisive in bringing Russia into World War I may well be doubted. The same result would very possibly have been achieved by the nationalistic tendencies now raging unchecked among the Russian bureaucracy, the military caste, and the upper classes generally, coupled with the tsar's strange weakness for military adventurism. To people still imbued with a strong conviction of the iniquity of the kaiser's Germany or Franz Josef's Austria, it may seem strange to hear it suggested that the Russian monarchy might have done better, in the interests of its own preservation, to remain aloof from involvement in a war against Germany. In the light of the prevailing nationalistic emotionalism of the time, it would no doubt have seemed preposterous to suggest that Serbia should have been left to Austria's mercy and that Russian prestige, just recently so painfully injured in the crisis over the annexation of Bosnia and Herzegovina, should suffer another and perhaps even greater reverse of this nature. The fact remains that in 1914 Russia was in no condition to participate in a major war—the experience of the war with Japan had demonstrated this; and neither the fate of Serbia nor the question of control over the Dardanelles really represented for her a vital interest, comparable to what she stood to suffer by courting another domestic upheaval on the heels of the one she had just experienced in 1904–05.

The Franco-Russian alliance served, in Russia's case, a financial interest but not really a political one. The kaiser's Germany may have been a threat to Britain; it was not in great measure a threat to Russia. Some of the more sober statesmen, Witte and even the otherwise nationalistic Stolypin, saw this, and would have tried betimes to avoid the catastrophe to which this alliance, which took no proper account of Russia's internal condition, was leading. But it was the pervasive nationalism of the age that defeated them; and I am inclined, for this reason, to attribute to that nationalism a major role in the causes of the final collapse of the regime. A tsarist autocracy that saw things clearly and wished to exert itself effectively in the interest of its own preservation would have practiced a rigid abstention from involvement in world political problems generally, and from exhausting foreign wars in particular, at that crucial juncture in its domestic-political development.

The third of the weaknesses of the autocracy that I should like to mention was the personality of the last Russian tsar himself. Poorly educated, narrow in intellectual horizon, a wretchedly bad judge of people, isolated from Russian society at large, in contact only with the most narrow military and bureaucratic circles, intimidated by the ghost of his imposing father and the glowering proximity of his numerous gigantic uncles, helpless under the destructive influence of his endlessly unfortunate wife: Nicholas II was obviously inadequate to the demands of his exalted position; and this was an inadequacy for which no degree of charm, of courtesy, of delicacy of manner, could compensate. It is ironic that this man, who fought so tenaciously against the granting of a constitution, had many of the qualities that would have fitted him excellently for the position of a constitutional monarch and practically none of those that were needed for the exercise of that absolute power to which he stubbornly clung. Time and time again, in the record of his reign, one finds the evidences of his short-sightedness and his lack of grasp of the realities of the life of the country interfering with the political process in ways that were for him veritably suicidal. True, he was the product of the vagaries of genetics; another tsar might not have been so bad. But the experience of his reign only illustrates the fact that these accidents of royal birth, tolerable in earlier centuries where the feudal nobility bore a good portion of the load, and tolerable again in the modern age wherever the main burden is borne or shared by parliamentary institutions, were not tolerable in the age of economic development and mass education and in a political system where the monarch claimed the rights of personal absolutism.

So much for the leading and crucial weaknesses of the autocracy itself in the final decades of its power. Mention must be made, in conclusion, of the Russian revolutionary movement. It was, of course, not the revolutionary parties that overthrew the autocracy in 1917. Nevertheless, there were indirect ways in which their existence and activity affected the situation of the regime; and these must be briefly noted.

First of all, by providing a somewhat romantic alternative to any association with the governing establishment, the revolutionary movement drew many talented youths into an attitude of defiance and revolutionary disobedience to it, thereby impoverishing it in talent, energy, and intelligence. Every time that a young person of ability was drawn into the ranks of its revolutionary opponents, the bureaucracy, deprived of these sources of recruitment, became just that more stupid, unimaginative, and inept.

Second, there was the effect the revolutionary elements had on the development of governmental policy. They obviously had no interest in seeing the modernization of the country proceed successfully under tsarist tutelage, and they did as little as they could to support it. I find it significant that more useful social legislation appears to have been passed by the two final and supposedly reactionary Dumas than by the first two relatively liberal, and partially revolutionary, ones. But more important still was the influence of the revolutionaries in frightening the regime out of possible initiatives in the field of political reform. These revolutionary parties and groupings had, as a rule, no interest in seeing genuine progress made in the creation of liberal institutions. Their aim was generally not to reform the system but to cause it to fall and to replace it. For this reason, the more the regime could be provoked into stupid, self-defeating behavior, the better from their standpoint. They often found themselves, in this respect, sharing the same aspirations and purposes as the extreme right wing of the political spectrum, which also— though for other reasons—did not wish to see any liberalization of the autocracy. And in this respect one has to concede to the revolutionary movement a series of important successes. In one instance after another where there appeared to be a possibility of political liberalization or where the pressures in this direction were intense the timely intervention of revolutionary activity of one sort or another sufficed to assure that no progress should be made. One has only to recall, as examples, the effect of the Polish uprising of 1863 on the policies of Alexander II or the effect of his assassination in 1881 on the projects then being entertained by Loris-Melikov.

THE WAR AND THE FINAL CRISIS

So much, then, for the major weaknesses, failures, and strains that entered into the undermining of the tsarist system of power.

It remains only to note the manner in which the effect of all of them was magnified by the world war that began in 1914: magnified to a point where the system could no longer stand the strain. Wartime patriotic fervor, engulfing the liberal-parliamentary circles even more hopelessly than the government itself, brought them in at this point as critics of the government on new grounds: on the grounds that it was not *sufficiently* nationalistic, not *sufficiently* inspired and determined in its conduct of the war effort. And to this there was now added the quite erroneous but heady and dangerous charge that it was pro-German and even treasonable in its relations to the enemy. These charges were utilized by the liberal-parliamentary circles as the excuse for setting up new organizational entities, such as the various war industry councils, which were able to function as rival authorities to the governmental bureaucracy, to provide channels for political activity hostile to the regime, and eventually to contribute significantly to the circumstances surrounding its collapse. Meanwhile, the strictly military aspects of the war effort had a whole series of effect—such as the weakening by losses in battle of the loyal portion of the officers' corps, the stationing of undisciplined garrisons in the vicinity of the capital city, the removal of the tsar himself to field headquarters, and so on—that were to have important connotations, unfavorable to the security of the regime, at the moment of supreme trial. In a number of ways, furthermore, the war effort exacerbated relations between the government and members of the national minorities, who for obvious reasons did not always share the Russian emotional commitment to the war. Finally, not perhaps as a consequence of the war (this is hard to judge), but certainly simultaneously with it, there were the grotesque developments in the tsar's own personal situation, particularly the ripening and the denouement of the Rasputin affair—developments that finally succeeded in alienating from his cause not only large elements of the immediate bureaucratic and military entourage that had constituted his last comfort and protection, but even a portion of the imperial family itself, thus completing his isolation and removing, or disqualifying, his last potential defenders.

CONCLUSIONS

Prior to the undertaking of this review, I was inclined to feel that had the war not intervened, the chances for survival of the autocracy and for its gradual evolution into a constitutional monarchy would not have been bad. On reviewing once more the events of these last decades, I find myself obliged to question that opinion. Neither the tardiness in the granting of political reform, nor the excesses of an extravagant and foolish nationalism, nor the personal limitations of the imperial couple began with the war or were primarily responses to the existence of the war. None of the consequences of these deficiencies were in process of any significant correction as the war approached. The spectacle of the final years of tsardom prior to 1914 is that of an impressive program of social, economic, and cultural modernization of a great country being conducted, somewhat incongruously, under the general authority of a governmental system that was itself in the advanced stages of political disintegration. The successes in the field of modernization might indeed, if allowed to continue, have brought Russia rapidly and safely into the modern age. It is doubtful that they could for long have overbalanced the serious deficiencies of the political system or averted the consequences to which they were—even as war broke out—inexorably leading.

Suggestions for Further Reading

There are two recent collections of interpretative essays dealing with the last years of Imperial Russia: *Russia in Transition, 1905–1914. Evolution or Revolution?* edited by Robert H. McNeal (New York, 1970) and *Russia under the Last Tsar* edited by Theofanis George Stavrou (Minneapolis, 1969). Both books have ample bibliographies. Two general survey histories of the period have been written by Richard Charques, *The Twilight of Imperial Russia* (Oxford Paperback, New York, 1965) who concentrates on politics and the failure of Russian liberalism, and Lionel Kochan, *Russia in Revolution, 1890–1918* (New York, 1966) who presents a broader synthesis. Robert K. Massie's *Nicholas and Alexandra* (New York, 1967) is a popular biography of the last emperor and empress. Sidney Harcave's *Years of the Golden Cockerel: The Last Romanov Tsars 1814–1917* (New York, 1968) has an excellent account of the reign of Nicholas II. Bernard Pares' *The Fall of the Russian Monarchy* (Vintage Books, New York, 1961) remains a classic analysis of the reign. Henri Troyat's, *Daily Life in Russia under the Last Tsar* (London, 1961) is readable and informative. Jacob Walkin's *The Rise of Democracy in Pre-Revolutionary Russia: Political and Social Institutions under the Last Three Czars* (New York, 1962) offers an optimistic view. Harold W. Williams' *Russia of the Russians* (New York, 1914) is a mine of information otherwise difficult of access. Donald Mackenzie Wallace's *Russia on the Eve of War and Revolution* (Vintage Books, New York, 1961) is a standard contemporary description. A useful recent collaborative work edited by George Katkov is *Russia Enters the Twentieth Century* (London, 1971).

The Memoirs of Count Witte (New York, 1921) present his point of view. Thomas Riha has written *A Russian European: Paul Miliukov in Russian Politics* (Notre Dame, 1969) and Arthur P. Mendel has edited Miliukov's *Political Memoirs 1905–1917* (Ann Arbor, 1967). Maklakov's *The First State Duma* (Bloomington, 1964) is of value.

Edward Chmielewski's *The Polish Question in the Russian State Duma* (Knoxville, 1970) is a recent study of Russia's principal nationality problem.

There are several specialized articles that throw light on various aspects of Imperial Russia's political life. Alfred Levin's "June 3, 1907: Action and Reaction," in *Essays in Russian History* (Hamden, Connecticut, 1964), edited by A. Ferguson and A. Levin, pp. 233–273, is invaluable. C. Jay Smith's "The Third State Duma: An Analytical Profile," *The Russian Review, XVII*, no. 3 (July, 1958), pp. 201–210 is illuminating. Important aspects of Stolypin's career have been examined by Edward Chmielewski in two articles, "Stolypin's Last Crisis," *California Slavic Studies, III* (1964), pp. 95–126, and "Stolypin and the Russian Ministerial Crisis of 1909," *California Slavic Studies, IV* (1967), pp. 1–38.